Theo Hobson's previous books include *Milton's Vision: The birth of Christian liberty* (2008), *Faith* (2009) and *Reinventing Liberal Christianity* (2013). He has worked as a teacher, copywriter and journalist. He is presently working as a librarian at a comprehensive school near where he lives with his wife and three children in Harlesden, London. He is very interested in religious art, and sometimes tries making some himself and getting his local church to display it.

GOD CREATED HUMANISM

The Christian basis of secular values

THEO HOBSON

First published in Great Britain in 2017

Society for Promoting Christian Knowledge
36 Causton Street
London SW1P 4ST
www.spck.org.uk

British Library Cataloguing-in-Publication Data
A catalogue record for this book is available from the British Library

ISBN 978–0–281–07742–7
eBook ISBN 978–0–281–07744–1

Typeset by Graphicraft Limited, Hong Kong
First printed in Great Britain by TJ International
Subsequently digitally reprinted in Great Britain

Produced on paper from sustainable forests

To my wife Tess, who must love me

Contents

Acknowledgements

I am grateful to those who have encouraged me in various ways during the writing of this book, including Rowan Williams, Francis Spufford, Alain de Botton, Brendan Walsh, Rupert Shortt, and my vicar Michael Moorhead. I am also grateful to Philip Law and the rest of the team at SPCK, for their friendly enthusiasm. And I suppose my family has been fairly tolerant of my brooding obsession with big ideas, on which any brief moments of recent moodiness can be blamed.

Introduction

Let's begin at the beginning. This is the thing we seem to find hardest when thinking about the moral and political basis of our society – simply beginning at the beginning; easier to get stuck into this or that debate (in which we're very sure we're in the right), and to evade first principles. Let's try to begin at the beginning.

We in the West believe in something; something more than shopping and pleasuring ourselves. Really, we do.

Is it liberal democracy? Not quite: that's a form of politics (and quite complicated to articulate). We need to talk about the world view, or ideal, that underlies it. It might sound hopelessly naive or vague or earnest, but it is the belief that all human lives matter and should flourish, and that part of such flourishing is the freedom to express one's core beliefs; it of course entails 'human rights'. I think we must call this ideology 'secular humanism' – despite great risk of being misunderstood. It is secular in that it expresses itself in non-religious terms, which doesn't mean it's anti-religious but that it seeks to include those of all faiths and none. This is important to underline because 'secular humanism' is often used to mean the rejection of religion: a softer term for atheism. I'm suggesting that secular humanism is the outlook that underlies 'liberal democracy', which is a more complicated phenomenon, referring to a form of politics in which certain basic individual rights are protected, and in which participation through regular elections is guaranteed. The average Westerner would struggle to define liberal democracy, but has a visceral sense of what secular humanism is.

I suggest that we need to be clearer, and prouder, that this moral ideal underlies the West. It is a core part of our more concrete allegiance, to the nation. (If a Western nation were taken over by a regime that rejected secular humanism, it would lose most citizens' allegiance – one hopes.) In reality, of course, this ideal blurs with mundane pragmatism and national self-interest, and personal self-interest – but worldly-wise people who dismiss this ideal as nebulous and naive are themselves being naive (without the redeeming idealism). For it is there, this moral vision, at the heart of our politics and culture. In our public discourse it is taken for granted that all human lives are valuable and of equal worth, and that all human suffering is a matter of urgent concern. This assumption is our form of the sacred, in a sense (thus we have various taboos about saying things that go against it).

But there's a problem. It seems that secular humanism is too vague, too broad, too thin to function as a strong, emotive creed. It feels empty until we add more detail. And so we angrily disagree about what is the right detail to add – socialism, atheism, the free market, national security, whatever. And in the bitter spats, common ground is eclipsed; we fail to affirm the core basic ideology, the shamefully vague humanist ideal. It slips away; or we somehow do not quite get round to reflecting on it, affirming it. It is still there, quietly underlying our culture, but invisible. The attempt to focus on it seems rather foolish to opinion-formers on all sides. Left-wingers see secular humanism, on its own, as too weak to challenge an unjust system, and therefore as a useful fig leaf for powerful elites. Right-wingers see it as nebulous, corrosive of firmer social bonds, prey to trendy causes and political correctness. All these people wonder whether there's anything here worth discussing, let alone celebrating.

Why are we so inclined to avoid dwelling on, and affirming, this basic common ideal? It is because this thing is so amorphous, elusive, unclassifiable. It is hard to say what sort of thing we're taking about when we talk about secular humanism. This intersection of politics and morality is awkward. When we say that everyone is equal, is that a statement of fact or a moral aspiration? It must be a moral aspiration, but it's so built into the culture that we don't really link it to personal morality: we are in the habit of seeing secular humanist morality as *just normal*, the default position of civilized people, not a moral commitment one has to think about, work at. It's a sort of morality that is public rather than personal; a morality that society does for us, perhaps, for it is built into our politics. Is it a form of moral idealism? Yes and no: for it is ordinary, expected of us, and we think of 'idealism' as something more than that.

There are other causes for evasion, and faint praise. We don't want to sound naively optimistic, as if we think that history is inevitably moving to a happy conclusion: in the past, secular humanism was closely associated with such a belief in rational progress, and it's still haunted by it. We must dispel the old association, insisting that secular humanism is not the rational solution to history that inevitably triumphs, but simply the *right moral ideal*, whether or not its influence is spreading. Also, we don't want to sound arrogantly imperialistic, telling all the peoples of the world how to live. Maybe secular humanism is right for us, but we shouldn't try to push it on others – so we mute our affirmation of it.

But the thing that makes secular humanism really tricky is religion, for this moral idealism overlaps with religious idealism in a very problematic way. For many people, religion is the real source of this moral vision, and a secular version is suspect. And many atheists say that this moral vision can only be clarified and completed if it is explicitly anti-religious. In other words, the humanist ideal is divided by the question of religion. This is chiefly why secular humanism is so difficult to think about: its relationship to religion is powerfully unclear.

Was it ever thus? Yes and no: this tense relationship was, until rather recently, softened by a liberal religiosity that fused with national identity. In the twentieth century, the big ideological battles did not expose this tension; rather fascism and communism could both be fought by a vague alliance of religion and secular humanism. But the principal ideological enemy of our day, militant Islam, is different. By accusing Western freedom of being godless and selfish, it drives a wedge into our creed. It sows opposition between believers and non-believers. The former want to say: 'Don't call us all godless, many of us dissent from secularism'; the latter want to say: 'Yes, our creed certainly does reject religion, thank God.' (And more moderate Islam has the same effect: it makes the old fusion of liberal religion and national identity seem unsustainable; for many Muslims want their religion to be expressed in public life in a way that makes the average agnostic recoil from the whole concept of religion being expressed in public life.)

I suggest that we must get beyond this internal rift, this religious–secular civil war, and affirm secular humanism as the basic public creed of the West. This means challenging a deep-seated assumption: that this sort of discussion, about our core political morality, should make little or no reference to religion. Instead, I suggest, secular humanism can only be strongly affirmed if its positive affinity with religion is emphasized. The task is to show that this moral idealism that quietly unites us has a vast amount in common with the religious tradition of the West. Secular humanism, despite being secular, is firmly rooted in Christianity. Its moral universalism is an adaptation, or mutation, of Christianity. Only if this paradox is acknowledged can we address our paralysing religious–secular split, and reaffirm our public creed.

To claim that Christianity is the primary source of secular humanism might sound excessive. But where else did secular humanism get its optimistic moral vision, its idea that human beings ought to seek the well-being of all other human beings? Is this just the morality that comes naturally to all human societies, the evolved instinct for altruism perhaps? No – that sort of instinctive morality certainly exists, but it is frail, ambiguous: it might come naturally to protect an orphan of one's own tribe, but it also seems to come naturally to see other tribes as enemies, and to treat their orphans with less care. Maybe a widening of morality comes with the development of rationality. But the morality of the brainy ancient Greeks was limited, hemmed in by fatalism, militarism, hierarchy, slavery (their rationality, as we'll see, was intrinsically elitist). 'Yes, but modern humanist thinkers overcame such limitations,' says the atheist, 'and discovered the great truth of human equality, of universal rights.' OK, so how did that happen? When one bothers looking into the matter, one finds that these humanists were almost all Christians, or semi-Christian believers in a rational God – 'deists'. Secular humanism very gradually emerged *within* Christian culture. Which means that the modern humanist principles of liberty and equality are rooted in Christianity. It does not come naturally to us to believe that we can move towards a world of ever-greater justice for all, that all lives are of equal worth, that oppression and discrimination must end. It comes far more naturally to us to see drastic inequality as inevitable, and distant others as inferior.

'Maybe Christianity played a historical role in founding secular humanism,' some might say, 'but that's all in the past.' No: secular humanism has continued to be shaped by its Christian basis, in recent times. Two examples: in the mid twentieth century the ideal of universal human rights was launched by mostly Christian thinkers and statesmen. And a bit later, Christianity was central to the civil rights movement in the United States, with its vision of future harmony. Before that movement, secular humanism did not entail the urgent commitment to racial equality it now does.

Am I saying that secular humanism is 'really' a form of Christianity without knowing it, maybe that it is the final expression of Christianity? No: it is something else, something distinct, but it has Christian roots. Christianity gave rise to a moral universalism that is in a sense more advanced than it – for secular moral universalism is capable of being more universalist, in that it overlooks religious difference in asserting fundamental human unity.

This strange dynamic has not been easy for Christianity: it has not really known how to relate to the new ideology that it gave rise to. The loudest Christian voices have always responded defensively to secular humanism, attacking it as spurious and shallow (and in recent decades such voices have held the intellectual high ground, due to a strong anti-liberal reaction in theology). This response is understandable, for secular humanism has been most strongly voiced by atheists, who say that religion gets in the way of the simple, objective rational good of human flourishing, that it fatally muddies the waters of humanism. It's the idea enshrined in John Lennon's song 'Imagine': if we all stop believing in heaven, the brotherhood of man is round the corner. Atheists define secular humanism in anti-religious terms, which gives it an aura of clarity and strength. Because secular humanism can be expressed in this anti-religious way, the Christian is likely to be wary of it.

Instead, I suggest, the Christian should affirm the secular humanist vision of universal human flourishing, for a public ideology must take secular form – and this is the best imaginable public ideology (by 'public ideology' I mean an ideology that underlies politics, that unites a nation, or aspires to).

Am I saying that Christianity should admit that it has been super-seded by secular humanism, and so throw in the towel? Absolutely not! This must be underlined from the outset, for a lot of modern Christian theology did suggest that a rational-humanist sort of religion was the way forward. Instead, Christianity should affirm secular humanism *as a public ideology* but also say that it is inadequate, it is limited to the practical public sphere, the surface of life; it has no strong account of life's meaning and purpose, but gravitates to an evasive shrug. Its universalism is fuller, in the sense that it can bypass the questionable particularity of religion, and theoretically include everyone irrespective of their belief. But it is also *thinner*: it cannot say why we should affirm this moral universalism, and it evades the full drama of this moral vision, which is its absolute and perfectionist desire for the good of all humanity – a desire that clashes with the fact of human fallibility.

So secular humanism has an element of dishonesty: it advocates an absolute good, justice for all, but finds it possible to do so on the cheap, without facing the fact that this ideal is indeed absolute, perfectionist.

It finds it possible to affirm this ideal in a muted, pragmatic, sceptical way, to believe in the good of all within reason, up to a point that is deemed sensible by the culture of the day. And it assumes that it is *normal* to espouse this ideal; it is what is expected of all rational civilized people. A huge, culture-sized, convention calls this a coherent enough position. But is it? I suggest that it's a timid dilution of moral absoluteness, and that the full and direct expression of Christianity is still needed, if one is seriously to affirm the fullest moral universalism, the fullest humanism. To the assumption that it is clear enough how to be good enough, we must say: 'No! Good enough isn't good enough.' Serious pondering of 'the good' involves us in awkward and embarrassing wrestles with absoluteness.

I am offering a new understanding of Christianity's relationship to secular humanism. They are two halves of the same vision, two opposing sides of the same coin. In other words, the religion–secularism split is overcome when we understand secular humanism to be based in religion. And yet the vision must remain unsynthesized, dialectical. Instead of forging a stable new Christian-based secular humanism, we must accept the endless creative tension between Christianity and the fuller but thinner moral universalism it has produced.

I am saying that we must affirm secular humanism with new vim, and I am also saying that secular humanism is not enough, that it is shallow and rather dishonest when severed from its religious roots. Is this a contradiction? No, it is a paradox. The moral-political tradition we inhabit is paradoxical: it is post-religious, yet incoherent when separated from its religious roots.

Arguing for the Christian roots of secular humanism means challenging the conventional story of modernity, which goes something like this: secular humanism emerged when people gradually dared to question religion and to see that morality could exist without it, on both an individual and a cultural level – they thus discovered the true universal morality, compatible with rationality. What's wrong with this story? It implies that this non-religious moral vision is natural, is just there, waiting to blossom forth once religion is replaced by rationalism. In reality, this universal humanism was *shaped* by the Christian centuries. Humanitarian ideals are not natural, nor are they rationally deducible; they are complex cultural traditions, brewed over centuries. And the main ingredient in this brewing was the story of God taking the side, even taking the form, of the powerless victim; and the promise that the humble shall be exalted, and the higher sort knocked from their glamorous perches. Only after centuries of this myth having a dominant cultural place did the idea of the equal worth of all human beings begin to seem axiomatic.

As we shall see, secular humanism emerged within religion; it came from religious reform movements of various types. But did it not then detach itself from religion? Well, yes and no. Its optimistic universalism is so fundamentally indebted to Christianity that its distinctness is somewhat fishy. Though it sidelines religion in its grand universalist narrative, it is not cleanly post-religious.

Someone might reply: 'This abstract theorizing is beside the point. *My* secular humanism is free of religion. I hope for a more humane future in which the rights of all are respected, and this is not based on religion, which feels irrelevant to me, and often seems a force for bad.' Am I claiming that such people have a superficial understanding of their own world view? Well, let's put it this way: such people express one aspect of secular humanism: its freedom to dismiss religion and to consider itself fully autonomous. I am inviting them to reconsider that assumption, to ponder their debt to Christian tradition.

Through discussing this strange dynamic I seek to persuade the agnostic reader that Christianity, despite its seeming mythic absurdity, demands to be taken seriously. If she values secular humanism, she should also value the source of this value. And I am also seeking to persuade the conservative believer that secular humanism paradoxically complements Christianity, that it is the right *public* ideology. ('Political' might be better than 'public', as Christianity is also public, but differently so.) Christians should affirm this post-religious ideology as well as spread the faith from which it flows. From a Christian point of view, this thin universalism is the proper icing on the thick religious cake.

This is my attempt to break the dull, dull deadlock that has dominated religion-discussion for a very long time. I'm tired of it, tired of religion that bigs itself up by bravely attacking secular humanism; and tired of secular humanism that knows how to sound impeccably concerned for humanity in a hundred with-it ways, but lacks the backbone to ask the simple – but hard! – question, of where its values come from. Enough already! Here's something new.

Here's how my argument unfurls. Chapter 1 asks why we are so inclined to take secular humanism for granted and to assume it comes naturally: why do we resist seeing that it is a particular *tradition*? It then focuses on the recent atheists, who are secular humanists with a strange lack of self-knowledge. Their insistence that morality comes naturally, as long as it's undisturbed by false ideas, is flimsy. This chapter also considers some recent agnostics, who awkwardly grasp that religion is at the root of their inherited moral values. Chapter 2 traces the secular humanist potential enfolded within Christianity and considers other ancient ethical perspectives; it then looks at the medieval emergence of a form of secularism and its development in the Reformation era.

Chapter 3 is particularly action-packed: it considers two developments, or mutations, of Protestantism: the rise of religious rationalism (influenced by classical Stoicism) and the reformism that rejected theocracy and separated Church and state. These, together, sowed the seeds of the Enlightenment. Chapter 4 shows how, in the nineteenth century, secular humanism gradually took on its current post-religious character – but also shows that various Victorian atheists and agnostics were recycling Christian idealism (a phenomenon first identified by Nietzsche). Then, in Chapters 5 and 6, we follow the story into the twentieth century: just as secular humanism seems on the verge of smooth triumph, a major reaction against it emerges, leading to the horror of the mid century. Secular humanism then recovers, in practical terms, becoming the firmly dominant ideology of the West – but its theoretical weakness becomes more obvious.

The faith of the West today, the Preliminary Conclusion then explains, is not simply secular humanism but *Christian-based secular humanism*. Only if this paradox is acknowledged can we strongly affirm our public creed. Christianity's difficult task is to affirm secular humanism, relating it to the absoluteness of its own vision – but *also* to call secular humanism inadequate; it must say that more meaning is needed, that human lives need to be founded in the good myth, from which secular humanism derives. Christianity is the engine of secular humanism – and also a critical questioner of it, a spanner in the works.

Finally, Chapter 7 is a surprising changing of the subject – for my main argument, large as it is, is not enough. 'Even if Christianity is the source of secular humanism,' the agnostic might reply, 'it remains impossible to believe in – for the thuddingly obvious reason that its myths are plainly irrational. We have to move away from roots that are not credible.' My approach to this – not small – issue is to argue that

Christianity is surprisingly able to accommodate rational scepticism. There is another paradox here, in the fact that authentic faith is an open conversation with unbelief. In this religion there is room for honesty about the clash between myth and rationality. I shall explain this partly with reference to Martin Luther, who insisted that Christianity is compatible with *honesty*: we must admit that this religion is impossibly morally demanding, and on one level impossible to believe in – this admission is central to authentic faith, for we must grasp God's otherness from us. In this way also, Christianity is surprisingly accommodating of our modern difficulties with religion. Its seeming weaknesses, when probed, oddly resemble strange strengths.

A further word on the term 'secular humanism'. My choice of it might seem odd, in view of its association with atheism. But I want to contest that association. I want to delegitimize the assumption that there is an affinity between the secular and humanist creed that unites us, and opposition to religion.

1

The ideology in the room

This creed that I say unites us – surely it is the prime subject of our discussions, surely it is endlessly admired and assessed, and weighed and measured, and prodded and patted? Surely secular humanism is as widely affirmed and as hotly debated as religion was until recent times? But this is not the case. Though its truth is assumed, it is seldom the focus of our attention. It is taken for granted, including in the sense of ignored. We avidly discuss secondary aspects of it but seem to lack a vocabulary for the thing itself – it is not even quite clear what to call it. It is the elephant in the room.

Our secular humanism is so deeply ingrained that it feels natural, part of the air we breathe, the landscape we inhabit. This might seem a good thing – for it's a good ideology. If this good ideology has become axiomatic, then isn't that a sign of our collective moral health? Yes and no: there's also a danger in seeing secular humanism as 'just there'; it means we are forgetting to see it as a tradition that needs conscious nurturing, and as a – rather complex – story we must strive to understand.

It cannot be doubted that secular humanism is taken for granted in our culture. For example, newspaper columnists decry the violation of human rights in a distant land but are highly unlikely to pause and ask why we are supposed to care about these far-off folk; it is assumed that we just do, or rather that we should. It is not widely wondered what 'human rights' are – such inquiries are dry academic affairs. Another example: a television presenter is forced out of his job when it emerges he has used a term with racist associations. It seems that equality is so sacred to us that even the slightest questioning of its authority is illicit. But this sacred aura is more likely to be expressed negatively ('You are not allowed to say x, y and z') rather than positively ('Here is what we think about equality, here is why we care'). To put it differently, the equal worth of all human beings is treated as a *fact*, denial of which puts one outside of civilized, sane society. This is presupposed in every news bulletin; indeed, 'the news', as well as informing us, upholds the unspoken creed we share: it assumes we care about these victims of child abuse, of police racism, and that we still care about the victims of a long-ago genocide. In other words, an assumption circulates like blood through our culture: we care about the good of all humanity and the principle of equality. This is our 'sacred' cause, our binding assumption – so why don't we reflect on it more?

Some might say: 'Secular humanism does not unite us in the way you suggest, for it is only the liberal left that really believes in this cause; the right, which hugely influences mainstream society, merely pays it some lip service.' But in most of the West, the mainstream right is fully accepting of secular humanism: it justifies its policies in terms of creating wealth that will benefit all, and of course it seldom or never rejects the principle of secularism. The semi-exception is the USA, where the right has in recent decades been strongly influenced by a conservative religious lobby that uses both 'secular humanism' and 'liberalism' as boo-terms. Yet even at its height, this influence has been balanced by the US right's acceptance of the political liberalism enshrined in the constitution; indeed, it has fetishized the liberal revolution that founded the nation. (In the UK there is a version of this: Tory thinkers tend to flinch at 'secular humanism' and 'universal human rights', as ideals that lead to the neglect of national traditions of well-being; but on close inspection their argument is with the application of these ideals, and there is seldom any substantial dissent from the principle of moral universalism.)

Of course, there are different interpretations of what secular humanism entails. Most obviously, left and right differ over how far government should promote economic equality. But there is surely no denying that this is our common creed. The neatest proof is that no British public figure can dissent from it without facing a media witch-hunt.

Then why does it receive so little attention? 'Because it is too obvious and too vague', many will say. Yes, we theoretically affirm universal human flourishing, but so what? It's a rather airy ideal that gets elbowed aside by murky pragmatism in a hundred ways – so isn't there something pretentious and falsely pious about taking it too seriously? Isn't it hypocritical to profess belief in equality but to accept a system that thrives on inequality? Also, isn't it arrogant to think that we in the West have a monopoly on such idealism? Doesn't it just come naturally to human beings to care about the well-being of other human beings, just as it comes naturally to us to need to eat when hungry or sleep when tired? Let us beware of claiming to be the morally superior civilization! Now more than ever we are aware of the crimes committed in the name of Western universalism. In the heyday of empire one could turn a blind eye – nowadays the descendants of the victims are eloquently among us, forbidding such evasions. Do such past abuses discredit Western universalism? No. It is in the language of Western universalism that they are condemned. But they do advise against a confident tone.

So there are strong reasons to downplay our secular humanist idealism. Above all, there is an embarrassing gap between our theoretical concern for every soul on the planet, and our self-interest, both corporate and personal. And it also looks likely that compassion for all humanity is a universal impulse that we in the West should not claim to own.

And yet these responses are evasive. There is something special about the core ideology of the West. This humanist vision is uniquely robust. Even if it is true that all humans have benign impulses and that many other cultures promote such good will, the vision of the West still stands out. It is a tradition that has promoted humanist principles through its political structures.

'But surely all cultures are evolving in this direction,' some might say, 'for at root all humans desire universal human flourishing. Once people can think clearly (which might mean attaining a certain level of material security), then surely their natural capacity for altruism will blossom.' But this is not the case. Humans do not naturally desire universal human flourishing, rather the strength of their own tribe. Yes, some civilizations have developed versions of moral universalism, but these ideals have been frail and limited. Only in the West did the humanist ideal find real political expression, and only there did it become authentically universalist.

In other traditions the desire for universal human flourishing is secondary to the will to promote a particular cultural order. This cultural order is deemed to have intrinsic authority: the right to think differently is severely curtailed. Islam, for example, espouses a universal moral vision in which compassion and justice are central, but this must be realized within a political order in which individual liberty is seen as a threat to social cohesion. And in ancient Chinese culture, compassion for all humanity was seen as a sacred duty, but had to be expressed through traditional rules that contributed to social order. A theoretical universalism was massively subordinated to political reality. (This model has basically remained the Chinese reality, but with more emphasis on the nation state: communism was a temporary mask for it.)

Only in the West did the humanist vision develop a robust concern for individual liberty – including the liberty to dissent from the dominant cultural creed. From this emerged the principle of secularism. This development – let us speak straight – makes the humanism of the West superior. Because of this, its desire for universal human flourishing is detached from the triumph of any particular cultural tradition. 'But surely the West wants everyone to be secular humanists, just as Islam wants everyone to be Muslims', you might say. The two desires are not comparable: the former entails the promotion of liberty; the latter does not.

It is secular humanism that is strange and different. Our creed certainly does *not* come naturally. Therefore, surely, it is something to be nurtured, kept in shape, celebrated. But we hardly know how to name this public creed, let alone celebrate it.

Am I suggesting that we should daily pat ourselves on the back for being so moral and civilized? Well done us for caring about the good of all humanity! In a sense, yes. I am indeed suggesting that there ought to be more reflection on the benign ideology that unites us, or at least provides our common denominator. As well as clashing over controversial policy details, we should affirm the basic principles that unite us. Look – we all affirm a vision of human flourishing; we want to see the rights of all people respected. Let's be proud of this public creed!

How naive this doubtless sounds. But maybe it is necessary to play the boy who comments on the emperor's clothes; only in this case, it is necessary to point out that the emperor is *not* naked. We have a public ideology, worthy of pride, but are too busy bickering over secondary aspects of it to see this.

What's going on? Is secular humanism, like the sun, too bright to look at directly? Is there something about this public ideology that makes it so resistant to affirmation? Something that makes one feel a soppy mug for wanting to cheer it? I have no simple explanation for this deep-seated evasion, only a complicated one. We have to look in detail at the whole story of our public ideology, its development over centuries, in order to understand what's going on here.

But a possible place to start, I think, is by probing the idea that secular humanism is the *natural* creed of civilized human beings, for this idea is central to our reluctance to reflect on our creed. Why is this idea so pervasive, despite being so easy to disprove? The merest acquaintance with history and current affairs tells us that most cultures do not subscribe to secular humanism in a serious way (though perhaps most do now pay it lip service to placate the West). So why do we persist in supposing it to be somehow normal?

Perhaps it is because secular humanism overlaps with something that *is* universal, or close to universal: natural humanity, compassion, benevolence. To feel compassion for one's fellow humans does seem to be a more or less universal impulse. We in the West should not claim to be especially compassionate or humane, we feel. We are right to feel this; we are right to see that we have no monopoly on morality. We need only peer into our own hearts to see that desire for the general good of humanity is a weaker force than selfishness. Alternatively we can look at the negative effects of certain Western policies in the world. Given these things, how dare we claim that the West has the moral high ground?

So we need to separate secular humanism from compassion, benevolence. This exists almost universally but is frail and fallible everywhere. Secular humanism is a crucially different thing. It is a tradition that structures benevolence. It says: 'Let us seek us the good of humanity in this organized, theoretical way – let us apply this rigorous principle.' It perceives that natural benevolence is too patchy and limited: we are apt to care far more for our own sort than for those who are distant and different. So it asserts a rule that all human lives are equally valuable and that people should be allowed to think and behave differently – even if this seems to threaten traditional social cohesion. This rule is somewhat against nature: we must force ourselves to learn, and keep learning, that all lives matter equally, that our habitual suspicion of otherness is deficient. Because it enshrines this principle, our tradition *is* special; it is a more authentic universalism. Other cultures simply lack this robust moral universalism that respects the rights of all, irrespective of race and religion.

But – again – we are hesitant about this. We fear that it is arrogant to claim moral superiority to non-Western people, unschooled in secular humanism. There is an element of admirable humility here, but also of evasion and conceptual muddle. We should dare to say that our creed is superior, although we ourselves are not – we are its fallible foot soldiers. It's a tricky balancing act, a slight paradox – our *creed* is morally superior, even though we individual people are as morally shaky and fallible as any in the world. (This surely echoes the logic of revealed religion: we serve a unique moral vision, but are sinners.)

Some might say: 'The West supposing itself superior is the root of so much global evil. Look at Iraq in 2003: the USA and others assumed the right to stride in and liberate a people from dictatorship, but only made things worse.' But there's another way of looking at this. The error that the invaders made was assuming that liberal democracy would naturally bubble up when Iraqis were freed from dictatorship. In reality, liberal democracy needs a particular ideological tradition in place. In this case, the West, or some of it, overlooked the uniqueness of secular humanism. A more 'arrogant' approach – which holds that liberal democracy is unlikely to flourish in a state without a tradition of secular humanism – might have resulted in more caution. In other words, there is also a sort of arrogance in denying that our tradition is unique – it leads to an assumption that our values are natural. This is incoherent, for it is evidently not natural for people to espouse human rights.

So there is a huge impulse to see secular humanism as just another manifestation of natural human benevolence, which comes naturally. And there is massive resistance to the alternative viewpoint, that it is a special tradition.

Why is it so unpalatable to us to admit that our public ideology is a tradition? I see two interconnected reasons. We remain, to a large extent, the children of the rational Enlightenment, who want to think we have risen free of anything so murky and suspect as a tradition. Traditions are particular, limiting – the autonomy of the rational individual is denied, for we are all dependent on our arbitrary membership of this particular historical story. We prefer to think that the truth is directly available to any individual who dares to criticize inherited habits and think clearly. We want to see our form of moral universalism as universally available – it sounds logical that universalism should be universal – but it is not. In reality, moral universalism has grown and spread through a few traditions (and only one of these traditions is robustly universalist, I suggest). Also, a tradition is a hard thing to think about. It means grappling with history, which is awesomely complicated and awesomely old. It means taking seriously the ideas of people who were very different from us, whom it is easier to write off. It means reckoning with the fact that our deepest values emerged in the misty dawn of civilization, amid embarrassingly crude mythological thinking. It would be neater to dismiss such thinking as an irrational irrelevance. But if our creed is a tradition, some very ancient and odd figures have a sort of authority, and the authority of secular rationalism wobbles disconcertingly.

I now want to demonstrate this in relation to the recent atheists. In their determination to present secular humanism as natural rather than a tradition, they tie themselves in logical knots.

Atheists

What was chiefly new about the 'new atheism' that arose following 9/11 was its stridency and its dogged refusal to reflect on its own basic assumptions. It seemed hardly even to notice its central assumption, the truth of secular humanism. This sort of atheism treats a certain moral agenda as natural, obvious: equality, justice, human rights and so on. It insists that religion is not just false but morally culpable because it tends to contravene these secular humanist principles.

Where do the atheists suppose these values come from? Of course, they hotly deny that such morality is rooted in religion: how can something good come from something bad? Where then? The dominant answer is that morality is just a natural human thing: the moral faculty is part of what it means to be human. Secular humanism is therefore seen simply as a fully up-to-date expression of *natural human morality*. To rational agents, it is clear enough how to be good enough.

There are two major problems with this. First, if morality were merely natural, it would be equally present in all human traditions everywhere, in all periods of history. There would perhaps be local variations, but there would surely be no long-standing cultural practices that could be called immoral. Also, it is hard to deny that human moral culture has almost always taken religious form – which makes it a bit absurd to present religion as a force for *immorality*. In other words, there is a contradiction between calling morality merely natural and claiming to represent a morally superior tradition that liberates us from the blockage of religion. The atheist wants it both ways: there is no special moral tradition, morality being natural; and yet the tradition that sees through religion has huge liberating power – in effect it's our salvation. If morality were just natural, as natural to humans as the possession of skin, or farting, there would be no such thing as moralistic discourse, or ethics (the theory of morality).

These incoherences are heightened – though superficially disguised – by the appeal that some of the most prominent atheists make to evolution. If evolution is the master key that explains the world to us, including the human world, then it must explain morality. In fact it very conspicuously fails to do so. Let's explore this in relation to the most famous Darwinian atheist.

Richard Dawkins made his name as an explainer of evolution, putting the emphasis on the gene as the agent of natural selection, or the survival of the fittest. As the title of his 1976 book *The Selfish Gene* suggests, he invested heavily in an anthropocentric metaphor, with a dark sci-fi aura: all individual creatures are the mere vehicles through which genes replicate themselves. Such a picture of the world would seem to reject traditional moral agency and affirm a form of determinism. But in fact Dawkins backed away from such a conclusion, and reaffirmed conventional humanist morality at the end of the book. We can and should defy our natures: 'we, alone on earth, can rebel against the tyranny of the selfish replicators'.[1] But how come we can? Why should we rebel? And, crucially, can this rebellion be understood in terms of evolution, or must we leave such science behind when it comes to morality and turn to other conceptual categories?

In his subsequent writing Dawkins did not squarely face this issue, to put it mildly. Instead he implied that evolution could in principle explain all of human life. He became an ever-stronger advocate of naturalism, the claim that there is nothing beyond the material world, all of which can in principle become scientifically intelligible. He therefore implied that evolutionary science is leading to a clearer understanding of morality. It has already shown us that altruism, as a facet of group loyalty, has an evolutionary function: the implication is that morality stems from this. But this contradicts what he admitted at the end of *The Selfish Gene*, that there is a tension between the dictates of natural selection and the moral imperative; that morality transcends, or is at odds with, the natural processes known to science. And he continued to restate this claim that evolution must be defied, that we humans have the unique power to choose *not* to be mere tools of natural selection.

In the introduction to a collection of essays in 2003, he explains that he advocates Darwinism as a scientist only: 'I am a passionate anti-Darwinian when it comes to politics and how we should conduct our human affairs.'[2] A contradiction? No, he insists:

> There is no inconsistency in favouring Darwinism as an academic scientist while opposing it as a human being . . . For good Darwinian reasons, evolution gave us a brain whose size increased to the point where it became capable of understanding its own provenance, of deploring the moral implications and of fighting against them.[3]

The first sentence is unobjectionable: one can affirm Darwinism as the key to biology but also insist that it is no guide to meaning and morality, which have other sources. But then, in the second sentence, he implies something else: that we have *evolved* to be able to see that defying natural selection is our moral duty. Soon he repeats the claim, telling us that evolution may not have made us the fastest or strongest creatures, but it has given humans the 'biggest gifts of all: the gift of understanding the ruthlessly cruel process that gave us all existence; the gift of revulsion against its implications'.[4] Here is a strong claim that the moral instinct is a product of evolution. To say that evolution has given us the ability to understand this 'cruel process' claims too much, for in reality evolution has no discernible role in our tendency to judge this process as cruel.

He wants to cling on to the notion of Darwinism as a total explanation, including of morality – even as he admits that Darwin's essential discovery, natural selection, merits moral censure. If this is not a contradiction I'm not sure what is. The claim is that Darwinism, by revealing nature's amoral workings (which if applied to human life are positively immoral), clarifies the whole issue of morality. By showing us what we naturally are, it crystallizes the need to be other. But in reality it sheds no light on why we should oppose the processes it reveals. To talk about this *why*, a totally different discourse is needed. But Dawkins very much wants there to be one master discourse. He wants to carry over the clarity he finds in Darwinism to the sphere of morality. This must be judged dishonest, despite his seeming sincerity. He fails to reflect with honesty on the difficult fact that morality must be discussed in terms other than natural science; he prefers to imply that it falls under the purview of science, as all things must.

Why does he not simply admit that morality is something that science, including Darwinism, can shed no real light on? Because he wants to express his strong dislike of religion. Its will to supply false explanations for things must be exorcised by a bold account of science as the explainer of everything. The notion of a realm beyond the reach of science must be denied. Of course, he admits that science cannot yet explain everything, but he insists there is no valid discourse that limits science's explanatory power: 'Optimists among scientists, of whom I am one, will insist that "That which we don't understand" means only "That which we don't yet understand".'[5] He denies the otherness of morality from natural science, sensing – rightly in fact – that this otherness strengthens the case for religion.

Incidentally, Dawkins's muddle about evolution and morality partly echoes his hero. Darwin started his investigations with a vague sense that God oversees evolution, with the emergence of humanity in mind. This idea lingers in the conclusion of *The Origin of Species*: the violence of natural selection is justified by the fact that 'the most exalted object which we are capable of conceiving, namely, the production of the higher animals, directly follows. There is grandeur in this view of life.'[6] By this time his belief in God had faded away, but as one commentator says:

> what he seems never to have abandoned is the ascription to natural selection itself of those properties of discrimination, power, and moral concern previously conferred on it by divine agency. These properties allowed the law of natural selection to lead to the end Darwin foresaw as the goal of the evolutionary process . . . namely, the natural creation of man as a moral creature.[7]

In theory Dawkins rejects the idea that evolution is teleological in Darwin's sense, that there is a hierarchy of life, with us at the top. In an early essay he criticized 'human speciesist vanity', even claiming that 'a chimp/human hybridization would provide exactly the come-uppance that "human dignity" needs'.[8] Later he called the notion of hierarchy in nature an 'unquestioned Victorian presumption' of Darwin's.[9] But in practice he awkwardly retains a deeply teleological view of evolution; as we have seen, he presents human morality as the culmination of evolution. He retains a form of Victorian providentialism to which he cannot admit. Indeed, he echoes Darwin's notion that natural selection is redeemed by the emergence of human morality. This is a muddled notion because it implies that morality emerges from this natural process, even though this is a logical contradiction.

We have strayed a bit from the issue of new atheism's relationship to secular humanism, but this detour into evolution is necessary if we are to understand where Dawkins is coming from. In his 2006 book *The God Delusion* he doesn't just charge religion with peddling untruths: he fuses this charge with another, that religion is immoral. This ought to involve discussion of what morality is but he sees no need for careful reflection on where his secular moral assumptions come from; he just gets straight on with portraying religion as scientifically false and therefore morally harmful. The pervasive implication is that morality just comes naturally. Significantly, he does not even acknowledge the conundrum we have just discussed, of amoral natural selection somehow producing morality. Instead he vaguely implies that science is beginning to sort the matter out; it has established that humans have evolved to be altruistic in certain ways, and is working on a fuller explanation. He is gesturing with his scientific expertise in a dishonest way rather than honestly reflecting on what it can and can't tell us.

His basic claim, which he does not even deign to state explicitly, is that morality is natural; it is a constant thing, stable throughout history – or would be if religion stopped perverting it. But then he explains that different ages have different ideas of morality, and says that in recent times there has happily been a major advance in our moral conventions. He explains that, whether they're religious or not, people nowadays tend to agree on the basics of morality. 'With notable exceptions such as the Afghan Taliban and the American Christian equivalent, most people pay lip service to the same broad liberal consensus of ethical principles.'[10] Most people in the world? Of course, he is really talking about the West; elsewhere there is less consensus. He speaks as if Western liberal values are universal, a matter of common sense rather than a complex tradition. He says that recent developments have strengthened this ethical consensus, especially the triumph of the idea of equality: these developments 'certainly have not come from religion', he snaps.[11] They have come through various factors, he says, such as inspiring leadership, for example that of Martin Luther King (whose Christianity is totally irrelevant, of course), and through better education leading to 'increased understanding that each of us shares a common humanity with members of other races and with the other sex – both deeply unbiblical ideas that come from biological science, especially evolution'.[12] But biological science, especially evolution, can be used to authorize eugenics and racism. The real issue is the triumph of secular humanism. Instead of asking what this tradition is, and where it comes from, he treats it as axiomatic. This is just the natural human morality, he wants us to think, and in our times we are fortunate to see a particularly full expression of it.

Let us briefly consider another 'new atheist', the late Christopher Hitchens. His 2007 polemic *God is Not Great* is more interested in the sound of its own digressive wit than in trying to state a clear position, but he actually has a lot in common with Dawkins. He too rushes straight in, full of urgent indignation, without pausing to reflect on his moral assumptions. These atheists seem to sense that such reflection might detract from the obviousness of atheism's intrinsic morality.

He admits that there seem to have been morally exemplary believers, but this is a sort of optical illusion: they are really serving secular moral ideals. So Dietrich Bonhoeffer did not resist Hitler from Christian conviction, but because his Christian faith 'mutated into an admirable but nebulous humanism' (this is untrue).[13] And Martin Luther King used religious imagery as mere metaphorical packaging for moral teaching: the Exodus story was just the myth that his audience knew; a Greek myth would have done as well, if similarly well-known.[14] Because King rejected the violent retribution that is – according to Hitchens – basic to Christianity, he was not a Christian in a 'real as opposed to nominal sense'.[15] What is one to say to this? It's just too jaw-droppingly juvenile for a serious response. Similarly he says that the charitable image of believers is irrelevant: 'charity and relief work, while they may appeal to tenderhearted believers, are the inheritors of modernism and the Enlightenment'.[16] In reality, religious believers launched most traditions of humanitarianism and welfare.

At one point he explains that the true basis of morality is the Golden Rule, which 'simply enjoins us to treat others as one would wish to be treated by them'.

> This sober and rational precept, which one can teach to any child with
> its innate sense of fairness (and which predates all Jesus's 'beatitudes'
> and parables), is well within the compass of any atheist and does not

require masochism and hysteria, or sadism and hysteria, when it is breached. It is gradually learned, as part of the painfully slow evolution of the species, and once grasped is never forgotten. Ordinary conscience will do, without any heavenly wrath behind it.[17]

He seems to be saying that morality comes naturally, to all human cultures, religious or not; it is axiomatic, obvious. But this doesn't really square with the claim that religion is 'positively immoral' due to its propagation of false myths and inhumane doctrines.[18] For almost all human cultures have been religious. Is the Golden Rule blotted out by their error? Here again is the atheist muddle about morality and tradition: on the one hand, it is claimed that morality is a natural human instinct and that there is no special moral cause or tradition; on the other, if religion's power to subvert morality is so great, then there is surely intense moral heroism in the tradition that attacks and exposes religion – atheism must be the true saving cause. But the latter narrative is groundless: modern history does not show humanist morality to be based in atheism. As we shall see, most pioneers of humanism advocated some sort of reformist religion, or deism; and atheism has a dramatically patchy relationship with humanism.

Finally let's look at A. C. Grayling. His 2013 book *The God Argument: The Case Against Religion and for Humanism* asserts a very strong link between atheism and humanism. He spells it out in his introduction:

> In my view, the argument against religion is an argument for the libera-tion of the human mind, and the possibility of at last formulating an ethical outlook that all mankind can share, thus providing a basis for a much more integrated and peaceful world.[19]

So humanism is the true moral universalism, and religion blocks it. As he puts it later, with the withering of religion, 'an ethical outlook which can serve everyone everywhere, and can bring the world together into a single moral community, will at last be possible'.[20]

But where does this benign universalism come from? Like his fellow atheists, he wants to suggest that this ideal is *natural*, that it arises from common sense. It bubbles up wherever there is unprejudiced thought about how humans should live. Humanism is 'the concern to make the best of human life . . . in the real world, and in sensible accord with the facts of humanity as these are shaped and constrained by the world'.[21] It is 'an attitude to ethics based on observation and the responsible use of reason'.[22] It derives from 'the tradition of ethical debate in philosophy' that was born in ancient Greece.[23] In the Middle Ages it was subordinated to Christian theology, then in the Renaissance it was 'rescued' from this subordination. The rescue was gradual: adherents of 'religious humanism', such as Erasmus, spread the light, yet also 'adher[ed] to the conventions of church faith'. Gradually, partly due to the influence of Cicero's noble freethinking, links with religion were broken, and 'secular humanism in the form we know it now was given its first full expression in the eighteenth-century Enlightenment'.[24]

He wants to persuade us that humanism is a coherent entity, from ancient times to today, and that it has an anti-religious logic. But the story doesn't stand up. The central ancient philosopher Plato was neither anti-religious nor a teacher of universal morality. All of Greek thought lacked universalist idealism, but was fatalist, tragic, severely hierarchical, slave-bound. It is only Christian and post-Christian humanism that is dominated by an optimistic universalism. Instead of admitting this, Grayling claims that ancient and modern 'humanism' is a coherent entity, clearly superior to religious morality. As he puts it, Judeo-Christian morality does not compare 'to the richness and insight of "pagan" Greek ethics, or to present-day concerns about human rights and animal rights, which are much broader, more inclusive, and more sensitive than anything envisaged in religious morality'.[25] In relation to Greek ethics this is highly doubtful – the Bible has a passion for social justice that pagan thought lacks. In relation to modern humanism, it is a meaningless comparison, due to the depth of modern humanism's roots in Christianity. It is impossible to compare Judeo-Christian morality with 'present day concerns about . . . rights', because they are not neatly separate things.

He claims that atheistic humanism is naturally universalist. It involves 'no taboos, no food and dress codes, no restrictive sexual morality other than what is implicit in the demand to treat others with respect'.[26] It considers the basic humanity of all people before whatever 'identities might overlay their humanity – the political, ethnic, religious, cultural, gender identities that so often trump the possibility of a straightforward human-to-human friendship that would cross all boundaries'.[27] In reality this sort of universalism was gradually spread by Christianity, with its rejection of old categories such as 'Jew or Greek' and in its severance of God from a particular moral code, and was then developed in a stronger form by Protestant reformism and its deist offshoot. It is easier to ignore this complicated story and claim that these principles come naturally to humanism, ancient and modern.

Grayling's core claim is that 'humanism' names an ancient tradition of rational thought, sceptical of religion, that has a vision of progressive human brotherhood and unity. There is no such tradition. Putting aside religious dogma and 'thinking clearly' does not lead people to see the truth of secular humanism. The ideal of equality cannot be rationally deduced.

The new atheism is of course a form of secular humanism – a form that seeks to define secular humanism in anti-religious terms. Let's be blunt: this entails telling a false story about modernity. It says that humanism is essentially anti-religious, when in reality it emerged within religion, indeed in religious form.

One can only really grasp the thinness of the new atheists if one is acquainted with the thought of an older atheist, Friedrich Nietzsche. His great insight was that to reject Christianity and remain a secular humanist is muddled, half-baked. For humanism is rooted in Christian morality – all ideas of equality, progress and social justice are derived from the Judeo-Christian myth. He attempted, with a sort of mad courage, to be a fully consistent atheist, one who rejected the whole moral tradition attaching to the Christian God. And he understood that there cannot be neutrality in the realm of values: to reject Christian morality is to embrace the older moral, or amoral, order – of pagan 'natural strength', militarism, power worship. As John F. Haught says, the new atheists have no sense of this dark tradition:

> The new soft-core atheists assume that, by dint of Darwinism, we can just drop God like Santa Claus without having to witness the complete collapse of Western culture – including our sense of what is rational and moral. At least the hard-core atheists [he includes Camus and Sartre along with Nietzsche] understood that if we are truly sincere in our atheism the whole web of meanings and values that had clustered around the idea of God in Western culture had to go down the drain along with its organizing center.[28]

Agnostics

Because it has something so strong and simple to say, atheism gets disproportionate attention. What does the less strident, more mainstream post-Christian non-believer, or agnostic, believe? Well, I have not asked them all, but here is my reading of the matter. Of course, he agrees with the atheist that religious belief and practice are not necessary to morality. But does he quietly think that secular humanism is morally superior to religion? Does he harbour this atheist assumption in muted form? Not exactly. Unlike the atheist, he acknowledges that Western moral tradition is deeply shaped by Christianity, which makes it dubious to disparage religion on moral grounds. This sounds like a huge admission, one that puts the autonomy of secular morality in question. But it is balanced by his assumption that secular humanism is an *advance* on religion. It inherits its basic moral framework from the Christian myth and improves on it, purifies it, liberates it from the obsolescence of supernatural belief; it discovers in this mixed bag of good myth and stale error something of truly sacred worth: universal moral values, detachable from their religious source. The average non-believer might not consciously think all this stuff, but I suggest that he nevertheless inhabits this story to a greater or lesser extent. Whether he knows it or not, he is heir to the deists, to Kant and to post-Christian humanists such as George Eliot.

So mainstream secular humanism is post-Christian rather than anti-Christian; it (vaguely) acknowledges its basis in this religion and (vaguely) sees itself as advancing or updating its morality.

Some might say that this tradition is no longer as mainstream as it was, that it has been in decline for some decades. There is some truth in this: a generation or two ago there was a coherent-seeming thing called Christian-based Western values – the sort of thing Winston Churchill lauded in his speeches. In the late twentieth century, the Christian basis of secular humanism was affirmed by various cultural traditions; for example, the British Labour Party often presented itself as largely Christian-rooted. This whole narrative has weakened a bit with rising secularization, and maybe lost its axiomatic aura. But it's still there; it hasn't really been ousted as the dominant view. Certainly, the creed of the new atheists has not ousted it. And in recent years some agnostic writers, prompted by the crassness of the new atheists, have acutely reflected on the persistence of the traditional view. Here are a couple of examples.

In his 2008 book about his fear of death, *Nothing To Be Frightened Of*, the novelist Julian Barnes describes himself as a non-believer who has a vague sense of cultural nostalgia for the Christian God – despite never having believed. 'Christian morality still loosely governs Britain, though congregations dwindle and church buildings make their inexorable transition to historic monuments . . . That sway extends to me too: my sense of morality is influenced by Christian teaching.'[29] And then he expresses a particularly interesting thought:

> My agnostic and atheistic friends are indistinguishable from my profess-edly religious ones in honesty, generosity, integrity and fidelity – or their opposites. Is this a victory for them, I wonder, or for us? When we are young, we think we are inventing the world as we are inventing ourselves; later, we discover how much the past holds us, and always did.[30]

The non-believers of his circle – and he himself – seem to have proved the detachability of morality from religion. But what morality? A morality largely defined by religious tradition: 'We live broadly according to the tenets of a religion we no longer believe in.'[31] Then, perhaps slightly wanting to row back from this, he raises the possibility that religious morality is just an example of the altruism that seems to come natu-rally to humans, that evolution has bred into us: 'individuals living in societies generally act in much the same way.'[32] But he can't shake the feeling that religion frames or enshrines morality in a stronger, more basic way than its secular replacement. So he conforms to the traditional secular humanist attitude, which is respectful of religion as the seeming prime source of morality, and yet resolved to express this morality in a more sophisticated, flexible, rational way.

A very different agnostic response to the new atheists is the Marxist (or Marx-ish) literary critic Terry Eagleton. Partly drawing on the thesis of the philosopher Charles Taylor (to which we'll return more directly), he explains that liberalism did not emerge in opposition to religion but was shaped by religion, as was science: 'It is not as though an eternal, universal rationality, having patiently bided its time through long centuries of darkness, was able finally to fight its way through the rubbish dump of religious credulity under which it had been buried.'[33] Instead, universal rationality gradually emerged within the Christian thought-world. This was largely due to the Protestant passion for criticizing religious tradition: 'the Enlightenment was deeply shaped by values which stemmed from the Christian tradition'. It opposed aspects of religion, yet:

> in a choice irony, it inherited its brave campaign against superstition partly from Christianity itself, with its rejection of all false gods and prophets, all idols, fetishes, magical rituals, and powers of darkness, in the name of human flesh and blood.[34]

He responds with disdain to Hitchens's claim that 'our [atheist humanist] principles are not a faith'. Are we really to think that such humanism involves 'no trust in men and women's rationality and desire for freedom, no conviction of the evils of tyranny and oppression, no passionate faith that men and women are at their best when not labouring under myth and superstition'?[35] To claim that one's own values are just neutral normality is a failure to understand what values are: 'The liberal principles of freedom and tolerance are dogmas, and are none the worse for that.'[36] In its belief that we must 'shake off a poisonous legacy of myth and superstition', liberal humanism is itself a myth.[37] To espouse any sort of values in any serious way is to have some form of faith, rooted in some form of mythology – and for us Westerners it will probably have a strong basis in Christianity. Eagleton accepts that his own socialism is a faith-based position, one that derives from Judeo-Christian tradition.

The new atheists have unwittingly drawn attention to secular humanism, reminded some of us of its profound importance as a concept. By stridently refusing to reflect on this tradition, and treating humanism as somehow normal, they have helped us to see the scale of the evasion that is ordinarily practised. Agnostics also evade the issue when they vaguely accept secular humanism's debt to Christianity yet inquire no further. There is a cultural convention that says that this debt is not worth exploring – for how can our self-understanding be enhanced by dwelling on the divisive and discredited business of religion?

An excessive claim?

My argument is based in the claim that secular humanist morality is strongly rooted in Christianity. I admit that this claim looks excessive. For no human society is without moral values. The very word 'society' derives from the Latin *socius*, friend or ally. In a sense society presupposes the Golden Rule; it consists of people one sees as like oneself, worthy of the respect that one feels entitled to – though of course this principle might coexist with class and gender inequalities. (Trying to establish whether this basic social morality is a version of evolved altruism, as found in ant colonies, seems pretty fruitless.) When someone helps a stranger in the street, this can be ascribed to normal, natural human behaviour.

'Well that's all that secular humanist morality is', the humanist might say: 'It is a return to this understanding of morality as normal, natural, rather than related to divine obedience or enshrined in some incredible ancient myth.'

But to argue this is disingenuous. For secular humanist morality has a universalist energy that is abnormal. It has an abnormal impatience with a morality that is limited to the tribe; and an abnormal impatience with a morality that is framed in terms of religious tradition, which limits it in another way. It demands moral values that are universally valid rather than ones confined to a particular tradition. And it has a deep sense that such values ought to spread and triumph. The culture 10,000 miles away that treats women as inferior ought to change, it ought to learn our universal values. This passionate desire to see the triumph of universal values is something different from the normal human impulse to treat those around one well – though of course it coexists with it. At root there is in secular humanist morality an absoluteness, or in plainer language a *perfectionism*, that it cannot squarely reflect on. There is a – half-buried – impulse to assert *total* justice against all traditions that dull and block it. It is difficult for those who reject religion to admit this; they prefer to imagine they are simply speaking up for 'natural morality'. They are not: they are muddled inheritors of the Christian universalist vision.

2

Sowing the seeds

I have said, against the atheists, that secular humanism is a tradition. It is not just the natural human morality. But it is reluctant to think of itself as a tradition, as an ideal with a particular story, with old and complicated roots. It prefers to see itself as modern and as clearly distinct from what is pre-modern. Well, it is modern, but that doesn't mean it doesn't have ancient roots. We must now look at these roots: we must first consider how a universal moral vision emerges in the Hebrew Bible and is developed in the New Testament. We must also cast a glance at other ancient religious traditions to determine whether this tradition is really so important.

You might ask, 'What does biblical monotheism have to do with *secular* humanism?' Of course, this tradition was not secular: its key authors did not for a second imagine severing morality from God. But on the other hand there is an unwitting step towards secularism in the passionate insistence that human justice is the supreme expression of the divine, beside which other expressions are dubious.

From around 700 BC, Israel began arranging its story, retelling its myths, writing law codes. This rewriting preserved a lot of primitive stuff, including foundation myths adapted from other traditions, and it gave central place to moral and cultic laws, attributed to God. Other ancient peoples ascribed moral commandments to the gods, or some-times to one supreme god, but something induced the Jews to do so with a new intensity and new sense of narrative drama. Israel's desire to tell the story of its morally ambitious national god gave rise to a new conception of history as meaningful.

In the early part of the narrative, God's idea of morality seems rather cavalier. Are we to trust his judgement that Noah and family are the only righteous people on earth, that everyone else merits wipe-out? When he makes a similar judgement in Abraham's hearing, concerning the cities Sodom and Gomorrah, Abraham nudges him to rethink, to look harder for signs of righteousness that would justify saving the cities from destruction. Here it seems that morality, or at least mercy, comes more naturally to humans than to God. Maybe it's something that's worked out by God and people together. But the great moral vision is presented as coming from God: he promises to bless Abraham's descendants and through them all of humanity. And in the book of Exodus he takes the entire initiative, directing the liberation from slavery, then giving his people a new identity: they are to embody the justice of which they were deprived in Egypt. They are to obey him through obeying his commandments. This law was not clearly morally superior to the law codes of other ancient peoples (for example it did not abolish slavery), but it differed in being so closely associated with a particular god and in having such a central role in national identity. The retelling of the conquest of the Promised Land preserves stories of God commanding violence, even genocide. To some modern minds, such holy violence utterly discredits the Bible's moral vision: God seems like a mafia boss or dictator who claims to defend the widow and the orphan but only cares about power. But this overlooks the fact that in the Hebrew Bible there is a movement towards a more consistently moral idea of God.

The key agents of this movement were the prophets. Prophets were originally a special caste or sect of ecstatic religious performers, shaman figures; from this tradition emerged spokesmen for a morally reformist idea of God. They presented God as yearning for Israel to be a beacon of practical justice and as unimpressed by the cultic side of religion.

In Isaiah's mediation of God's voice, the central message is quickly delivered: sacrifices and special festivals are hateful while the worshippers neglect justice: 'Stop bringing meaningless offerings! Your incense is detestable to me . . . Learn to do right; seek justice. Defend the oppressed.'[1] Isaiah was prophesying in the southern Israelite kingdom, Judah, while it was under intense threat from both the Assyrians and the Egyptians. The threat of extinction led him to articulate a defiant faith: God will make Jerusalem the hub of a new peaceful world, with all nations obeying his law. It's a vision of invading cultures being ultimately overcome by Israel's cultural influence, its 'soft power'. In this vision practical political hope merges with supernatural imagery: not only will there be peace, but even natural violence will end (the lion will eat straw, the wolf will befriend the lamb); death will be destroyed and all tears will be wiped away.

The crisis passed, but a generation later it returned, with Babylon now threatening to conquer. Jeremiah called Israel to look beyond current affairs and have faith in its ultimate destiny, modelling divine justice. This meant a new rejection of pagan religion, a new sense of the nation's 'marriage' to God. Through such obedience Israel will enable a new world order in which God's moral law will triumph, Jeremiah said; God will transform all humanity and a new era of peace will dawn, beginning in Israel and spilling out to the world beyond. This is simultaneously a fantasy of national triumph and a vision of world peace. Through a fully obedient Israel, the whole world will be made new. This time the disaster happened: Babylon conquered Israel and forced a large proportion of the population into exile. But this tradition of prophecy continued, with the announcement that God's plan still stood and that the new conqueror on the scene, Cyrus of Persia, was God's tool: his empire would prepare the ground for God's true and final empire of moral obedience and peace.

Paradoxically, Israel's weakness and defeat led to a new conception of her god's strength. It seemed to the prophets that he must be using these other powers to create a new order, in which his moral law would triumph. Never had any god been credited with such international scope. In its weakness, then, Israel learned to see its tribal god as *the* God, of all the nations. Monotheism in the full sense was born: the idea of one God whose moral law was binding on all humanity. Of course, the chief focus remained on peace and social justice in Israel – a land in which none will be poor but everyone will sit under his own vine and fig-tree – but the possibility was also raised of peace without borders. For the first time, universal human harmony was seriously imagined and yearned for.

Were the Jews unique in associating the divine with a universal moral vision? Yes and no: the concept of universal compassion existed elsewhere but it tended to coexist with conservative pragmatism, and lacked revolutionary energy.

At a broadly similar time to the Jewish prophets (the 'Axial Age'), other civilizations were also reforming religion in the direction of practical morality. Confucius was reordering Chinese religion in a practical moral direction: he was seemingly the first to articulate the principle known as the Golden Rule, that people should treat others as they would like to be treated. But this coexisted with a conservative, hierarchical world view. Indeed, he taught that compassion (*ren*) is subordinate to ritualized social order (*li*). Without a stable social world, in which different ranks are properly demarcated, the exercise of compassion is impossible, for all is chaos. Harmony depends on knowing who is in charge of whom. 'Let a ruler be a ruler, a subject a subject, a father a father, a son a son.'[2] And he also set out more detailed distinctions in relationships, such as older friend and younger friend. The unifying principle was of dominance and submission, yin and yang. *Li* also referred to the ritual tradition of sacrifice to ancestor spirits, overseen by the ruling class. In its fusion of ritual and moral law and its infusion of every aspect of life with sacred significance, it resembled the Jewish law.

A century later, about 400 BC, the reformer Mo Tzu put more emphasis on universal compassion, asserting the Golden Rule with greater radicalism, implying that it should challenge traditional structures. But his teaching didn't widely catch on (and he too taught the necessity of an authoritarian state keeping order).

This dynamic of a reform movement challenging a hierarchical religious tradition also occurred in India. The huge baggy tradition that has fairly recently been summed up as Hinduism emphasized moral duty (*dharma*) within a ritualized social order, with rigid class distinctions. It also emphasized the individual quest for enlightenment (*moksha*), meaning the penetration of illusion (*maya*). This theme was placed centre stage by a reform movement, Buddhism. It emphasized compassion and had a reformist agenda against traditions that obscured this principle. All the inherited stories of the gods were recast as metaphorical illustrations of this central adventure of the soul. It's an escape story: the aim is to escape from the bonds of fleshy desire, a bondage identified with ignorance. There is a sort of universalism here: anyone can seek this spiritual freedom; the traditions that restrict enlightenment to a priestly caste are implicitly rejected (though a direct, polemical confrontation with such traditions is largely avoided). But there is no substantial idea of *corporate* human flourishing, of hope for universal justice; the focus is on the individual's achievement of enlightenment through serene escape from worldly pain (*Nirvana*). This obviously lacks the Jewish sense of historical and cosmic transformation, a totally new era of justice, the restoration of creation. Also, there is strikingly little hope: almost everyone is condemned to a grim cycle of rebirth into a new form of suffering.

What about Greece? Despite its precocious rationalism, Greece was actually slower than these other civilizations to put the morality of the Golden Rule in the foreground. The Homeric ethic of military heroism kept it at bay. Gradually though, philosophers began to focus on the question of how to live, what sort of character (*ethos*) to nurture – the root of 'ethics'.

Socrates, as presented in the writings of Plato, associated morality with a purist pursuit of rational truth. He opposed the self-serving pragmatism of the Sophists, for whom concepts such as justice were malleable, mere human constructions. Rather, he said, they are fixed objective realities, independent of our will. He associated his rational morality with the divine and challenged religious and moral traditions to some extent (enough to get condemned to death, in fact). But he had no decisively new conception of religion; generally he seems to have affirmed cultic tradition and the centrality of the city state, the polis. And Plato's thought was firmly bound by the polis; he had no clear idea of universal humanity, nor did he express divine morality in social, historical terms, as the demand for a new order of justice. His imagined ideal state is a place of chilly efficiency and Nietzschean power worship. Order is everything; it depends on the rule of an elite, authorized to tell 'noble lies' to maintain social harmony. Instead of rejecting old-fashioned religion, with its myths and cults, Plato thought it could be reinterpreted, demythologized, nudged in a rationalist direction, made into metaphorical support – very like Buddhism's attitude to its mythological inheritance.

Aristotle developed a smooth version of this vision; a rational account of how the individual's pursuit of fulfilment or flourishing squares with the health of the polis – again, there is no vision of fundamental moral transformation, of a new era of justice. He put huge emphasis on the concept of nature, which meant idealizing the existing order of things. To be 'good' is to be what you are meant to be, which is a good citizen, which of course meant affirming the social structure, including slavery. Humans can't step outside of their political context: only a god or a beast has no need of a city, he said.

In a sense this idealization of the polis was progress, for in previous centuries one's loyalty belonged to smaller tribal units and above all to the family, which was the central religious institution. The city was the joining together of many family-cults, the forging of a new common allegiance. It provided the stability in which various 'civilized' habits took root.

After Aristotle, Greek rationalism took on a religious aura in the form of Stoicism. It developed Plato's assumption of the superiority of spiritual rationality to bodily life and put great emphasis on social duty. It resembled Buddhism in its rejection of passionate emotion of any sort and in its cool awareness that all material things pass away. In the Roman era it was the dominant philosophy among the ruling class and it developed universalist and humanist aspects: 'reason' was seen as the essential human faculty that all might cultivate, in theory (in practice it was the male citizen, with a share in governing the polis, who expressed this universal faculty to the full). Understanding this, the rational man is a 'citizen of the world', in Epictetus' phrase. The Stoic thinker Hierocles envisaged a series of concentric circles, beginning with oneself and one's family and radiating out to humanity: one should seek to widen the sphere of one's concern. But this sort of universalism is compatible with conservatism: one's primary duty is to one's city, the rest is rather abstract. (You could say that Christianity smashes up this nest of circles, to give the outermost band, universal humanism, new force.) Similarly, Roman intellectuals idealized 'liberty' but they did not quite mean that all people should become free; rather they meant that the citizen, who participated in politics and so defended the liberty of the republic, was the best sort of person.

The most famous Stoic is the emperor Marcus Aurelius; his *Meditations* have found many modern fans. At one point he ponders the idea that, if reason is common to all humans, then humanity is one big family or one big 'city': it is our 'common government'.[3] This sounds admirably humanist, but in fact this noble-sounding notion coexists with the assumption that only superior people are capable of living rationally and that 'the inferior exist for the sake of the better'.[4] Very often he tells himself that moral action is rational and natural – it is as natural to us as greenness is to an emerald.[5] But of course this is protesting too much: in reality it is surely more natural to pursue sensual pleasure, as he seems to admit elsewhere. So his narrative feels rather brittle: there is an elite capable of self-mastery; this elite sees that all humanity is one family. This is not a message of universal humanism in the modern sense, which entails a passionate desire – the Stoics rejected desire – for justice for all.

So classical morality and classical rationality were both utterly defined by the enlarged tribal entity, the polis. To Plato and Aristotle, an egalitarian universalism was literally unthinkable since it would threaten the order of the polis. Roman Stoics glimpsed its possibility because the rational faculty was seen as theoretically present in all, but it was an impossible possibility as only male citizens could fully develop and exercise this faculty.

Back to the Jews: Jesus of Nazareth was obviously in the tradition of the prophets – he suggested that their new era of total justice was already underway. He announced 'the kingdom of God' – a sort of utopian revolution. His teaching primarily addressed Israel but there are strong hints of universalism: the parable of the Good Samaritan suggests that all fellow humans are to be treated equally, that looking after one's tribe or caste is not enough. And like earlier prophets, he clearly put practical morality above cultic practice. This is perhaps most clearly expressed in the parable of the sheep and the goats. God seems indifferent to religious observance, even to belief: it is those who feed the hungry and clothe the naked who win divine approval, and some of them seem not to have intentionally been serving God at all. To the modern reader this seems to raise the question of whether, if charity rather than piety is God's will, we can do his will just by serving our fellow humans and do without the religious trappings. But of course this question was unimaginable at the time: God is assumed to be the framework for moral action. Indeed, according to the Gospel writers, Jesus' ministry has intensely unsecular features: exorcism, miracles, expectation of an imminent apocalypse and, in the case of the Fourth Gospel, unworldly metaphysics. The historical Jesus remains obscure in some ways, but it's clear enough that he was no secular humanist before his time. He has little grasp of utilitarianism – for example, he scorns the idea that the expensive perfume used to anoint his feet is a waste of money that could be spent on the poor (an idea ascribed to Judas). So although Jesus is in the tradition of envisaging practical peace and justice, he does so with an apocalyptic absoluteness that disrupts the tradition of practical moral rules. In Judaism, all must conform to certain standards if justice is to flourish; God's will must be expressed in actual laws. Jesus seems to affirm the goal to which these laws point, but to suggest that excessive focus on the laws can obscure that goal. We must serve justice with a new flexibility and absoluteness, and treat all rules as secondary. Of course, this means offending moral convention: for example, Jesus' teaching often rejects normal familial loyalty. This directly defies the sort of morality taught by Confucius (and others), which makes the Golden Rule of universal compassion subordinate to respect for the family and other hierarchies. True morality is potentially disruptive of all authorized social orders, Jesus says.

So Jesus uniquely associates the divine with an absolutist moral vision, disruptive of all moral systems. Instead of teaching a set of practical moral rules as the means to realizing this vision, he suggests that all rules and traditions are inadequate to it. But before we start thinking of him as a radical humanist, we must remember that he framed this in fully mythological terms, talking of battling Satan, awaiting God's rule and so on.

Jesus has often been seen as a teacher and exemplar of morality, Paul as the dubious genius who constructed a theological system around his life and death. This won't do: Jesus launched the theological themes that Paul sought to tie up. Paul's thinking was obviously formed by the earliest Christian community, which was formed by its direct experience of Jesus. And yet there is a difference of emphasis in Paul's writing: a new sense that humans are unable to do God's will, except by the miracle of grace.

In his letters, Paul insists that all human beings are called to a new sort of life, which participates in the risen Christ and in the coming cosmic consummation. This new life is marked by a moral perfectionism – meaning what? Paul understands morality as that which the Jewish law seeks to express but also fails to express. But he doesn't set out new and better rules for Christians to follow. The emphasis is on a new state of freedom: Christians are beyond rules. This is a mark of the universalism of the new creed – the old cultural barriers that separated the godly from the rest are declared dead. As has often been said, including by some modish thinkers in recent years, Paul invents the radically free individual who is not defined by his inherited moral culture. All humans are equally capable of responding to the good news, serving God – this is the root of the idea that they are equal.

Incidentally, Paul in a sense makes Jesus' teaching more coherent – or more humanly accessible. For he confronts the fact that the new moral perfectionism is impossible for us – Christians remain sinners. But it is miraculously made possible by God. Christianity is not a new moral system but a new language of morality as the miraculous action of God in us (there will be more on this in the final chapter).

So the Bible's ethical universalism puts certain ideas on the table that will feed into secular humanism. It associates God's will with social justice and criticizes cultic tradition that neglects this. But of course this ideal can't be separated from the narrative of God's agency and authority. One aspect of this is that the vision of divine justice is assumed to be difficult, costly, tied to sacrificial suffering. Justice is not an abstract principle, as secular humanism would have it (and Plato too); rather it is part of a story of gift, risk, costly commitment. This is basic to the prophets' message: Israel *suffers* this vision, and the individual prophet embodies this suffering (as well as risking physical persecution, one could say that the vision gives him psychological issues, judging from the dramatically eccentric behaviour of Jeremiah and others). Christianity generalizes this: every believer must share in this logic of sacrificial suffering to some degree, take up his or her cross.

'What gloomy mysterious nonsense!' says the non-believer: if human flourishing is the highest good, there is no place for this pathos of holy suffering; it will cause all sorts of neurotic problems and cast doubt on the goodness of ordinary human life, implying that we are sinfully complacent if we don't somehow suffer for the truth. So this is a crucial paradox relating to the relationship between God and the good: God wills human well-being, but this is not the whole story; this vision does not function in a blank abstract way, in a way amenable to human reason. Instead there is a sort of sub-plot: the religious vision of universal well-being is maintained, or energized, by costly commitment to it. This sub-plot has a stubborn air of mystery: we cannot map it out, know how it works.

So at the heart of Christianity is a dynamic, energetic universalism. A new order is arriving in which old divisions are swept aside, in which the equal sacredness of every single human soul is asserted. As Larry Siedentop puts it:

> By emphasizing the moral equality of humans, quite apart form any social roles they might occupy, Christianity changed 'the name of the game'. Social rules became secondary. They followed, and in a crucial sense, had to be understood as subordinate to a God-given identity, something all humans share equally.[6]

The Jewish ideal of universal justice is refreshed through this new iconoclasm against traditional cultic practices. And, crucially, this new order is distinct from a political order that can be created through violence, due to the centrality of the suffering of its saviour and the idea that it is God who brings his own kingdom. In order to spread within the ancient world, did this radical new moral vision have to be 'compromised' – especially its non-violence? Yes and no: at the core of this religion is material that can't really be compromised. Salvation comes through a man who rejected worldly power, wealth, security, and died as an outcast. On one level this message is compromised if it is taught by a fat rich bishop who does the emperor's bidding. But on another level it is not, for the core Christian images, icons, texts are still there, and will do their work, permeate their culture, in spite of the institutional compromise. (It is worth noting that this religion of moral perfectionism is always being compromised in some way.)

We must now start grappling with the word 'secular', which is obviously an important part of secular humanism. It only very gradually – and confusingly – comes to mean 'non-religious'. It comes from the Latin *saeculum*, meaning 'the present age'; it gradually slipped into meaning 'the temporal realm' or the worldly political realm, as opposed to the spiritual realm, the realm of the Church. Christianity gave rise to this distinction between worldly and religious realms. The distinction is not total: the realms overlap because the Church needs political protection, and politics can have religious authorization. And yet this distinction ran very deep in the early Christian psyche and it is central to the developments of modernity.

Where did this dynamic come from? The idea seems alien to Judaism, with its assumption that God's rule must be expressed in the world. It is also alien to mainstream classical thought, with its location of value in the polis or the empire.

But maybe it's not entirely alien to Judaism: its seeds are there in the idea of God's total rule that will iron out all human divisions, bring permanent peace. In relation to this prospect, no currently existing rule is fully godly. This is especially clear when the Jews are subject to pagan rule – a situation that inspired the apocalyptic form of prophetic writing, and one that firmly obtained in Jesus' time. It seems that Jesus saw Rome's rule as a frail temporary reality on the verge of being overturned. Its authority must on one level be respected: tax must be paid to the regime, he said, with the famous sound bite, 'Give back to Caesar what is Caesar's and to God what is God's.'[7] An integration of religion and politics is not presently possible. There is a tension here that can only be solved by the coming of God's kingdom.

This is more explicit in Paul's writing: until the kingdom comes, Christians should accept the political authority of pagan Rome. Despite its idolatry and violence, God authorizes it, for now. The early Church was apolitical, unintegrated, just 'residing', or camping, in the world. This was a totally new development of 'religion', this sense of careful separateness from the political order. All other ancient cults melded with their political setting: Roman paganism was all about local tradition and civic pride, and the power of the 'divine' emperor. Only Christianity stood apart from this, and located true religion in something other than the public ceremonies. To observers, it was this negative, critical attitude that stood out: the Christians seemed 'atheists'.

But as it grew, this subculture couldn't really remain apolitical; it became a force in the world. As conversions increased, Christian communities edged into the public square, and some bishops began to resemble mayors. Then, with the conversion of the Emperor Constantine (a gradual event that began in 312), a far larger public role for the Church became possible. Though it became official, established, the Church retained its distinction between spiritual and temporal realms. This distinction was more fully expressed in the Western Empire, where politics was less stable: the Church retained a bolder sense of its authority. For example, Ambrose, Bishop of Milan, dared to excommunicate Emperor Theodosius for war crimes in the late fourth century. This impressed his younger contemporary Augustine, who remained slightly sceptical about the new 'Christian empire' in Constantinople: a supposedly Christian civilization does not change the fact that there are 'two cities, the earthly and the Heavenly ... mingled together from the beginning to the end of their history'.[8] The two realms ought to overlap – worldly politics should ensure that the Church is culturally dominant, and the Church should in turn transform worldly politics – but they should not merge into a unitary theocratic ideal. He argued that Christianity transforms civilization through its condemnation of such practices as bloody spectator sports, excessive military violence and abortion, but also insisted that such transformation can only go so far – the world cannot be cured of its worldliness.

Augustine glimpsed the fact that this duality of realms enabled the Western Church to survive the fall of the Empire in the West, the rise of the barbarians. It had to assert itself as a clearly distinct site of authority, to avoid being conscripted by this highly unpalatable form of worldly power. This model underlay the rise of the papacy and the conversion of Western Europe. In the 490s, Pope Gelasius explained that spiritual and political authority constituted separate spheres, of which spiritual power was superior. This model was gradually accepted by the new kingdoms of Europe, which came to recognize the pope's authority over them in a theoretically united Christendom.

Before returning to the concept of secularism, we should consider the question of the Church's moral influence. This can hardly be overstated: it was steadily transforming the habits of the ancient world. In many cities, bishops modelled a new sort of civic rule, in which concern for the poor was central – they set up a sort of welfare system – and the old cultic celebrations, with their enshrining of elitism and militarism, were replaced by the more egalitarian performance of the sacraments.

But didn't the Church condone slavery and continue the ancient world's denigration of women? It condoned slavery but only just: it gradually undermined it and made it seem an aberration, through its teaching of the equal status of all souls in God's eyes. Paul's insistence that the gospel was equally available to 'slave and free' raised the status of slaves, made their abuse seem inhumane. As Rowan Williams puts it:

> The Christian attempt to think through the implications of slave and slave-owner as equal members of the same community inevitably qualified what could be said about absolute ownership and offered minimal but real protection to the body of the slave.[9]

A related development was better treatment of criminals: in 316, Constantine forbade the practice of branding them on the face, for 'man is made in God's image'. Later in the century some bishops spoke directly against slavery: Gregory of Nyssa condemned slave-ownership as a usurpation of God's role, and again appealed to the doctrine that man is made in God's image.

The subjugation of women was similarly challenged. This was primarily through a new idealism surrounding marriage: husband and wife were placed under equal, mutual obligation to be faithful to each other, implying the equality of the sexes. Also, the assumption that women were chattels of father or husband was challenged by a new role that the Church offered: they could opt to be dedicated virgins. This was a rebuke to the patriarchal assumption that they were fully subject to the will of their men. Indeed, the Church attacked patriarchal habits in various ways, most obviously by asserting the authority of the priesthood, a hierarchy detached from the normal hierarchy of family and tribe. Yes, this was another form of male authority – but it gradually weakened the primary ancient mode of male authority, the family, and spawned an individualism from which women gradually benefited too.

So when the papacy managed to persuade the barbarian kings of its authority, from about 500, it was ensuring the rise of a new morality. It insisted that there was a higher law than their warrior ethos, a divine moral law. A determined insistence on the separation of spheres was needed, if the rulers were to allow Christianity into their cultures (like a Trojan horse). The otherness of the Church was typified by its major new expression, the monastery, so different from warrior culture as to seem unthreatening to it. In these little islands of order, impractically high standards of morality were protected, incubated. But of course the culture of the monastery leaked out, partly through kings valuing the bureaucratic skills of monkish scribes. Kings were offered a grander conception of their rule – they could be like King David, overseeing a godly people and suppressing idolatry, and also like a Roman emperor; and through trying on these roles they began to echo Christian rhetoric about concern for all human souls, made in the image of God. Although this did not mean the sudden spread of human rights, the seeds of change were sown and soon a few little shoots appeared. For example, in the sixth century, King Chilperic of the Franks decreed that his daughter should have equal status as an heir, being no less God's creation than her brothers. Of course, such shoots were weak in the face of the brutality of dynastic squabbling, but when trampled they regrew.

Islam

Islam is somewhat separate from our story of the emergence of secular humanism; rather, of course, it seems to be its most obvious 'other'. But in fact it has huge common ground with Christianity in its dynamic vision of moral universalism: both this common ground, and its crucially different conception of politics, must be carefully assessed.

Around 600, Christendom still principally meant the 'Roman' Empire, based in Constantinople. Constantine had launched the close alliance of Church and state, in which orthodoxy was upheld by imperial decree. In particular, the difficult doctrine of the Trinity was enforced – against thinkers who wanted to give Christ secondary status or deny his divinity altogether. But an intense dispute continued about whether Christ had two natures – human and divine – or whether they merged in him. It seems odd, but this rarefied-sounding dispute caused a very long civil war. It seems that the paradox was almost too much to take – that God, the ruler of all, was fully incarnated in a vulnerable man. It seems that the divinity of Christ was the hardest idea that humanity has ever got, or half-got, into its head.

On the fringe of the Empire was Arabia, home to uncivilized nomads called Saracens. They were traditionally seen as sons of Ishmael (Abraham's illegitimate son), second-class Jews. They echoed some Jewish habits, such as circumcision and the avoidance of pork. In fact they were on the fringes of two empires: to the East was the mighty Persian Empire. Around 600, a major war broke out between the Christian and Persian empires, and a plague also ravaged the region. Then something unexpected happened: amid the chaos, the Saracens, famous for their tribal infighting, formed a united force and started expanding into both empires. Their original leader was Muhammad – he was an inspirational general and the founder of a new federation, the *ummah*.

And of course he was the founder of a new religion, but in a sense this is secondary: only about 50 years later does any written source present him as such; the new religion emerged gradually, during these decades of explosive Arab expansion and the emergence of a new superstate. This 'new' monotheism didn't drop from the sky: it was composed of Jewish and Christian strains; in particular it echoed some fringe forms of these faiths that had been banished to the desert centuries earlier.

The key point for our purposes is that it completely did away with the Christian distinction between religion and politics. 'Muhammad was, so to speak, his own Constantine', as one historian says.[10] This distinction was somewhat obscured by the strong Byzantine establishment of religion, but it was still there under the surface. Consciously or not, Muhammad wanted to imitate the mighty monotheistic empire to his West, but on simpler purer terms. That principally meant uniting religion and political rule more completely, but it also meant developing a purer monotheism. One of Christianity's design faults was that the Jews were still around, convincingly claiming to be purer monotheists. Also, Christianity allowed itself to be divided by an overcomplicated teaching about this paradoxical divine human, who supposedly triumphed through weakness and death. Islam rejected this complication, which is of course tied to Christianity's religious–secular split. In Muhammad's view, a religion that worshipped a suffering leader, a victim, a political refusenik, was bound to run into practical problems, to become incoherent, divided, weak. He saw that a Christian political order is in the tortuous position of admitting that it is at odds with its force-rejecting source. Islam has no need for such awkwardness. It simply asserts that there is a godly form of rule, whose truth must find expression in power. It is theocratic, in the sense that it supposes that politics and culture should directly and fully reflect God's will. It does not even see the need for a priesthood or a religious entity like the Church – that would obstruct the simple unity of the godly state and the assumption that the caliph is God's representative. The most important religious professionals that emerged were the lawyers, the interpreters of God's revealed law.

Does its birth amid military state-building mean that Islam is an intrinsically violent religion? It is better to call it a *realistic* religion: the new godly order must be armed to survive and triumph. This militarism is balanced by its civilizing impulse: it wants to create a stable peaceful order, which involves making peace with Jews and Christians and implementing justice. So its founding texts are famously ambiguous: they combine a commitment to peaceful persuasion (deriving from Muhammad's original ministry in Mecca) with a more militant approach (developed after his move to Medina). This coexistence of belligerence and peace reflects the ambiguity of every actual empire ever. Compare the British Empire or the American semi-empire. That's the thing about Islam: it has to be assessed as a religious empire, not simply as a religion.

On one level this empire simply reflected the Christian empire it was rivalling, for that empire had for centuries been waging holy war against those on its fringes and heretics in its midst, claiming to have God's blessing. The difference is that in Christianity there is another, contradictory dimension beneath the violence of a Christian empire: there is a story about God's full revelation in the form of suffering non-violence. True, this might be scant consolation to a Jew or pagan being butchered by a Christian soldier – but it is nevertheless the case that the religion has a logic apart from such violence. It might find itself deeply allied with military power, but it can plausibly claim not to be defined by that alliance. In Islam, on the other hand, there is no such pacific hinterland, away from its success or failure as a political force. So Islam is not more violent than other civilizations, including Christian ones, but it is more accepting of violence, more realistic about it, than Christianity – for it is not a religion that can be separated from the imperial expression of that religion.

It should also be noted that Islam brought a moral universalism that was in some ways unprecedented. It was egalitarian in the sense that it gave authority to every male believer: it unsettled or even overturned aristocracies, caste systems and monarchies within the immense caliphate that emerged, stretching from Spain to India. It declared that social status could be earned through piety rather than being fixed by birth. On the other hand it set in stone its limited egalitarianism by claiming unshakable divine sanction for the inferiority of women, and slavery. Similarly, its huge stability and self-confidence generally allowed it to be quite tolerant of Jews and Christians in its midst, as long as they kept to themselves and accepted their outsider status. Christendom was at this time less tolerant – but its attitudes were less fixed.

Islam might be summed up as a new version of Judaism.

> It makes no sense historically to classify Muhammad's core doctrines as anything but essentially Judaic – evident in the indivisibility of the one unseen omnipotent God . . . ; the coming of the Last Days . . . ; the hatred of idolatry; the righteous commandment of charity; the strict prohibition not only against pork but also against consuming meat with its living blood still in the flesh; the insistence on ritual washing and purification, especially before prayer.[11]

But this new version has two major differences. It seeks the conversion of all. And, more subtly, it lacks the eschatological tension of Judaism, in which God's rule is (partly) seen as yet-to-come – a tension that Christianity makes central.

Towards modernity

Returning to Western Europe, the contrast with Islam's merging of religion and politics is strikingly clear. The rulers of the Franks and other such kingdoms were the polar opposite of Muhammad and his heirs in their acceptance that religion was strange, other – a form of power awkwardly at odds with their secular strength, one that had to be mediated by a totally different sort of institution with a different sort of elite. They accepted that this institution was authorized to teach them a superior sort of rule.

The greatest king of the Franks, Charlemagne, got behind the idea of Christian rule with boyish vim, launching crusades against pagans and Muslims (who were pushing up from Spain). He also demanded an oath of allegiance from everyone within his borders. This might not sound very progressive but in fact it signalled a new view of all his subjects, however lowly, as separate moral agents rather than mere chattels of their lord. From this time on, feudalism began to be gradually challenged by the basic individualism of Christianity, the idea that, at least on one level, a peasant was as important as his lord. For would not all souls face God's judgement after death?

Brutal militarism was not reformed away, nor was the lord's claim to own his serfs. And yet the principle that all souls were of equal worth gained strength. As Larry Siedentop writes, the revolution of the New Testament was finding political expression:

> Paul's conception of deity . . . laid a normative foundation for individual conscience and its claims. In the ninth century this moral universalism began to impinge on the . . . conception of the proper relations between rulers and the ruled.[12]

Once Christianity had entered the bloodstream of the Franks (and Anglo-Saxons and others), the Church faced a new danger of becoming too closely integrated with the world around it. It had to reassert its otherness lest it end up in the pocket of a semi-Christian king and dilute its moral teaching to please him. In the tenth century a new monastic movement arose, stemming from the abbey of Cluny. It sharpened up the Church's claim to distinct authority. In the next century, this reform movement was stepped up: the papacy took control of it and started forging an ambitious new conception of its role. It developed a bold new account of its own authority and expounded this in a new legal discourse – canon law. The Church was determined to prove that kings and lords had no right to seize Church lands or meddle in its affairs, for example by appointing a wayward nephew to a bishopric. In defending its rights, the Church had to explain, and to a large extent invent, the concept of rights.

'Rights' originally referred to the rights of rulers to rule. A lord had the right to command his peasants – a peasant didn't have rights, except perhaps over his family. The Church now said that it also had a legitimate 'right' to exert authority. This was a different sort of right, based in its function, the care of souls. So it began to insist that it had the 'right' to enforce the doctrine of the equal worth of all souls.

> In developing a distinctively Christian legal system, popes and canonists based their arguments on the equality of souls in the eyes of God, with its implications for the claims of morality. They sought to establish that there is a moral law ('natural' law) superior to all human laws, and, consequently, that the spiritual realm cannot be made subject to the secular sphere.[13]

The concept of natural law was adapted from classical thought. But as we saw, Aristotle's notion of nature was tied up with an aristocratic rationalism. Now, in the twelfth century, it began to be defined by biblical morality: one central text, Gratian's *Decretum*, explicitly rooted natural law in 'the Law and Gospel by which each is to do to another what he wants done to himself and forbidden to do to another what he does not want done to himself'. As we have seen, various religious cultures affirmed the Golden Rule. But this was new: to declare it to be the true basis of law, capable of overriding traditional practices. Feudalism's days were numbered once the idea spread that true authority to rule must take account of the equal worth of each individual. It was the Church that upheld this principle of the rights of the common man – sometimes it had the opportunity to force it into new political documents, such as the Magna Carta of 1215.

Rather paradoxically, the Church became increasingly authoritarian and monarchical just as it was affirming the equality of all souls with new force. And soon its claim to full 'sovereignty' over the spiritual sphere affected secular politics. In response, kings began to claim fuller sovereignty over the secular sphere, and the intermediate entities of feudalism, the lords, began to lose power. 'The example of the Church as a unified legal system founded on the equal subjection of individuals thus gave birth to the idea of the modern state.'[14]

We can now return to the concept of secularism. We have seen that the Church emphasized its own otherness from secular power and that this enabled it to stand up to brutish rulers and spread a new morality. But as culture became imbued with Christian principles, the landscape changed. The old institutional separateness of the Church became questionable: new movements demanded that Christianity be expressed beyond the sphere of the Church – in the 'secular' sphere. So 'secularism' emerged as a *religious* impulse to dismantle the old distinction of Church and world.

This impulse was influenced by the Cathar heresy and related movements that stressed the idea of the simple Christian life and condemned the institutional Church. While suppressing these heresies, the Church developed movements that somewhat echoed their concerns: the Dominicans developed a more lay-focused spirituality and launched a new engagement with philosophical rationalism, culminating, around 1250, in Aquinas' work. But the really potent new movement was the Franciscans. It developed practices that implied criticism of a rich, authoritarian Church. And its thinkers sharpened the idea of the moral equality of all individuals.

Such thinking overlapped with a less idealistic sort of secularism: kings wanting to rule without interference from the pope. In the early Renaissance the two motivations blurred, with Italian city states leading the way. In the early 1300s, the poet Dante attacked the Church's involvement in the politics of Florence and other city states, and hoped that a strong Christian emperor would emerge to put it in its place. Soon after, Marsiglio of Padua put the case in more systematic terms, arguing that Christ forbade his followers from exerting worldly power. The Church should be a voluntary society within the state; its ministers should be ordinary citizens, not exempt from secular law. He anticipated the idea of a state that excludes religious institutions from political power.

The new religious mood was world-affirming: Dominicans and Franciscans proclaimed the goodness of creation against the Cathar heretics' flesh-scorning dualism. There was a rise in artistic representations of Jesus as a human being, one of us, our brother (statues of his mother also became popular). There was also a boom in depictions of heaven and hell, and purgatory (a newly invented idea). This sounds archetypally Dark Ages, but there was actually a powerful form of proto-modern universalism in the insistence that all human souls will be judged, on equal terms.

So there was a new mood of secular spirituality, meaning a desire to see religious truth expressed in lay rather than churchy forms. Though outwardly loyal, the Franciscans spread criticism of the worldly power of the Church and emphasized Christlike service to the poor. (They were partly influenced by Joachim of Fiore's suggestion that a new historical era was dawning, the Age of the Holy Spirit. Worldly institutions would gradually become unnecessary as humanity became directly enlightened by God before the Second Coming.)

By the mid 1300s, Christian culture had become wider than the institutional Church – many felt that the Church, with its power and wealth, could not truly express the spirit of Christ. Lay piety was especially strong in the Netherlands, where a movement emerged known as 'the modern devotion'. The essence of Christianity was holy living, it said, and laypeople were called to such a life. Indeed, there was criticism of mendicant (charity-dependent) friars; one should earn an honest wage and also pursue the godly life. It was calling for a new unity of the spiritual and practical: piety should be expressed in the world.

According to the theorist Charles Taylor, this turn to worldly spirituality opened the door to the multiple revolutions of modernity. It was therefore 'the mother of revolutions'.[15] The key impulse was a rejection of other-worldliness, a will to see God as involved in the human realm and creation as precious in all its particularity. Giotto brought such particularity to painting, depicting biblical scenes populated by seemingly real human beings rather than generic icons. This turn to the world was partly inspired by the doctrine of the Incarnation: through becoming human God had affirmed *this* world. One version of this vision is Dante's *Divine Comedy*. As one of its great interpreters, Eric Auerbach, explains, although this epic poem

> describes the state of souls after death, its subject, in the last analysis, remains earthly life with its entire range and content; everything that happens below the earth or in the heavens above relates to the human drama in this world.[16]

Dante achieved a new intense representation of human beings, in their historical individuality – and he did so not by turning aside from a religious framework but through that framework. The more worldly focus of the later Renaissance, Auerbach argues, derives its energy from this vision of physical and spiritual unity. Another aspect of Dante's importance is that he dared to elevate sexual love to the heart of the Christian myth. As A. N. Wilson says:

> almost from the beginning, Christianity had feared the body and downgraded sexual emotion or indeed any feelings of human love beyond generalized 'charity' . . . Dante . . . believed that what he felt for this Italian teenager [i.e. Beatrice] was part of, or identifiable with, the Love which moved the stars.[17]

It was in this context that Renaissance humanism dusted down classical literature in the fifteenth century and expressed a new concern for human flourishing in this world. In the case of Desiderius Erasmus, humanism was firmly rooted in religious idealism. He found the academic study of theology intolerably obfuscating, and saw classical thought as a useful broom (he commended Socrates for bringing philosophy down from heaven to earth). In very readable prose he taught that the essence of Christianity – the spiritual and moral teaching of Jesus and of Paul – had been obscured by the Church, which had allowed semi-pagan practices to clog things up (he criticized the cult of the saints in a largely rationalist way). He pointed out things that seem axiomatic to modern Christians: Jesus would not approve of a power-loving, persecuting Church, nor of military culture. This was perhaps the point he argued most forcefully: Christianity tends towards pacifism and sees war as deeply regrettable rather than a cause for religious excitement. How dare combatants use religious language, he asked:

> 'Our Father'? What impudence, to dare to call on God as Father, when you are making for your brother's throat! 'Hallowed be thy name.' How could the name of God be less hallowed than by your violence towards each other?[18]

The Christian should use Scripture as a guide to morality and think for himself: one should try to be loyal to the Church, he explains, but 'sometimes it is none too clear where the church is to be found. I shall take care never knowingly to write anything that Christ would disown.'[19] This was a subtly new approach to Christ: seeing him primarily as a moral guide, asking 'What would Jesus do?'

Like other humanists, he criticized Christian asceticism, gloomy other-worldliness (he had briefly been a monk, and hated it). But he also criticized those humanists who implied that all Christianity tended in this direction; he was adamant that true Christianity was world-affirming, healthy-minded, the key to a happy soul. (He thus argued that Epicureanism was in tune with the gospel; Epicurus had rightly considered the peace of the soul to be the greatest good, Erasmus said.)

He was the inventor of a major form of liberal theology, which deeply assumes that the point of Christianity lies in its moral influence. If we really attend to the gospel, surely we will become progressively peaceful: 'if all Christians were such as Christ wished them, there would be no war amongst them, nor even quarrels'.[20]

Erasmus' influence in the sixteenth and early seventeenth centuries was immense: his moral and rational optimism inspired generations of humanists. Some of these would sow the seeds of modern secularism through questioning the necessity of revealed religion. But in a sense modern secularism is already underway, once Christianity has begun to turn against its sacred–profane dualism, and to emphasize the goodness of creation. This could be called Secularism Stage One: in which late medieval Christianity discovers its world-affirming side, which means criticism of a powerful Church and emphasis on the humanity, and moral vision, of Jesus, and the goodness of creation. To some it also means affirming the rights of the state against the claims of the papacy, and to others it also means criticism of ritual traditions that obscure the moral and spiritual teaching of the New Testament, and also a willingness to draw on aspects of classical thought. There's a lot going on, many different strands of a huge glacial movement. But all of it is going on under the Christian umbrella. There is not yet any part of this broad movement that wants rid of revealed religion.

The Reformation

Luther's rejection of Rome has often been seen as the first step in the creation of modern secular culture. But this underestimates what we have just discussed: the long slow reform movement that began in the 1200s. As we saw, one aspect of this related to Church and state: some thinkers argued that religion should be subject to local political control. This was a form of secularism, but it did not entail saying that the state should be non-religious; instead it was assumed that the state should enforce religious unity. Luther enabled the sudden advance of this way of thinking about Church and state. He renewed the claim that the Church should have no political power but rather be subordinate to local secular power. He gave this perspective new theological underpinning by his forceful rejection of the whole concept of religious law, his insistence that the state was the only authentic lawgiver.

So the state, in Luther's thought, was handed huge new power over religion: it had the right, indeed the duty, to ensure the health and strength of the Church within its borders. When he first set out this vision, Luther sounded wary of coercion: the state should not force people to shift allegiance, for true faith cannot be forced. But such qualms came to seem irrelevant: in practice, rulers had to impose religious uniformity and crack down on religious dissent, which was inextricable from political dissent. A new respect for toleration was not on the agenda. England followed this model in the 1530s: Henry VIII's new Church inherited the monopoly of the old Church, and enforced it with new rigour. In other words, Luther's revolution did not inaugurate an early form of liberalism, but in the long run it did prepare the ground for the liberal state: it was in nations that got rid of Rome that toleration gradually took root, as we shall see.

The other main form of Protestantism, the Reformed tradition, launched by Zwingli in Zurich and developed by Calvin in Geneva, shared Luther's assumption that political uniformity was necessary: it insisted that a more tolerant attitude would open the door to chaos, leading to Rome regaining total mastery of Europe. A few Protestant thinkers were more liberally inclined, but not many.

So mainstream Protestantism did not bring any sudden shift from an authoritarian religious society to a more tolerant one. One sudden shift it did bring related to sexuality and the family. As a young monk, Luther obviously saw sex as a barrier to holiness. Then he decided that the monastic life was fraudulent and that marriage was the normal human state, fully to be affirmed. And he married (a former nun). To the worldly modern mind, it seems obvious that he had an acute personal interest in moving to this conclusion: who wouldn't prefer to conclude that sex was on the table, so to speak? But in fact he had to talk himself into seeing marriage as a positive thing; he retained a deep sense that celibacy was the serious godly option. He decided that this sex-averse position was tied up with legalistic habit; therefore he proudly claimed to have married in order to defy the devil. To marry was a statement of commitment to his new world view. Fortunately, marriage and family life brought him joy, and he saw joy as the chief means of warding off Satan's attacks, beside prayer. So he could heartily recommend larking around with kids, playing games and music. In the Lutheran Church he became an icon of worldly piety, family values, the culmination of religion's long-brewing secular turn. (In reality he was probably a gloomy so-and-so half the time.)

Even the prickly prig John Calvin submitted to the logic of marriage. And it was he above all who intensified the late-medieval desire to see piety expressed in the world, in the structures of secular life. People with normal jobs were not excused from taking religion fully seriously: holy living was not the pursuit of an elite but demanded of everyone.

Therefore Geneva's laws should directly reflect God's commandments, and traditional sources of fun and games should no longer be tolerated.

The spread of Protestantism caused a major social revolution that historians call 'the reformation of manners'. For the first time, the ordinary lives of the masses were deemed worthy of close attention, regulation, improvement. Without huge grass-roots changes in habits of living, and notions of public decency, religious reform was felt to be frail, impermanent. Unless ordinary farm labourers were weaned away from wasting time – and indulging appetites – at the local semi-pagan festival, the new religious culture was in doubt. Through such reformism the social world became subject to a new sort of rational control. Clear new rules were established about the duties individuals owed each other. Work relationships gradually became ruled by contracts, with fixed hours and fixed pay rather than vague traditional agreements formed by ancestral habits and hierarchies. This is generally seen in sinister terms, as the imposition of cold capitalist logic on a merry carnivalesque culture (Malvolio ousting Sir Toby). But it was also morally progressive in its claim that even lowly sorts should be taken seriously as moral agents, ushered into civilization, treated as responsible individual citizens. This revolutionary new attitude to society prepared the ground for the more strictly rational reformism of the Enlightenment era. Indeed, this reform movement already had a rational aspect. The motivation was religious but a major consequence was rational disenchantment. The creation of a more orderly world meant the imposition of new objective standards, measurements, currencies, languages. A degree of scientific rationalism was indirectly imposed in the battle to wean the masses from ungodly disorder.

Montaigne

After Erasmus, literary humanism spread fast among the elite. Well-born young men modelled themselves on eminent Romans. The dangerous passions of the Reformation led many to glimpse a calmer, saner world in classical texts. A new confident style of humanism was born, free from the shadows of monasticism and scholasticism and quietly sceptical of traditional religion.

Michel de Montaigne lived in Bordeaux, which was partly Protestant. He said that as a youth he was 'tempted' by the radical aura of Protestantism, as he witnessed the persecution of Protestant thinkers, but he decided that the reformist cause brought unnecessary disorder, and Protestant zeal as much violent intolerance as the old order it opposed. He opted for conservatism, sat in Bordeaux's parliament and later served as mayor. While France descended into civil war, caused by Protestant rebellions against the Catholic monarchy, he began his career as a man of letters – of an unprecedentedly worldly sort.

In his cheerful, world-affirming *Essays* religion is often blithely ignored in favour of classical literature: 'When I am attacked by gloomy thoughts, nothing helps me so much as running to my books.'[21] He doesn't mean the Bible and the prayer-book. In an essay on his vulnerability to fluctuating moods and contradictory states of mind, there is no reference to sinful thoughts – that sort of religious seriousness is banished:

> No man living is freer from sadness than I, who neither like it in myself nor admire it in others. Yet the world is pleased to honor it, and say it is a mark of wisdom, virtue, and conscience. A silly and ugly mark![22]

This is similar to the world-affirming cheer of Luther – but of course Luther's rhetoric of good cheer belongs to the narrative of struggle with Satan. That whole aspect of psychology is now declared unnecessary, the obsession of a previous age. It is now possible to be proudly self-accepting, healthy. In an essay on approaching death, Montaigne states his almost complete lack of regrets: 'I rarely repent: my conscience is satisfied with itself, not because it is the conscience of an angel or a horse, but as the conscience of a man.'[23] This superficially echoes conventional Christian anthropology, which urges us to remember that we are sinners. Montaigne undermines this by *affirming* moral frailty as the normal human condition rather than repenting of it, striving beyond it.

In his essay on his approach to religion, he expresses a desire to leave theology aside in his writing, as he is offering 'merely human ideas', 'matters of opinion, not faith'.[24] He wants literature to be a secular space, a place of respite from the politicized faith-war of the age. Instead of expressing reformist theological ideas, it is wiser to accept the religious status quo.

He seems to be one of the first secular minds of modernity, but at the same time his mind is deeply coloured by Christianity. His world-affirming cheerfulness is a significant departure from most ancient philosophy, which has an essentially tragic idea of the soul trapped in the body, and the need to do battle with one's passions – an idea that lasted from Plato to the Roman Stoics and beyond. 'I love life, and cultivate it such as God has been pleased to bestow it on us . . . I do not wish the body to be without desires and titillations: that would be wicked and ungrateful.'[25] It is a poor philosophy that 'preaches to us that it is barbarous to wed the divine with the earthly; that pleasure is a brutish quality unworthy to be relished by a wise man'.[26] On one level this sounds like someone who is quietly ditching traditional Christian assumptions, but on another it reflects the long tradition of emphasizing God's affirmation of his creation. It is in the tradition of Dante's vision, of the divine significance of the human world.

So Montaigne's seemingly secular world view is founded on a confidence in the goodness of creation and the dignity of humanity; it is rooted in the *Christian* appropriation of classical humanism, with its sacred agenda of taking religion beyond churchy confines, applying it to secular life. Although Montaigne is a pioneer of the coming secularism, of the affirmation of this world and the sidelining of religious concerns, a Christian-based confidence in the goodness of creation underlies this very world-affirmation.

3

Mutations of Protestantism

It is often said that Protestantism made a decisive contribution to the rise of secularism, and it's true. But attempts to elaborate often recycle misleading assumptions, in this sort of way: after daring to throw off Roman Catholicism, thinkers in Protestant lands dared to go further still; they gradually dared to think rationally and to question religion itself, and so to launch the era of secular humanism.

This story, which is of course the orthodoxy, is too hungry for a clean break between the era of religion and the era of secular humanism. And it tends to view rationalism as the agent of this clean break, which as we shall see is very wide of the mark. The more paradoxical, more interesting – and truer – story goes something like this. After the Reformation, the basic principles we know as secular humanist – rational scepticism, moral universalism and a rejection of authoritarian religion in favour of the liberty of the individual – gradually emerged *within* religious thought. In fact 'within' is too weak; it could mean something alien growing within religion's body (as in that scene in *Alien*). These things emerged as new forms of Protestantism. So this is the strange thing I am trying to narrate in this chapter: the essential features of post-religious thought emerged within religion, as *mutations* of Protestantism.

The conventional story has no need for this paradox; it sees secular humanism as the 'natural' ideology, which is progressively revealed as religion's power declines, like rocks on a beach are revealed when the tide goes out. This fails to see that secular humanism is *constructed*, and principally from Christian material. Yes, classical philosophy plays a role, and yes, the rise of science also plays a role, but the core energy and purpose, or *telos*, of secular humanism comes from its secularization of Christianity's ethical universalism.

The new God

A rational version of religious reformism had grown alongside Protestantism. For example, Calvin's contemporary and enemy, Sebastian

Castellio, had argued for a liberal rationalist sort of Protestantism that drew on classical philosophy, especially Stoicism. 'Reason is, so to speak, the daughter of God', he explained. 'She existed before all works and ceremonies and before the creation of the world.'[1] As the reference to 'works and ceremonies' suggests, there was a reformist energy to religious rationalism, a will to refute the perceived superstitions of Catholicism. This partly derived from Erasmus but was intensified by the Reformation in two ways: on the one hand it was inspired by the reformers' full-scale attack on ritual; on the other it saw the need to counter *Protestant* dogmatism, particularly Calvin's doctrine of predestination. This doctrine was to provoke rationalists for centuries to come, and most of these were religious rationalists, wanting to rescue God from the appearance of tyranny.

The influence of Stoicism on Protestants such as Castellio was immense. Stoicism inherited and adapted Plato's view of religion: the myths about the various gods, with their transparently human features and foibles, should not be taken seriously; true religion was rational reflection on the Good, the supreme divine principle animating the cosmos. We all have a spark of this divine rational principle (*logos*), which we can cultivate through philosophizing and behaving morally (the two activities are seen as one). Instead of rejecting old-fashioned religion, with its myths and cults, Plato thought it could be reinterpreted, demythologized, nudged in a rationalist direction, made into metaphorical support. Ancient Stoicism echoed all this and was more inclined to talk about this supreme divine principle as 'God'. It agreed that religious observance was a social good, despite the redundancy of literal belief in traditional myth and ritual. This became the basic stance of all educated Romans.

Stoic-influenced Christianity quietly spread during the Renaissance – as we saw, Erasmus was sympathetic yet also wary of its capacity to marginalize Christ. Then, after the Reformation, it gradually dared to express itself more openly. Various thinkers, especially in the Netherlands, espoused it around 1600. Such thinkers downplayed its difference from traditional religion; rather they presented it as a reformed version of traditional religion. Their emphasis on reason's ability to perceive the divine rationality of the created order was soon boosted by the inductive revolution in scientific method announced by Francis Bacon.

It was also boosted by the sense that traditional religion led to violence. The Thirty Years War (1618–48) comprised countless bloody

Catholic–Protestant skirmishes. A new basis for religious truth, away from both the papacy and the Bible, seemed a good idea. In the 1640s, René Descartes announced the key principle of this new approach: the rational capacity of the individual was the foundation of all knowledge, including theological knowledge. What we really know of God corresponds to what we know through reason. Claims to know God through external authorities should be distrusted. In effect, Descartes defined God in Stoic terms – as the rational principle, linking the thinking individual with the laws of nature. He implied that reliance on revelation was unnecessary.

Why was such a plainly unorthodox idea of God tolerated? How did it become culturally dominant in Protestant lands in the next generation or two? It's a big question. To answer it we have to consider the big picture, of how theology relates to rationalism.

Theology had pursued a smooth synthesis of faith and reason since the third century, when it incorporated Greek wisdom so enthusiastically, right up to Aquinas' great synthesis that incorporated Aristotle's rationalism. After Aquinas this synthesis broke down – it was challenged by nominalism, which emphasized God's otherness from human reason; this critique was intensified by Protestantism. As a result, the Protestant world found itself without a big theory that harmonized faith and reason. It seemed faced with a choice between Protestant dogmatism and total scepticism. In this context, the Stoic approach to religion was deeply attractive; it promised to recover the old harmony of Christianity and reason – without recourse to Catholic thought. Of course, it did so at the cost of downplaying or denying Christianity's basis in faith and revelation. But this issue was evaded by the religious rationalists, who focused on the need to move away from the era of post-Reformation factionalism and violence. And soon this shift seemed to bring cultural stability, peace, the flourishing of civilization and advances in science: here was an ideology that worked, that promised a more peaceful and harmonious future – in contrast to the traditional creeds.

So this new religious rationalism can be explained by two factors. It spoke to the age-old impulse to harmonize religion and reason, at a time when the more orthodox synthesis, which affirmed revelation, had become unavailable (to Protestants). And it spoke to the spirit of reformism that the Reformation had unleashed. By making strident Protestant noises about the need to oppose ritual and superstition, this creed was able to seem essentially Christian.

It should be seen as a mutation of Christianity in which the basic themes of revelation, faith and grace were sidelined, or even ousted, by a determination to see God in terms of a rational universe, and his implanting of rational morality in humanity. It was a *heretical* mutation, the Christian historian of ideas is obliged to say – for when Christianity forgets its basis in faith and cult it has begun to commit suicide. But one should also get down from one's high horse and admit that this mutation of Christianity produced a new sort of moral universalism that transformed the world in a not entirely terrible way. In a sense, the Christian historian needs two voices: one to say, alas, authentic Christianity was undermined; another to say, *felix culpa*, a new moral universalism was born.

Secular politics

But Christian rationalism was not the sole agent of secularizing change in the mid seventeenth century. Radical Protestantism also played a role – especially in inventing the ideal of secular politics, the separation of Church and state. It was not rationalists but *religious radicals* who first dared to call for an end to theocratic tradition and a new sort of liberty-protecting state. In effect they called for a new sort of reformation, embracing political liberty.

This was a decisive departure from previous Protestantism. Starting with Luther and Zwingli, mainstream Protestantism assumed that religious uniformity was necessary – everyone should be baptized at birth into the national Church. It seemed obvious that no state could cohere without imposing an official religion. An alternative view emerged among religious radicals, who said that state-imposed religion was wrong and that the true Church consisted of adults who freely chose to belong to it. This 'sectarian' idea of religion was seen as subversive – even by relatively freethinking intellectuals. It seemed inseparable from fanatical extremism, the idea that all politics was evil, that we should stay pure and wait for Christ's return (the Anabaptists exemplified this).

Then something happened to combine this marginal radicalism with a more practical political reformism. During the crisis of the English Civil War, a liberal wing emerged in the anti-monarchical Puritan movement: it reconciled the anti-theocratic idealism of the radicals with political reality.

A new form of Anglicanism emerged under Charles I around 1630. It tightened up laws about how to worship and what ideas were permissible – it tightened things up in a Catholic direction. This was another version of Roman Catholic tyranny, said the Puritan opposition, whose MPs turned militant. But when the Puritans won the war they were split between those who wanted to impose a tight Calvinist order and those who wanted fuller toleration. People had talked up toleration for many decades but that usually just meant urging the official Church to be a bit softer on Dissenters. Now a new vision was promulgated by a small but influential network of thinkers: they said that the state should stop trying to impose an official religion on people altogether, but should allow various Protestant churches to coexist and should protect religious liberty. This was the origin of liberal – and secular – politics.

John Milton set out a strict separation of Church and state. The ideal politician (whom he idealized in terms of Roman republicanism) was a defender of liberty – and that meant battling every form of theocracy and protecting a space for people to think freely about religion (he assumed this would be Protestant religion). He sounds like a modern 'secularist' but his position was based in intense Protestant faith. In fact he was one of the boldest religious thinkers ever. He announced a new era in religion (and politics), 'the reformation of the reformation'. Like Luther, he appealed to Paul's rejection of religious law – Christians should not impose holy rules on each other. But he went further than Luther, who had assumed that the state must uphold an official religion. No it must not, said Milton, because that involves it in religious legalism; it means bossy bishops issuing moral and cultic rules. The only valid law is secular law – religion should be left to the individual to decide about. He therefore used the principle of Pauline liberty, or freedom from religious rules, to refute the legitimacy of an established Church and to demand a new era of religious liberty.

In the chaotic aftermath of war, 'freedom of conscience' was trumpeted by a major movement, the Independents. But most Puritans were opposed, feeling that only a strict Calvinist system could bring order. Rather surprisingly, the powerful leader who emerged, Oliver Cromwell, favoured liberty – in theory. In practice he had to appease the Calvinists and also play the dictator, to stop them taking over Parliament. He employed Milton as his chief propagandist: his tracts tried to establish religious liberty as England's public creed.

Did Milton therefore advocate total religious liberty, for Catholics and atheists? No, not even for Anglicans (as they wanted the old establishment back). He advocated liberty for different sorts of non-episcopal Protestants. But before you cry 'Hypocrite', consider the political situation: Anglicans were fighting, literally, to regain their monopoly, and in the wider world Catholics were stamping down on any talk of toleration. Such political enemies had to be proscribed if a new culture of liberty was to have a chance of taking root.

It is important to note that this original vision of secular politics, this rough blueprint for the liberal state, was based in a radically Christian movement and not in the semi-Christian rationalist movement, which was mostly conservative. It was the influence of the edgy sectarians that put religious liberty on the political map so dramatically. Though the English Revolution failed after a decade, it changed the ideological landscape: its idealization of 'liberty' put the old unity of Church and state in question. Only after this *religious* radicalism had caused a rupture with the past did a more rational form of liberal political theory emerge – principally that of Locke.

Spinoza

But let us first consider Locke's exact contemporary, Baruch Spinoza (both were born in 1632). He was the most radically rationalist thinker of the seventeenth century. Only he issued a clear call for a break with traditional revealed religion. But the assumption that he was therefore an atheist is wrong: he exemplifies the religious roots of rational humanism.

He was the son of Jewish immigrants to Amsterdam, refugees from the Spanish Inquisition, who belonged to a tight, authoritarian subculture. Soon after his bar mitzvah, Spinoza questioned synagogue teaching. He denied that Jews were set apart by any special revelation, for all humanity was essentially the same. For saying so he was expelled from the community. This was the beginning of his rationalist opposition to traditional religion, but it's important to see that this rationalism echoed the liberal Protestant critique of superstition and empty ritual, which was very much in the cultural air. In Holland, liberal Protestantism was an underground force; it had been decisively expelled from the Calvinist Church decades earlier. The original liberals were the Remonstrants, who strongly denied predestination as irrational and inhumane;

there was now a wider liberal movement known as the Collegiants. Many of these moved to a wider critique of revealed religion, but it remained a very religious movement, emphasizing the God-given spirit of reason, or inner light, as the key to holy living. It was influenced by Castellio and other religious-rationalist reformers such as Sebastian Franck. Spinoza began to move in such circles, whose thought chimed with the Hispanic-Jewish mysticism with which he was familiar, and he began to be known by the less Jewish name Benedictus.

In his treatises of the 1650s he argued that truth must be universal, available to everyone, as all truth has the objective character of geometry. This principle was contrasted with the biblical theme of revelation: miracles should be seen as primitive packaging surrounding authentic moral insights. Influenced by his Protestant friends, including an off-shoot of the new Quaker movement that was attempting to convert Amsterdam's Jews, he often spoke of Christ as the bringer of universal enlightenment or 'inner light': 'I do not believe that anyone save Christ alone ever attained to such superiority over others as to have had the precepts of God which lead to everlasting life, revealed to him immediately, and without the intervention of words or a vision.'[2] He therefore did *not* say that Christianity should be jettisoned in favour of a purely secular morality. He said that true Christianity entailed this purging of all outward religion. 'In one sense Spinoza's critics were right: he . . . was reducing, even diminishing, the status of scripture, theology, and clerical authority. But Spinoza understood this as the fulfilment, not the desecration, of the Christian faith.'[3]

Were he a gentile, he would surely have fitted right into such rational-liberal Christianity. But his residual Judaism led him to keep thinking, to seek fuller clarity: why should a truly universal form of religion give such prominence to Christ? Belief in his divinity meant reliance on revelation and disparagement of reason, and this was a poor basis for a unifying form of religion. This was his stated aim: the pursuit of 'a very simple universal form of religion'.[4] He was not using 'religion' as a mere veneer for atheist rationalism, as some recent interpreters imply. He actually understood himself in avant-garde *religious* terms. This is reflected in his lifestyle: he adopted Quaker habits of dress and speech but devoted himself to a solitary personal quest, the pursuit of a divinely pure rationalism that could bring universal enlightenment to humanity. He broke with Descartes, who had argued that a transcendent God underwrote human reason; instead, he said, there is no rational basis for a God who is independent of the laws of nature. But he continued to speak of 'God, or Nature'. And he echoed an austere traditional religious morality, warning against love of what is corruptible (he seems to have steered clear of sexual relations). So he remained a religious thinker, of sorts: his rational universalism was clearly rooted in monotheism. (Like Marx, his adaptation of Judaism entailed a strong aversion to actual Jewish practice, which seemed a direct denial of the universalism at the heart of the faith.)

In his *Theologico-Political Treatise*, Spinoza argued that rationalism enabled an optimistic view of politics: reasonable people would restrain their selfish appetites and seek the common good. Real lasting social harmony would not come until everyone 'must have firmly resolved and contracted to direct everything by the dictate of reason alone'.[5] This quietly reverses the assumption that religion underlies social order. The real unifying faith is rationalism, and revealed religion must be marginalized, as a threat to social harmony. In other words, the truly liberal state must be based in rational religion. He repeats that his motivation is 'the love of God, or the supreme happiness and blessedness of man, and the highest object and aim of all human actions';[6] in his subsequent works he often identifies his rationalism with the 'intellectual love of God'. He seems to have experienced his core conviction, that universal reason could unite humanity, in mystical terms, as a sort of (naturally available) revelation.

So this pioneer of secular rationalism was a Jewish mystic, deeply influenced by rational Protestantism. He was inspired by one aspect of Judaism, its universalism, to oppose another, its particularity, meaning its basis in revelation and its attachment to ritual practices. Some forms of liberal Christianity had been defining 'true religion' in opposition to supernatural belief and ritual practice for decades, but it took a Jew to announce a total opposition, to say that God favoured reason over all traditional religious forms.

All subsequent rationalism is coloured by Spinoza's approach: it is not neutral but endowed with the aura of religious reform, loaded with a claim to be the true agent of universal salvation in place of the old religious forms. It's a paradox: Western rationalism, even as it attacks religion, echoes the spirit of religious reform.

The term 'deism' had been in use for a few decades to refer to a rational form of theology. Spinoza gave it new definition: after him, the term normally referred to a religious rationalism that rejected the concept of revelation. Such extreme deism was tantamount to atheism, critics said. They were both right and wrong: yes, it certainly meant rejection of the Christian God; yet Spinoza and others sincerely believed in a rational God, or divine rationalism.

Locke and deism

John Locke's advocacy of toleration is perhaps the single most important ingredient of liberal political thought, which is inseparable from secular humanism. Writing after the restoration of the English monarchy, he turned away from the radical religion of Milton but shared his goal to a large extent: a state that has moved away from the theocratic past and instead enshrines liberty of religion.

He based his argument for toleration in a neat theory of the respective functions of politics and religion. The state should be seen in secular terms, as an association for mutual protection, for the securing of material goods (especially the protection of property). Here he adapted Thomas Hobbes's theory that we accept the government's authority because it delivers peace and order – which includes accepting the ruler's enforcement of an official religion. Yes, said Locke, the state serves the secular ends of peace, security, prosperity. But the only sure way to this is religious liberty, for a ruler's refusal to tolerate religious dissenters will lead to conflict, even civil war. Rather than seeking to save people's souls by establishing the true faith, which can't work, as faith can't be forced, the state should let people worship as they choose, as long as this does no public harm.

The other side of the coin is that religion should be seen as a voluntary matter – churches are just clubs one can choose to join. Here Locke points to the New Testament, showing that Christian truth must be freely assented to rather than imposed by state power. We can now move away from the long era of theocracy towards a purer, more spiritual understanding of religion.

Once it is understood that politics and religion are separate in this way, toleration will come naturally – it is the rational religious policy for a state to follow. But doesn't society need religious cohesion? It only needs a minimal form of it, said Locke: profession of belief in God. He thought that public expressions of atheism would undermine people's trust in each other – and also that the state's claim to authority should be rooted in theism.

Should all forms of religion be tolerated? Yes – unless there are political grounds for excluding them. And he judged Roman Catholicism – and, more theoretically, Islam – to fall foul of this, to entail loyalty to a foreign power. Essentially, this echoed the vision of Milton and others a generation before, but Locke presented the vision as more rational than religious. Instead of saying, 'True Christianity demands this new sort of politics,' he said, 'This new sort of politics is the rational means to lasting peace.' This shift of emphasis is one of the founding moments of secular modernity. A Christian-based vision is presented in terms that move away from Christian particularity – towards rational universalism.

Locke's account of religion and politics found gradual acceptance and remains a basic plank, perhaps the basic plank, of political liberalism. This is still essentially how the liberal state deals with religion: instead of telling us what to believe and how to worship, it protects our freedom to do as we choose, within the limits of the secular law. The difference nowadays is that the state does not think it necessary to uphold a unifying theism, though the ghost of this aspiration persists in various ways (such as the USA writing 'In God we Trust' on its money, and the UK's official retention of religious establishment).

How dependent on Protestantism is this liberty-affirming form of politics? It's a tricky question. At the time of its invention, the dependence was massive. It plainly derives from the liberal Puritanism of the civil war era – the claim that God wills the overthrow of theocracy and the creation of a new sort of liberty-loving state. In Locke's day, absolute monarchy and Catholicism were still threats, and he was involved in the liberal Protestant opposition to them. But because he shifts this vision into deist terms, the link with Protestantism is semi-broken: the tolerant state is presented as the rational option rather than the godly option. But the link with Protestantism is only semi-broken: it is still there a century later, in the American Revolution, as we shall see.

Though a religious rationalist, Locke condemned the more extreme rationalism of Spinoza and his deist imitators in the 1690s. These writers attacked revelation and 'superstition' (focusing on Roman Catholicism in order to evade censure), and affirmed a strictly rational idea of God. The Church of England of course condemned a movement that disparaged most of the core Christian doctrines, but it looked favourably on a wider, softer form of religious rationalism. Locke's book of 1695, *The Reasonableness of Christianity, as Delivered in the Scriptures*, was of this type. It aimed to present a simplified version of Christianity, based in the moral teaching of Jesus, which is 'conformable to that of Reason'.[7] This was the mood of the age, defined by the scientific advances of Newton, which seemed to confirm a rational deity presiding over the universe. Indeed, for the next century a restrained form of deism was the public face of the national religion.

Let's sum up these reflections on the absurdly eventful seventeenth century. A new religious rationalism emerged within Protestant culture, which drew on classical Stoicism. It was partly inspired by the Reformation (it too wanted to purify religion from ritual and superstition) and partly arose in opposition to its dogmatism (especially that of Calvinism). At the same time, political secularism emerged from liberal Puritanism: it demanded an end to theocracy and establishment, in favour of a new sort of state that enshrined religious liberty. And then, with Spinoza, religious rationalism developed a more robust, revelation-denying form. And Locke, through semi-secularizing the previous generation's radicalism, launched the tradition of liberal political universalism.

So that's all clear then.

Voltaire, Rousseau

Deism, this strange mutation of Protestantism, was the dominant force in what's known as the Enlightenment. To call it the 'Age of Reason' is only accurate as long as reason has a capital 'R', for it was the age of religious reason. Atheism remained rare even in the later eighteenth century.

Whereas Protestant Britain tolerated the rise of deism, within certain limits, rigidly Catholic France suppressed it. (Louis XIV had officially forbidden the teaching of Cartesianism in 1671.) This put French deism on a post-Christian course. But in the first place French deism was strongly influenced by the Christian-based deism of England. This was thanks to the young rebel François-Marie Arouet, styling himself Voltaire. Banished for insulting the regent in verse, he spent a few years in Britain in the 1720s, where he read Locke, Newton and others, and was impressed by the tolerant Protestant culture and general air of bourgeois bustle. (His determination to reform France was partly economic: he hoped for the return of the enterprising exiled Huguenots.)

In the next decade he became the star spokesman for deism, explaining that Reason stood against all revealed religions: Christianity was just one muddled attempt to grasp the rational God. In order to show that Christianity was not unique, Voltaire turned anthropologist: the various primitive peoples being discovered around the world were not demonic savages but exhibited a natural morality that education would expand upon. But his Jesuit education showed through: he bitterly opposed the theology of the Jansenists (a French version of Calvinism), with its idea of God's arbitrary power. In a sense he sought to vindicate God from this slur. And though he denied that God was definitively revealed in Christ, his emphasis on God's mercy and compassion and hatred of authoritarianism was obviously influenced by the New Testament. He has a great deal in common with Erasmus, despite the latter's profession of orthodoxy.

Why did he not make the move to atheism, as a few of his friends did? Because, like Spinoza, he was convinced by the idea of a divinely ordered universe and the related one of God-implanted rational morality. The idea of Reason as a saving cause that could unite humanity seemed to require the existence of God.

> God has given us a principle of universal reason, as he has given feathers to birds and furs to bears; and this principle is so constant, that it subsists despite all the passions which struggle against it; despite the tyrants who wish to drown it in blood; despite the impostors who would employ superstition to bring it to naught.[8]

This expresses a contradiction at the heart of deism: if universal reason comes naturally to us, why does it resemble an embattled cause? Why has it not triumphed long ago? The main answer deists give is that institutional religion has ensnared humanity – deism therefore has an inbuilt conspiracy theory (which is inherited by today's atheists, of course).

France provided plenty of fuel for a view of organized religion as the engine of oppression. Conversion to Protestantism, and blasphemy, were crimes punishable by death. In the absence of a culture of liberal Protestant reformism, Christianity seemed synonymous with an illiberal Church, and radical deism seemed the true cause of reform. Voltaire did not urge a popular movement, an anticlerical revolution: he thought that Reason should be imposed from above, by enlightened aristocrats and monarchs, and that the masses would never really see the light.

He famously worried that, if Christian morality was to lose its hold over ordinary people, he was more likely to be swindled and cuckolded. Reform should be a slow, top-down affair, in which rational enlightenment slowly replaced traditional religion. (He remained impressed by the Church of England, as a liberal dispenser of traditional religion to the masses, to moralize them.) Though he never softened his opposition to organized religion, he began to be critical of atheists who denigrated Christian morality.[9]

Atheism was tentatively emerging into the open. When a priest called Jean Meslier died in 1729, the secret atheist diatribe he had written came to light – one of the first full avowals of atheism. This forbidden document emboldened Denis Diderot, founder of the *Encyclopédie*. He was impressed by the materialist turn in French science in the 1740s: the first inklings of the theory of evolution were surfacing. Deism's calm assertion of God's orderly creation no longer seemed tenable. But Diderot was an awkward, conflicted atheist, sometimes reverting to a vague faith in the divine. His friend Baron d'Holbach had no such misgivings. D'Holbach was the classic rational atheist; he tirelessly attacked the counter-rationality of faith and the immorality of the biblical God (almost all of 'new atheism' is already here). Such atheism is rooted in the deist assumption that rationality and morality are one and that there is therefore an intrinsic morality in attacking the supernatural. Of course, the Old Testament provided the main proof:

> [God's] conduct being so strange, cruel, and opposite to all reason, is it surprising to see the worshippers of this God ignorant of their duties, destitute of humanity and justice, and striving to assimilate themselves to the model of that barbarous divinity which they adore?[10]

It is taken for granted that every enlightened mind knows what duty, humanity and justice are: natural faculties, corrupted by religion. He was perhaps the first to express the new slogan of secular morality: government 'will be good when it will bring happiness to the greatest number'.

Alongside this humanist – essentially deist – atheism, a more sceptical variety emerged. Its main French exponent, Julien Offray de La Mettrie, started out with the conventional critique of religion as false and immoral but then observed that materialist atheism did not entail any moral, humanist agenda. Isn't the pursuit of hedonistic pleasure a more obvious response to the world, if we are just animals and if religion is false? Pleasure is 'the sovereign master of men and gods, in front of whom everything vanishes, even reason itself'.[11] This is the sort of thing atheists had always been accused of thinking. Diderot told him not to speak so openly. (Over in Britain, David Hume believed something pretty close to La Mettrie, but couched it in pragmatic, neoclassical terms – of which more later.)

But the debate between Voltaire's deism and the rising atheism was not the whole story. In the 1750s a new thinker changed the terms of the debate. Jean-Jacques Rousseau developed a new sort of deist idealism.

His father was a watchmaker from Geneva; his mother died in childbirth. Aged 16, he left his apprenticeship and wandered through Savoy, sometimes working as a servant, a role he resented. He found a patroness-mistress who was a *very* liberal Catholic; she helped him find work as a musician. He then moved to Paris in 1741 and did some writing for the *Encyclopédie*. Then, in 1749, he had an acute experience of vocation. It came as he saw the title of a journal's essay competition: 'Has the advance of the sciences and the arts helped to destroy or to purify moral standards?' Suddenly he knew that he hated his culture and that he was a great thinker. He won the competition, and fame, by arguing that modern culture was, for all its proud enlightenment, a mire of falsity, corruption, inauthenticity. And he showed that he meant it by refusing the identity of the urbane literary star and choosing to earn a living by copying out musical scores – no schmoozing with influential employers for him. (He also wore conspicuously cheap clothes, like someone choosing to wear nasty old jumpers from charity shops.)

What was his problem? Didn't he believe in rational progress towards a more humane world? Yes, but with an awkward intensity that made him see its other advocates as complacent, worldly, merely pragmatic. Conventional rationalism was conservative; it sucked up to the rich, flattering their (self-interested) interest in reform. Voltaire, so very at home in posh drawing rooms, embodied this. Rousseau saw the need for a bigger, bolder story about social transformation, about the restoration of true humanity.

So in the 1750s he put forward his big story. In his *Discourse on Inequality* he floated the idea of an original form of human life in which 'natural compassion' held sway, ensuring fundamental equality. With civilization, this primal equality disappeared, chiefly because property was invented. But the fall from grace is not complete – our essential nature remains good. So what did he want – a return to primitive living? No, he wanted to establish a new conceptual bedrock: the 'state of nature' was a thought-experiment. As he put it, it is 'a state that no longer exists, perhaps never has existed, and probably never will, of which one must nevertheless have an accurate idea in order to judge our present state properly'. Similarly, he coolly announces that we should begin 'by setting all the facts aside, for they have no bearing on the question'.[12]

If we want to reform our world, said Rousseau, pragmatic rationalism is not enough: we need this bold vision of full humanity regained. But what is 'full humanity'? How does Rousseau know that this potential exists? Ultimately it's a religious conviction: he insists that we are made in God's image. We know it by looking in our hearts, he says – but of course such looking is determined by religious thinking. Other deists talked of reason as a divine force in humanity. For Rousseau, it's humanity that's divine, not reason.

He continued to attack economic injustice, analysing the conspiracy of the rich to get ever richer. His response was to idealize the small, cohesive city state that instilled an ideal of the common good in everyone, from birth. This led, in 1762, to his bold theorizing in *The Social Contract*. The state originates in its citizens' decision to renounce their primal 'natural liberty' and seek 'civil liberty'. This means consenting to obey the 'general will'. This of course sounds sinister in the light of future totalitarianism, but it can be seen as a necessary aspect of his new theory of the state, which most of us can broadly affirm: the state exists to ensure the welfare of all its citizens, to pursue justice – which means that state power belongs to the people, exists to serve the common good.

This political vision was motivated by a moral idealism with clear Christian elements (social justice, concern for the poor, hostility to luxury, the equal worth of all human lives). But its practical side is derived mainly from Plato's *Republic*. It's a potent conjoining. Rousseau is a major pioneer of the idea that a more moral politics must be established and sustained through force – as all political order is.

The Social Contract includes a sketch of the place of religion in the ideal state. The state needs a high level of ideological unity, and Christianity is not well suited to this because it's unrealistic about worldly power. He proposes that there should be a minimal form of religion, or quasi-religion, concerned with loyalty to the state – 'civil religion'. The articles of this faith should be seen 'not precisely as religious dogmas, but as sentiments of sociability, without which it is impossible to be a good citizen or a faithful subject'.[13] Beyond this, people should be allowed to believe what they want, which will probably be some form of universal morality.

He expressed his religious views in his novel *Emile*, attributing them to an ultra-liberal priest, the original trendy vicar (in his youth Rousseau was deeply influenced by a real-life version of this figure). It's pretty standard deist stuff about God as the creator of the orderly universe, whose rules are written in our hearts in the form of conscience, and the need to criticize revealed religion as a source of conflict and error. The novelty lay in Rousseau's emphasis on the emotional appeal of this creed. By putting it in the mouth of a priest, he presented it as primarily a spiritual phenomenon, the key to the deepening of our humanity. On one level, deism was already 'humanist' – it talked of unlocking human potential through reason. But Rousseau brought a new idealism about humanity – that it was good, of sacred worth, *lovable*. In a sense he reached more deeply into Christianity than previous deists, seeing the need to recycle religious themes of personal authenticity, affirmation of creation, an emotional bond with fellow humans (*agape*). This gives him a good claim to being the founder of *humanism*, in our modern sense.

He understood that he could best expound this new humanism by talking about himself. In his *Confessions* he displayed a new sort of honesty about his emotional insecurities and moral lapses, confident that the reader would nevertheless love him as an embodiment of flawed but glorious humanity.

So his genius lay in seeing that religious vitality could be imported into deism. The impersonal God of nature could be related to in an ardently personal way (this prepared the way for the poetic faith of Wordsworth and others). On moving out of the city to a simple rustic home, he recounts: 'Losing myself in this immensity, I didn't think, I didn't reason, I didn't philosophize [but cried out] "O great being! O great being!"'[14] (Incidentally, Voltaire seems to have been piqued into competing with this sort of devotional deism. There's a story of him, after reading one of Rousseau's novels, making a trip to view the sunrise from a mountain-top and, as the glorious sight unfolded, prostrating himself and chanting, 'I believe, I believe in You. Almighty God, I believe!' He then explained to his companion that this was *not* a statement of faith in the Christian God.)[15]

Two revolutions

All the trends we have been discussing in this chapter coalesced in late eighteenth-century America and contributed to the founding of the new republic. Deism found classic expression in Benjamin Franklin, among others; political secularism was revived in a strong form, especially by Jefferson and Madison; and Rousseau's humanistic deism was in the air on the eve of the revolution.

Thomas Jefferson was a – nominally Anglican – deist who, before and during the revolution, was arguing for full religious freedom in the colony, then state, of Virginia, meaning the disestablishment of the Anglican Church. He was motivated by a Christian-based liberal universalism. He saw himself as representing the pure, reformist strain of the gospel, staunchly opposed to every vestige of superstition and theocracy (he was drawn to the new creed of Unitarianism, which insisted that Christianity needed a rational God in place of the Trinity and associated irrationalities). He is perhaps the most complete culmination of this entire era, combining Milton's anti-theocratic passion with Locke's focus on individual liberty and the more humanist and radical deism of Rousseau.

Of course, the classic expression of Jefferson's deism is the American Declaration of Independence; it appeals to 'the Laws of Nature and of Nature's God' in declaring that 'all men are created equal, [and] that they are endowed by their Creator with certain unalienable Rights, that among these are Life, Liberty and the pursuit of Happiness'. This echoes Locke's notion that the state exists to protect the individual rights of its citizens. But because these principles are asserted in the context of a nation gaining independence, the spirit of Rousseau is also present: it is implied that a new 'general will' has emerged among the colonists, necessitating revolution. The key point, however, is that Jefferson bases the new republic on a religious conception of humanity. (Incidentally, he had wanted to say: 'We hold these truths to be sacred and undeniable' – Franklin urged a more secular expression – 'self-evident'.)

Most of the other founders were similarly adamant that the new nation was rooted in religion, meaning their own Protestant-based deism and the more traditional Protestantism of the people. Thomas Paine was unusual, almost exceptional, in being a post-Christian deist, like Voltaire; the other major founders saw themselves as reformist

Protestants. For many, the essence of such reformism was the rejection of established religion, the ideal of the separation of Church and state. This principle was enshrined in the First Amendment, prohibiting establishment on a federal level, but this resolution was very blunt, for establishment was allowed to continue on a state level. And it did not challenge 'unofficial establishment', the persistence of a culture-bossing moral majority. The partial triumph of the separation of Church and state should not lead us to suppose that the republic's founding ideology was 'secularism'. It was Protestant-based deism (mixed with more traditional Protestantism). This allowed for an official ideology that was detached from any specific Christian creed, yet acceptable to the various Protestants who comprised the vast majority of the nation.

There was almost no anti-religious sentiment among the main founders. They saw the various churches as crucial to the health of society and worthy of nurture and protection. Religion was assumed to foster civic-mindedness, social morality. Thus Jefferson:

can the liberties of a nation be thought when we have removed their only firm basis, a conviction in the minds of the people that these liberties are the gift of God? That they are not violated but with his wrath?[16]

As Benjamin Rush put it:

the only foundation for a useful education in a republic is to be laid in religion. Without it there can be no virtue, and without virtue there can be no liberty, and liberty is the object and life of all republican governments.[17]

By contrast, France's revolution was a fuller rupture with the Christian past. It was driven by French deism, which as we have seen was post-Christian due to the lack of a 'bridging' culture of Protestant deism. During 1789 the National Assembly began to demand the French Church's subordination to the state, the nationalization of its property (there was an echo of England's Reformation). The motivation was a deist-influenced belief in the need for a united, rational state. A new, state-subordinated Church was attempted, with priests swearing an oath to the nation, but was blocked by Catholic conservatism. In response, the anticlericalism of Voltaire and Diderot was spread with new vim, as were Rousseau's ideas of 'the general will' and 'civil religion'. In a pamphlet published on the eve of the Revolution, *What is the Third Estate?*, the Abbé Sieyès wrote: 'The nation is prior to everything.

It is the source of everything. Its will is always legal; indeed, it is the law itself.'[18]

The Declaration of the Rights of Man and the Citizen, France's version of the American Declaration of Independence, was treated as the core of a new national religion. In 1793–4, Catholicism was comprehensively replaced by this new official creed. The atheist Jacobins promoted a 'cult of Reason' but some, including Robespierre, called for a stabilizing deism that might keep moderate Catholics on board.

So France became the first European state to break with Christianity, the first ever state to enshrine a creed that might be termed 'secular humanism' – though it understood this creed in national rather than global terms. This was soon mitigated by Napoleon, whose concordat of 1801 recognized a weakened Church as the national religion, but this assertive secularism remained France's dominant theopolitical tradition.

One result of the French Revolution was the emergence in Europe of a rather simplistic polarity between religion and secular liberty. This was strengthened as other Catholic countries gradually followed France's plot of the anticlerical pursuit of liberty. Britain was affected by this narrative: because it retained an established Church, radicals could convincingly paint religion as intrinsically illiberal – a half-truth at most.

America largely disproved this polarity of conservative religion versus progressive secularism: its progressive politics was rooted in religion, as Alexis de Tocqueville later explained. But the Atlantic was wide at this time: it was France's revolution that dominated European thought. This meant that the Christian roots of liberty and humanism began to be neglected. To put it polemically, there was a delicate, nuanced tradition of Protestantism giving rise to modern humanism – and the French messed it up with their crude, simplistic polarity of religion versus secular humanism. (The French had a few helpers, such as Thomas Paine, who was adamant that only a strictly post-Christian deism could contribute to political progress and 'the equality of man'.)

Kant: rational moral perfectionism

In the realm of more abstract thought, the triumph of deism seemed secure. For over a century it had asserted a triple alliance of God, rationalism and morality. Reason is a divine force through which we know of God's existence, of his ordering of the cosmos, and of true morality. This makes traditional religion superfluous: we don't need revelation to tell us what is good and true; our God-given rationality tells us. This was basic to the thought of Spinoza, Voltaire, Rousseau and Paine, and many Christian deists echoed it also. As we've seen, this approach was influenced by Plato and Stoicism, but the content of 'divine rational morality' was determined by Christian moral universalism.

Like the boy who calls the emperor naked, David Hume called this vision a huge sham. Reverting to the empirical theory of knowledge (the claim that real knowledge can only come from sense experience), he rejected the notion of this grand abstract rationalism that unveils the true morality, and substantiates the existence of God. Religion and morality are matters of 'preference', 'custom', social convention, he said. Morality means contributing to social order, the cultural health of the nation – abstract notions of moral truth, justice and rights might be socially useful ideas but they have no objective reality. This is a pragmatic and relativist idea of morality: different cultures have different moral traditions; it's folly to seek universal moral truth.

Most thinkers ignored this sceptical perspective, repeating the mantra that religion and morality must be rational. But over in Prussia, Immanuel Kant admitted the force of Hume's thought. Philosophy needed a new basis – or Hume's cynicism would triumph.

Kant was raised in Pietism, the Protestant movement that emphasized moral reform, inner sincerity. He had moved towards a less observant, more deist faith – which he now saw needed radical rethinking. He put all the emphasis on this question: what is morality? Is it just a bunch of hunches and habits or is there something objective here, some hard-core principle? In his first major work, of 1785, he argued that it's not enough to analyse particular actions and their results; we have to look beneath the surface at the question of motivation, or will. We have a sense of moral duty. Isn't this just a vague matter, shaped by tradition and habit? No, we can rationally establish that some duties are objectively valid. A moral duty is objectively true if we can honestly will that everyone should act on it. For example, my sense of obligation to help the poor is authentic because it would be good if everyone did so. By contrast, to say that everyone should look out for himself rather than help the poor is an objectively bad attitude, for we cannot wish that everyone shared it.

Why not just say that actions are good if they make the world better, enlarge human happiness? Because we can't really adjudicate this, we can't trace the results of actions; and so we can't find a rational principle here. It's only the phenomenon of duty that reveals morality's objective, rational core. Away from this principle, morality is too amorphous to be systematically understood.

Kant rejects the normal deist assumption that morality comes naturally (if so, why don't we all behave perfectly?). Instead he develops the religious assumption of a conflict between moral duty and one's fallen nature. We know what our rational moral duty is but we are prone to selfishness. How do we know our duty? All rational beings have an innate 'idea of moral perfection'.[19] (This is how we can recognize the divinity of Christ, who exemplifies this moral perfection, he suggests.) Only in relation to 'the principle of perfection' can morality be a rational system.[20]

So we naturally know what perfect morality consists in (as long as we are rational beings). The problem is doing it. And it is this experience of moral duty that gives us a sure sense of God's reality; we know him as the author of this perfectionist moral call, Kant explains in a book of 1793: 'Morality thus leads ineluctably to religion, through which it extends itself to the idea of a powerful moral lawgiver, outside of mankind.' And religion remains rooted in rational morality: 'A moral religion . . . must consist not in dogmas and rites but in the heart's disposition to fulfil all human duties as divine commands.'[21]

In other words, if we honestly reflect on morality, we see that it is an absolute obligation to seek the good of all, the perfection of human life. And it is in this context that God is credible – sort of (Kant implied that we should move away from literal belief). To put it differently, God is reinvented as the necessary principle upholding an absolutist form of morality. He doesn't conceive of a moral duty to be good enough, decent, to abide by the social norms (Hume's idea of moral duty), but to be perfect. This absolutely demanding morality is the core of Christianity – the mythical or creedal aspect grows up around it. We must believe in eternal happiness as the reward for obeying the moral call. Even if we struggle to believe in the old fashioned way, we must at least propagate religion as the means by which this sense of moral duty reaches the masses.

Although Kant claims to be analysing morality in an objective rational way and discovering its perfectionist structure, his approach is in reality coloured by his residual Christianity. In a sense he brings a new Christian intensity to deism. Deism had said that rational morality is the essence of religion, but in a vague pragmatic way. Kant tightened this up by introducing absoluteness, perfectionism (and a corresponding notion of fallenness, or 'radical evil' in humanity). Only such absoluteness can make morality a rational, coherent system.

Kant did a rather paradoxical thing: he gave humanist morality a new rational aura. But he did so by drawing on Christianity's moral perfectionism and in a sense secularizing it. This perfectionism is part of the structure of reality rather than a myth-based tradition, he implied.

After Kant, ethics tends to begin with the unexamined assumption that moral perfectionism is *normal*. Of course we all desire universal well-being, it assumes – the question is how we get there. This assumption is, I suggest, completely bizarre! We need to learn to begin at the beginning and ask where our basic idea of morality comes from.

A brief conclusion on a long era

In this chapter we have seen that, in the Enlightenment era, secular humanism slowly emerged from Protestant reformism. This was made possible by the fact that Protestantism developed two mutations: one in which rational universalism came to seem the essence of religion; another in which the separation of Church and state seemed a sacred duty. These mutations gave rise to various forms of secular humanism, which emerged in dialogue with traditional religion. Some hotly rejected religion; others half-affirmed it; all were shaped by it. In Charles Taylor's summary, 'exclusive humanism' (which he defines as humanism that sees 'no final goals beyond human flourishing') 'crept up on us by intermediate form: Providential Deism – both were made possible by earlier developments within Christianity'.[22]

Perhaps a note is in order on the term 'secular humanism'. In a sense it is misleading to say that something called secular humanism slowly emerged in the Enlightenment era, for of course various positions emerged, and they did not begin to coalesce into a single movement, let alone one calling itself by this name – 'humanism' only gained currency in the mid nineteenth century. But this simplifying umbrella term is warranted because these various positions shared a belief in universal humanism (which, after Rousseau, had a more emotive aura, replacing the colder rationalism of previous deism); and they also shared an opposition to traditional religion, especially its exertion of political power. However, we must bear in mind that there was no single, coherent, self-conscious movement. Indeed, the incoherence of secular humanism remained surprisingly extensive throughout the next century, to which we now turn.

4

Struggling to be born

In the nineteenth century, the same story continues: secular humanism continues to emerge from Christian tradition. Even when religion is boldly rejected, the influence of some form of reformist Christianity or deism is evident. So in this chapter, I want to continue to show that secular humanist ideas are not just 'there' when religion is removed but are shaped by centuries of religious thinking. (Ironically, the thinker who most acutely analysed this deep bond between Christianity and humanism was the sworn enemy of both: Friedrich Nietzsche, whom we'll consider at the end of this chapter.)

In this period, secular humanism became far more prevalent as an expanding intelligentsia adopted and developed the ideas we have traced. But rather surprisingly, it became no more coherent: no firm new ideology arose to replace traditional religion – instead, new secular humanist perspectives, such as communism, and new thinking, such as Darwinism, complicated things. We see it as the age of boundless reformist confidence but in fact most secular humanists seem to have been rather uncertain about the ideological future. Despite the apparent death of the old religion, the new creed was struggling to be born.

In discussing the emergence of secular humanism we should not overlook the fact that most actual, practical humanitarianism was still firmly religious. The anti-slavery movement is an obvious arena of this. The abolition of the slave trade in the British Empire in 1807 was due to a Christian-based movement that highlighted the ideal of universal human brotherhood. In the same way, later in the century, American abolitionism was a Christian-based cause. But both movements downplayed their Christian roots and spoke in largely secular terms; they therefore helped to found a Christian-based secular moral universalism. Also, it was chiefly Christians who protested at the working conditions thrown up by the Industrial Revolution, and who battled for social reforms. Christian socialism was not a marginal hybrid but was central to the gradual emergence of democratic socialism. And of course, especially in Britain and America, liberal politics was inextricable from Protestant idealism in the age of Lincoln and Gladstone.

Christian humanitarianism

In the Enlightenment era, humanitarianism remained principally Christian-based. Amid all the talk of rational progress, it fell to religious reformers to insist that the poor be treated as fully human. This was part of John Wesley's agenda in founding the Methodist movement: the established Church seemed stiffly incapable of ministering to the poor with real energy. He said to the Church: 'the rich, the honorable, the great, we are thoroughly willing . . . to leave to you. Only let us alone among the poor.' He saw ministering to them and improving their lot as basic to his calling, as 'Christianity is essentially a social religion.'[1]

Wesley was also more keenly opposed to slavery than the average rationalist. Even Voltaire held back from attacking slavery; he wanted to appear a realistic reformer, and opposition to slavery seemed a matter of sentimental excess (rather like animal rights to most of us today). Sensible men of the world accepted that slavery was just part of the fabric of reality. It 'has hardly any possibility of being abolished', said Adam Smith in 1763, for it 'has been universall in the beginnings of society, and the love of dominion and authority over others will probably make it perpetuall.'[2] Wesley, by contrast, denounced the racism underlying slavery as an intolerable denial of our common humanity: 'an African is in no respect inferior to the European', he said; he is just deprived of 'all opportunities of improving either in knowledge or virtue.'[3] This deep assumption of common humanity was most clearly and bluntly propounded by Christians: rationalists were more equivocal, on the one hand affirming that 'savages' were fully human but on the other implying that their lack of rationalism made them effectively sub-human, for the time being.

Wesley's opposition to slavery echoed the Quakers, who tried to raise the issue in colonial New England. (In an early form of protest theatre, one of the campaigners, Benjamin Lay, gave dramatic sermons in which he stabbed a Bible that seemed to bleed. He also stood outside a Quaker meeting house with a bare leg deep in snow, to give a taste of what slaves endured, and on another occasion kidnapped a slave-owner's child for a few hours.) In the next generation, Quakers tried to persuade the republic's founders to confront the issue, but deist pragmatism was unswayed (though Franklin was won over to the cause). It came naturally to Quakers to argue for abolition in general moral terms – for this form of Christianity put all the emphasis on Christlike action rather than Bible-based theorizing. This determined the language of abolitionism: it was a cause that did not draw attention to its Christian motivation; rather it appealed to moral universalism. It spoke in secular humanist terms, despite its mainly religious motivation.

The British campaign against the slave trade began in 1783, when a Quaker pressure group was formed for the purpose. It was gradually joined by Anglicans – notably the young trainee priest Thomas Clarkson – and relaunched in 1787. Soon the Evangelical MP William Wilberforce was on board. The cause was boosted by the famous icon, designed by Josiah Wedgwood (a Unitarian Christian), of a kneeling slave asking 'Am I not a man and a brother?' It was the first ever campaign invoking universal human rights. And this was understood in religious terms: 'brother' of course referred to the common fatherhood of God, but in a broad, undogmatic way.

The movement provided a platform for the freed slave Olaudah Equiano (a keen convert to Protestantism), whose autobiography and lectures refuted assumptions of heathen inferiority. The group's decisive publication, *The Abstract of the Evidence*, was carefully sober, objective; it resisted preachifying and made no references to the Bible. Again, it shows Christian-motivated humanitarianism opting to speak in general secular terms.

The argument was largely won by the early 1790s, but war with France and a slave rebellion in the West Indies slowed things down. And even after the vote to end the trade in 1807, the fight went on to ban slavery itself in the British Empire. This further fight was largely led by women's abolitionist groups; a leading figure was Elizabeth Heyrick, a Quaker convert. Such female leadership was a new thing, sparked by the slavery issue. It was in the midst of the campaign against the slave trade that the first great feminist tract appeared, Mary Wollstonecraft's *Vindication of the Rights of Women*. 'Is one half of the human species', she asked, 'like the poor African slaves, to be subjected to prejudices which brutalize them?'[4] So the Christian-based agitation against slavery was a major ingredient in the birth of the feminist movement. (Wilberforce was dismayed to see female leadership springing up even among Evangelical abolitionists.)

Was British anti-slavery a religious movement? Yes and no. Adam Hochschild ends his (excellent) account of it thus:

> All of the twelve [founders of the movement in 1787] were deeply religious, and the twenty-seven-year-old Clarkson wore black clerical garb. But they also shared a newer kind of faith. They believed that because human beings had a capacity to care about the sufferings of others, exposing the truth would move people to action . . . [They saw that] the way to stir men and women to action is not by biblical argument, but through the vivid, unforgettable description of acts of great injustice done to their fellow human beings. The abolitionists placed their hope not in sacred texts, but in human empathy.[5]

Hochschild is a bit too keen to separate the 'newer' faith from the old. Yes, they trusted in the power of human empathy, but saw such empathy as deeply rooted in Christian morality. It was because their culture was Christian that they had confidence that it would respond to their message.

Romantic humanism

We previously suggested that 'humanism' might be traced to Rousseau's emotionally inclined renewal of deism, his narrative about the restoration of humanity's true potential. This inspired practical politics, as we saw – but also the less practical business of poets attending to daffodils and so forth. Literary Romanticism was a new expression of deism, but some writers went further than Rousseau in rejecting traditional religion. Goethe made neopagan noises as, more tentatively, did Wordsworth. But Wordsworth is good evidence that Protestant-based deism remained the central influence: his poetry is dominated by a confidence in natural morality, known through communing with nature. Witnessing the French Revolution, he was attracted to a more radical form of humanism but, sensing its danger, backed down and moved towards affirming Christianity as central to British freedom. Coleridge's course was broadly similar, though he was more inclined to theological speculation. Most younger English Romantics were less theologically inclined: Keats and Shelley echoed Goethe's pursuit of a post-Christian humanism, combining neopaganism with secularized Nonconformist Protestantism. Shelley's atheism is in the tradition of the deism of Voltaire and Paine – God might be rejected but a belief in divine providence is effectively retained. Also, for Shelley and Keats, poetry is elevated to quasi-religious status – it enables the recycling of the themes of devotion, mystery, vocation, sacrifice. (Romanticism can be seen as a fusion of secularized Protestantism, secularized Catholicism and neo-pagan primitivism – a complex mix.)

In the 1830s, Romantic thought began to be influenced by a German thinker who had just died: G. W. F. Hegel. His grand philosophy of history, in which freedom emerges through a huge process of internal cultural struggle, inspired some post-Christian thinkers to a new bold Promethean sort of humanism. But Hegel would have been aghast to know this: his historical theory aimed to establish the truth of Christianity in new terms.

To begin with, Hegel – sounding like Rousseau – criticized Christianity as insufficiently social: it did not bring people together in communal joy and national togetherness; and Protestantism seemed worse than Catholicism in this respect, being overly individualistic. But then he decided that such a judgement was overhasty. In fact Protestantism was slowly brewing up a superior form of social religion, one in which rationalism and individual liberty were allowed to develop to full fruition. Only temporarily was there a tension – or dialectic – between rational individualism and social cohesion: a superior form of political culture was arriving, in the form of the liberal state. For it is through national culture that rational humanism emerges: universal humanism is a potential distraction from this.

Theology must be reinvented, said Hegel: instead of fighting dated battles with sceptics or appeasing them in the form of deism, it must explain what God is doing in history. This is how religion can be rational, without abolishing itself: it must show that rationalism is a movement that it owns. The so-called Enlightenment, 'that vanity of understanding', fails to see its rationalism as part of this religious story.[6] The proper business of theology is the history of ideas, showing how God works through 'the cunning of history'.

Did Hegel *believe* in Christianity? Like Kant, he thought that the intellectual elite would see religion in rational and moral terms and be ambivalent about its traditional ritual and creedal expressions. These should not be dismissed: God must express himself in popular cultural terms, not just in philosophy books. But these old forms are problematic in that they uphold the irrational, other-worldly aspect of religion from which Christianity is progressively moving away. 'He sounds like a post-Christian agnostic', some will say, 'who wants the masses to remain religious.' But that's not quite right: he sincerely proclaimed modern thought to be basically Christian. True philosophy, he said, must show 'that the truth in the most all-embracing sense of the term is deposited in religion'.[7] He sincerely felt that Christianity was the only source of modern thought's coherence and unity.

My own argument is in a sense Hegelian, for it has an idea of divine purpose working through a huge historical movement – secular humanism – that seems opposed to religion. I suppose I also share his belief that the history of ideas is the central business of theology, the way we can justify the ways of God to man. But I do not share Hegel's liberal Protestant idea that traditional religion – ritual, doctrine, faith – is becoming redundant, transforming itself into rational humanism. And in fact I would claim that my position is more dialectical. For Hegel, the dialectical movement of religious history moves towards a synthesis (as Christianity loses its other-worldliness and morphs into liberalism). As I see it, there is a *continuing* tension between Christianity, with its particular cultic forms, and post-Christian universalism.

Various philosophers and artists were drawn to Hegel's emphasis on history and its dramatic internal ructions, but wanted to de-Christianize this – or post-Christianize it. The vague and paradoxical idea emerged that religion had to be reinvented, turned inside out. Humanity must dare to become itself, in opposition to tradition, maybe to God (Goethe's *Faust* gave this classic poetic expression).

Thomas Carlyle, the Scottish-born sage of London, laboured in this direction. He warned that post-religious humanism was shallow, banal, flimsy against Mammon; the task was to recycle the bold, history-sculpting force of religion for a new age – he tried to be the authoritative prophet of this (despite lacking a clear positive message). This influenced the American writer Ralph Waldo Emerson (who visited Europe in the 1830s). He had trained as a Unitarian minister, and his thought is a heated argument with Christianity, seeking to liberate its world-affirming, incarnational aspect from its irrelevant dogmatic aspect. In 1838 he told the graduates of Harvard Divinity School that each should think of himself as 'a new-born bard of the Holy Ghost', scorning all conformity.[8] This aversion to tradition surfaces in his essay 'Self-Reliance':

Man . . . dares not say "I think," "I am," but quotes some saint or sage. . . .
These roses under my window make no reference to former roses or to
better ones; they are for what they are; they exist with God today.[9]

But this world-affirming, tradition-disdaining philosophy is patently
an offshoot of Protestantism.

A major strain of Romanticism, then, was 'post-religious' in a particular sense: instead of just rejecting religion as false, it saw the need to
rechannel the energy of religion in the cause of human liberation. This
idea was given philosophical expression by Ludwig Feuerbach. In 1841,
in *The Essence of Christianity*, he explained that when religion talks of
God it is really telling the truth about humanity: that it is sacred. The
divine must be pulled down from heaven and located in the human.
Atheism in this specific sense is the 'secret of religion itself';[10] for
Christianity, 'while lowering God into man, made man into God'.[11]
So it is missing the point to say that Jesus was merely human: 'I accept
the Christ of religion, but I show that this superhuman being is nothing else than a product and reflex of the supernatural human mind.'[12]
It's reminiscent of Rousseau, this idea that 'divine humanity' must come
to expression; but now there is a stronger animus against traditional
religion. This was soon to influence Marx's theory of humanity's hid-
den or alienated potential that only political revolution could liberate.

A different approach to the issue was proposed by Auguste Comte.
He started out as a disciple of the utopian socialist Saint-Simon, who
was openly seeking to reinvent Christian morality in secular terms (one
of his books was called *Nouveau christianisme*). Comte developed his
own brand of humanism in the 1830s and 40s – indeed it was he who
popularized the word 'humanism' (though it seems to have been coined
by his German contemporary Arnold Ruge). He announced that the
truth of rationalism, which he called 'positivism', could utterly remake
society. But this force must not just be written and talked about.
It must be enshrined in a new religion, the Religion of Humanity.
This proposed secular religion resembled Catholicism in its passion
for communal public expression and its detailed plans for temples
and liturgies, devotion to saints and so on. This echoed the French
revolutionary tradition of festivals of the Supreme Being, in a more
universalist, less political way.

It is common for today's agnostic humanists to smile at the earnest
folly of this, but in a sense Comte was more honest than they are. He

confronted the fact that humanist idealism has a religious character, as the universal creed that tacitly claims to unite humanity. The average agnostic of today half-believes this but keeps quiet about it, shelves the issue, doesn't go there, shrugs – which is cowardly evasion dressed as worldly wisdom.

The emergence of the term 'humanism' was not a major turning point. This creed was just updated deism, incorporating the emotional enthusiasm of Rousseau and others.

In a sense these philosophers were marginal exponents of secular humanism. Its primary form was the new politics of liberal nationalism that had been pioneered by France and now inspired liberation movements in Italy, Latin America and elsewhere. Though anticlerical, this tradition continued to be influenced by Christian-based deism (like the French Revolution itself). Of course, in all these movements the abstract principles of the universal rights of man and so on jostled awkwardly with violent political necessity. The whole issue of secular humanism was therefore too politicized to be carefully pondered. In Britain especially, the idea of a post-religious moral universalism was inextricable from the threatening politics sporadically erupting on the Continent.

Common humanity?

We have seen that the British abolitionists convinced the nation that slavery was a violation of common humanity, securing its full abolition in 1833. But in fact the debate went on: many felt that 'common humanity' was a pious aspiration that a sober study of human biology, and culture, disproved. The debate increasingly touched on the question of human origins – a question that fused science and moral ideology. Slavery was wrong because of the unity of humanity under God, the abolitionists had been saying for decades. And some left God out, just asserting the axiomatic unity of humanity. But was it axiomatic? Defenders of slavery, especially of course in America, were now using science to contest it, to show that the races were distinct, that physical differences, such as differently shaped skulls, determined their cultural separateness. Slavery defenders sneered at the myth of humanity's common derivation from Adam and Eve as the source of unrealistic sentimentalism – let us treat Scripture with enlightened scepticism, and stick to the fact that some races are evidently superior to others.

We are accustomed to assume that one of the big stories of this era was Science Disproving the Bible – particularly Darwin's science. But in relation to this issue it's more complicated: the counter-intuitive reality is that it was the Bible that drove the idea of humanity's common origin – and science only gradually backed this up. Most science pointed the other way: it put the idea of a common species identity in doubt. The orthodoxy was 'pluralism', meaning the belief that each race originated separately, that the myth of common ancestry was bunk. When Charles Darwin began amassing evidence to refute this, he was not setting out to defend the Bible, but nevertheless he was following a moral hunch that there was symbolic truth in the biblical picture.

He was the grandson of Josiah Wedgwood, the Unitarian pottery magnate who had designed the famous abolitionist icon; he was raised amid the conviction of human unity – a religious-based moral conviction. His voyage round the world in the 1830s showed him slavery up close, and his hatred for it sharpened. His observation of nature was coloured by his desire to disprove pluralism, to find a scientific basis for the common descent of humanity. And, of course, he found more than this: humanity's commonality with other animals. He found ammunition for the abolitionists, yet this ammunition was surprising and disturbing – in two ways. It challenged the biblical notion of humanity's uniqueness (and of course went against a literal reading of Genesis), but his discoveries also seemed to confirm the assumption that some races were destined to triumph over others. He was influenced by Robert Malthus's notion of competition for resources producing a fitter breed of humanity; this was a basic ingredient of his notion of natural selection. When he heard of white settlers displacing and ultimately exterminating native peoples, he was inclined to see this as a fact of nature. His thought was 'ideologically messy'.[13] In a sense his animosity to slavery was rooted in a desire for moral clarity that generally eluded his thought. We *must* see it as wrong, for we're in danger of seeing it as natural.

So his science supported universal humanism with one hand – disproving the racist idea of separate human origins – yet undermined it with the other, giving new justification to the ideology of competition between races.

And he complicated the question of whether morality comes naturally. As we have seen, deists and atheists implied that it does – we just need to be enlightened, freed from superstition and prejudice, and we will behave as we ought. This now seemed flimsy – the most basic natural impulse is to compete, fight for space, dominate. Darwin observed that some red ants enslave black ants, and called it 'an extraordinary and odious instinct'.[14] This is a muddled phrase, as it contradicts his belief that no animal instinct can be morally judged. What he surely means is that it is odious for humans to do likewise and to blame it on instinct. The problem is that he provides no means for distinguishing between what is natural in human behaviour and what is subject to moral condemnation.

Darwin hoped that his work would aid the cause of American abolitionism by disproving the racist science of plural origins. But the abolitionists had little time for science. Their concern was to turn vague Christian humanism into a militant cause. Again, this was a Christian-based movement that expressed itself in largely secular terms. Its main architect was William Lloyd Garrison; he blended biblical and republican rhetoric in semi-secular preaching, from around 1830. The movement's basis was 'Divine Revelation and the Declaration of our Independence', he announced.[15] He sometimes implied that the movement was a sort of religious reformation, the emergence of a fuller Christianity that refused all pragmatic compromise with moral evil. He resembled deists such as Jefferson: he too was a Christian who put all the emphasis on moral action. But he rejected the cautious rationalism of the deists and spoke in more enthusiastic terms, echoing the language of religious revivalism and biblical eschatology. The cause demanded absolute commitment, even if it meant breaking with one's church, even if it meant withholding loyalty from a tainted nation, civil disobedience. (The notion of civil disobedience, famously formulated by Thoreau, derives from radical Protestantism.)

The freed slave Frederick Douglass offered very similar rhetoric: the American ideal of liberty for all must be rescued from falsity, he said, and the Fourth of July must be made into a day worth celebrating. In his memoir (published in 1845), Douglass presented Southern Christianity as a kind of inversion of true faith, in which the rest of the country is currently complicit. '"Shall I not visit for these things?" saith the Lord. "Shall not my soul be avenged on a nation such as this?"'[16]

Such rhetoric about the need for national renewal and the fear of divine disfavour won over the progressive mind: Abraham Lincoln spoke of slavery being at odds with America's liberal destiny and the sacred principle of equality in the Declaration of Independence. In 1860, just before the war, he quoted Frederick Douglass: 'It is written in the sky of America that the slaves shall someday be free.'[17] Yet he remained deeply uncertain whether blacks could live among whites as equal citizens – he still flirted with the idea of repatriating them to Africa. But the conviction of the ungodliness of slavery led him to galvanize the North against the expansion of slavery into the West.

So abolitionism was a Christian-based movement, from the eighteenth-century Quakers, and British Evangelicals, through to Garrison and Douglass. Some might say, 'Well, it had to be, as it had to win over public opinion, and the vast majority in Britain and America were Christians.' That's a bit facile: in fact Christianity shaped the ideal of human unity – and post-Christian rationalism was often inclined to be evasive and fatalist on the issue.

We should be wary of the idea that it comes naturally to abhor slavery and racism, that such abhorrence is rational. Most scientists were inclined to credit the idea of different origins for different races. In opposing this, Darwin did not just follow his rational nose: Christian-based abolitionism prompted him to look for a theory of humanity's common origin. His career suggests that scientific discovery is, at times, not merely neutral but shaped by a moral framework.

Mill

In the second half of the century it became possible for British thinkers to advocate something like 'secular humanism' without seeming too dangerously radical. John Stuart Mill led the way. On one level he was a key inventor of 'secular humanism' as we know it – a sensible, moderate, idealistic creed with individual liberty at its heart. On another level, he is very different from the blasé secular humanist of our day: he confronted the creed's intensely demanding moral basis.

He was the son of James Mill, who worked closely with Jeremy Bentham, known as the founder of the rational reforming creed of utilitarianism, the pursuit of the greatest happiness of the greatest number. This was a new force in British public life, from around 1830, but the theory was not so new: for a century or two many thinkers, mostly Christian ones, had promoted a 'teleological' form of ethics (which calls actions good on account of their results), and criticized traditional natural law and deontological (duty-based) ones. This approach was favoured by atheists – including, as we saw in the last chapter, D'Holbach. But some Christian thinkers, such as William Paley, had also argued for something like utilitarianism.

Bentham was firmly in the tradition of eighteenth-century deism and atheism but he put more emphasis on practical reform than abstract speculation. He was serenely confident that he had found the rational principle of morality that could transform the world. If an action led to the overall increase of happiness it was good. This principle had to replace religious morality, he declared – he made utilitarianism a distinctly post-religious creed. Such rational reformism became hugely influential in Britain, especially in relation to the law, and its influence was generally benign. Yet in theoretical terms, Bentham deepened the problem that we noted in relation to Kant. Secular ethics unhelpfully assumes the obviousness of the goal of universal human flourishing; it blithely skips over the question of *why* we should pursue this morally demanding vision. The deists had said that divine rationality demands it: Bentham implicitly continued this assumption but replaced the language of divine truth with natural humanism, assuming that it comes naturally to us to pursue the general good. This was a humble development in a way, but on another level a dishonest one, a dubious bracketing of the question of motivation, a pretence that the humanitarian impulse is axiomatic.

Mill Senior, having rejected his Scottish Presbyterian upbringing, taught his son that religion was 'a great moral evil' because it detracted from the greatest happiness of the greatest number by spreading 'belief in creeds, devotional feelings, and ceremonies, not connected with the good of human kind'.[18] And yet the ghost of Protestant zeal lingered on: he also taught his son 'to take the strongest interest in the Reformation, as the great and decisive contest against priestly tyranny for liberty of thought'.[19] Like today's atheists, he was full of indignation at the notion of an all-powerful creator who allowed the world to contain such suffering, not to mention sending people to hell (another example of predestination-prompted atheism).

Mill Junior sought to soften and humanize his inherited creed, to emphasize that it was not just a rejection of religion but a positive vision, full of moral purpose; perhaps it could be seen as a new sort of religion, he ventured.[20] Bentham had claimed to be motivated by 'love of humanity' but his work exuded little warmth – and Mill Senior failed to see that such love begins at home; he was a cold fish of a father. So Mill Junior was drawn to the more enthusiastic humanism across the Channel: he looked favourably on the utopian socialism of Saint-Simon and the quasi-religion of Comte (he also saw the poetry of Wordsworth as a crucial resource in the emotional deepening of secular humanism). He soon decided that Comte was scarily dogmatic but he retained the idea that rational morality needed new humanist warmth. His basic framework remained utilitarian but he tried to add nuance. He confronted a subtle contradiction: we should see general human happiness as the criterion of morality but we should not be motivated by the pursuit of *our own* happiness. We should hope to find happiness in the service of humanity, in noble moral action. A happier world depends on people putting the general good before their own good.

But why should they? He seems to fall back on the idea that moral idealism is in our nature. So is selfishness of course, but rational thought will show that our true desire is for the good of all. This is very like Kant's idea that clear moral thought will perceive the 'principle of perfection'. He says that many non-believers 'have that which constitutes the principal worth of all religions whatever, an ideal conception of a Perfect Being, to which they habitually refer as the guide of their conscience'.[21]

He comes surprisingly close to admitting that humanist morality comes from Christianity. In a sense he does admit this: it is in the form of Christianity that the highest moral teachings are first expressed; but once they have been expressed, he argues, they can be detached from religion, for they are 'strong enough in their own evidence' to retain our allegiance:[22]

> [Jesus' teachings] carry some kinds of moral goodness to a greater height than had ever been attained before . . . But this benefit, whatever it amounts to, has been gained. Mankind have entered into the possession of it. It has become the property of humanity, and cannot now be lost by anything short of a return to primeval barbarism. [Jesus' teachings, including] the reverence for the weak and humble, which is the foundation of chivalry; . . . that of 'he that is without sin let him cast the first stone'; the precept of doing as we would be done by . . . are surely in sufficient harmony with the intellect and feelings of every good man or woman, to be in no danger of . . . ceas[ing] to be operative on the human conscience, while human beings remain cultivated or civilized.[23]

So Christian morality is an early discovery of *the objective moral truth*, which is now built into 'civilization'. This is a slightly more intelligent version of today's atheist claim that morality just comes naturally. It is something civilization has learned, so that it now comes naturally to civilized people. Traditional religion is no longer needed, but this moral idealism must be nurtured – in a sense it should be seen as 'religious', he says, so perhaps we should speak of a 'Religion of Humanity'.[24] Perhaps, replacing the worship of God, we need 'adoration of abstract moral perfection'.[25] This is rather different from the secular humanist assumption that we just need to be ourselves, let our natural moral instincts do their stuff. He felt that we must be quasi-religious in our humanism. The earnest intensity is reminiscent of Spinoza, whom Mill rather resembled in his unworldly way of life. He was an almost lifelong bachelor: late in life he had a platonic relationship with a married woman; they married when she was widowed and it's unclear whether it stayed platonic. He saw sex as deeply disruptive to moral progress and hoped that it would gradually become subordinate to rationality – as he supposed it already to be in well-bred women.[26]

Towards the end of his life he returned to the subject of religion. He argued that it is infinitely important that we imagine:

> a morally perfect Being, and [are in] the habit of taking the approbation of such a Being as the *norma* or standard to which to refer and by which to regulate our own characters and lives. [This is possible] even when that Person is conceived as merely imaginary.[27]

Christianity has rightly propagated this ideal, though it has muddled it by confusing it with a morally dubious creator and judge. And Christianity has done well to present us with an actual historical embodiment of moral perfection: 'Religion cannot be said to have made a bad choice in pitching on this man as the ideal representative and guide of humanity'[28] (there is something comical about this faint praise for Christianity). To see Jesus as our moral ideal 'can aid and fortify that real, though purely human religion, which sometimes calls itself the Religion of Humanity and sometimes that of Duty'. It can inspire us in 'cultivating a religious devotion to the welfare of our fellow-creatures as an obligatory limit to every selfish aim, and an end for the direct promotion of which no sacrifice can be too great'.[29] Such devotion to humanity is 'destined, with or without supernatural sanctions, to be the religion of the Future'.[30]

It is surprising to see such an influential secular humanist speaking in such quasi-religious terms. He almost says that authentic humanism should retain Christian shape. On one level, today's secular humanism concurs with Mill, seeing universal morality as axiomatic to civilization. *Of course* our deepest desire is seeking the good of all humanity, it says. But it has quietly ditched the other assumption, that this desire is an arduous ideal that must be nurtured in quasi-religious terms. Such thinking sounds comically dated – like the idea that moral universalism is a facet of 'civilization'. But what's today's alternative? The issue is just ignored – until the atheists come along, with their far less intelligent notion that moral universalism comes completely naturally.

Marx

Karl Marx developed a post-religious vision of human morality that was deeply shaped by Judeo-Christian tradition. Early in the century, socialism was a frail tradition, eclipsed by liberal nationalism. There were a few movements that resembled sectarian religion, focused on building a little vanguard of utopia (the cultish industrialist Robert Owen was such a pioneer). Such movements hardly impinged on politics.

In the 1840s, socialist thought was gaining currency, but to Marx, as a student, it seemed too close to airy religious aspiration. What changed his mind was Feuerbach's call to regain humanity's alienated essence. This gave 'socialism a philosophical foundation'.[31] He therefore inherited the idea that the Christian vision of human unity must be realized in this world. He then adapted a prophetic, apocalyptic rhetoric that he found in his fellow Jewish socialist Moses Hess, and his polemical political vision was born.

Throughout his writing he obviously secularized the prophetic tradition of demanding justice, denouncing greed, proclaiming human unity. Did he pause to ponder the religious roots of this? No. He wanted to sideline the whole question of moral motivation and launch an objective progressive science that would make all talk of 'humanism' and 'morality' unnecessary, beside the point. Action was what mattered, not warm words. This action was socialism, understood in a new hard-nosed way. Conventional socialism was just 'vain dishonest playing at preaching'.[32] His preferred term, communism, had a tougher association with the Jacobins of the French Revolution and their grown-up aptitude for violence. When he joined a London communist group he demanded that it drop its slogan, 'All men are brothers', with its echo of Christian-based abolitionism, in favour of 'Proletarians of All Countries – Unite!'[33] In one of his pithy sound bites, he called Christian socialism 'the holy water with which the priest consecrates the heart-burnings of the aristocrat'.[34]

Marx's demand for a clean separation of socialism from religion was a classic case of protesting too much. The reality was that socialism had various deep Christian roots – one tradition harked back to a medieval Catholic vision of social harmony, before the advent of capitalism (this was particularly clear in France, where socialism was nurtured by sections of the Catholic Church). In England, the radicalism of the Civil War-era Levellers had been revived by the Chartists, a movement demanding the vote for workers that resembled a secularized Methodism. It sparked a Christian socialist movement within the Church of England, which gained huge influence in diluted form through writers such as Dickens. More widely, the Judeo-Christian ideal of social justice and a final, eschatological, reckoning plainly drove all socialist idealism. Marx was uncomfortable about these religious roots; he wanted a clean distinction between religion and socialism rather than a messy overlap. His insistence that communism was a science arose from a sort of embarrassment at its moral idealism. In order to effect this distinction (and maybe partly to try to convince himself of it), he renewed the most virulent atheist rhetoric of the previous century, with an emphasis on religion's corruption of a healthy, manly attitude. For example:

> The social principles of Christianity preach cowardice, self-contempt, abasement, submission, dejection, in a word all the qualities of the *canaille* [rabble]; and the proletariat, not wishing to be treated as *canaille*, needs its courage, its self-reliance, its pride, and its sense of independence more than its bread. The social principles of Christianity are sneakish and the proletariat is revolutionary.[35]

This is strikingly like Nietzsche's approach to religion – except that Nietzsche says that it's the aristocracy whose natural strength is undermined by Christianity.

In seeking to deny the semi-Christian character of socialism in favour of a purely scientific version, Marx created a new sort of secular religion. And he also revived the narrative of radical deism: superstitious religion must be smashed, for enlightened morality to triumph. Of course, he presented this as atheism rather than deism, but any atheism that is so deeply convinced of the providential shape of history is certainly an offshoot of deism.

Secularism

As we saw, Britain – or at first England – adopted a semi-secular constitution in the late seventeenth century, a compromise in which an established Church was answerable to Parliament and in which there was limited toleration for non-Anglicans. This toleration gradually became a bit fuller, in a de facto way. But popular fears of popery and atheism kept the old order in place through the eighteenth century: the French Revolution produced a conservative reaction against Dissenters, or Nonconformists. This group comprised traditional pious Protestants and also radical deists (generally the children of pious Protestants). The latter began to call for a fuller secularism, in new bolder terms. They demanded an end to restrictions that made them second-class citizens and they revived the call for disestablishment. Jeremy Bentham and Mill Senior emerged as leading opponents of the Church of England in the 1820s. They swayed moderate opinion, and the Church's establishment was significantly softened around 1830 (fuller toleration was granted to Catholics as well as Protestant Dissenters). But dissenting opinion was not placated: calls for the complete separation of Church and state continued, indeed intensified. To complicate matters, such calls tended to accompany the rising ideology of free-market liberalism – many industrialists were from a dissenting background. This alliance of free-market capitalism and the desire for a more secular state allowed the Church to present itself, with some reason but also some humbug, as the great defender of the traditional social fabric, the defence against society's fragmentation into capitalist selfishness.

From mid century, the boldest calls for the separation of Church and state came from non-Christians, influenced by French anticlericalism. It was in this context that the term 'secularism' came into use. It was first used in 1851 by George Holyoake, a follower of the utopian socialist Owen and also of Comte. He attacked religion in his public lectures but was careful to avoid the term 'atheism', which he felt still had an amoral aura. He had been convicted of blasphemy in 1842 but not sentenced – a sign of England's waning will to impose its semi-theocratic constitution. What did he mean by 'secularism'? He explained in his book *The Principles of Secularism*:

> Secularism is the study of promoting human welfare by material means; measuring human welfare by the utilitarian rule, and making the service of others a duty of life. Secularism relates to the present existence of man ... [it is] a series of principles intended for the guidance of those who find Theology indefinite, or inadequate, or deem it unreliable.[36]

In effect, then, he identified 'secularism' with 'post-religious humanism'.

His younger colleague Charles Bradlaugh, who founded the National Secular Society in 1866, rejected his qualms about the term 'atheist'. He said: 'the logical consequence of the acceptance of Secularism must be that the man gets to atheism, if he has brains enough to comprehend.'[37] It is Bradlaugh who lacked the brains to comprehend that secularism is a complex, paradoxical tradition with roots in Christian reformism.

These thinkers raise an important semantic issue. Because he coined the term 'secularism', it might seem that Holyoake had the right to define it. But of course he didn't coin it from scratch: 'secular' had been in use for centuries, subtly shifting its meaning – putting an 'ism' on the end of a term does not give one the right to redefine it, ignoring its nuances. He was out of his depth in trying to pin down this complex paradoxical tradition.

As we saw in Chapter 2, 'secular' originally meant 'of the present age' and shifted to mean something like 'separate from the sphere of the Church', and had no anti-religious edge. Instead, reformist religion was proudly 'secular' in the sense of relating religious truth to the everyday world. For example, the Calvinist layman praises God through his *secular* vocation, meaning that he is not employed by a religious institution. Then came a major development: Milton and Locke, and later Jefferson and Madison, wanted the state to have a clearer *secular* character, meaning that it should disentangle itself from religious institutions. They understood secularism in this sense to be an aspect of Protestant reformism. So in this Protestant tradition there is a paradox: secular, or non-religious politics was mainly promoted by believers who wanted to see religion purified of worldly power.

This delicate tradition was shunted aside by the new, brash, post-religious use of 'secularism', which implied that religion stood in the way of true humanism. (Similarly, 'humanism' began to imply that the true morality was post-religious.) Mill was a relatively clear thinker on this issue. He argued for a fuller separation of Church and state, but unlike the above-mentioned campaigners he was careful not to present this as an anti-religious cause. Defending secular education, he wittily put it this way: 'To say that secular means irreligious . . . is very like saying that all professions except that of the law are illegal.'[38] In other words, he tried to associate secularism with a strict neutrality.

Disestablishment became an increasingly hot issue in the last decades of the century, thanks to both Nonconformist Protestantism and post-Christian secularism. (In subsequent decades, Nonconformism began to wane, making the issue less widely cared about.) In 1869 the Anglican Church in Ireland was disestablished – a belated admission that it was unjust to try to subject Roman Catholics to an official religion they rejected. The reform was led by Gladstone, who started out as a Tory defender of the Church's establishment, opposed to greater toleration for Catholics and Dissenters, but came to see that Britain's liberal tradition necessitated a more flexible approach. In effect he saw that the established Church must be reformed according to liberal principles – but not reformed out of existence; he held that it was the source of true, socially unifying liberalism.

In 1880, Bradlaugh caused a stir when he was elected to Parliament but refused to take the religious oath. The issue dragged on for eight years. Gladstone came to support Bradlaugh's cause. This was a major milestone in the hollowing out of the establishment – from now on atheists were acknowledged to be valid members of society.

By this time non-believers could describe themselves more politely than 'atheists': Thomas Henry Huxley proposed the new term 'agnostic' in 1869. He rightly saw that 'atheist' was an overcharged word since it carried the baggage of opposition to Christian morality. In effect an agnostic is a non-believer who makes no direct claim about whether religion is a force for good or ill (whereas an atheist is a non-believer who claims moral superiority to religion).

Despite his famous belligerence over evolution, Huxley was a far more nuanced critic of religion than the new atheists of our day. He tried to clarify that his fight was not with religion as such but with its exertion of political power. Agnosticism was not necessarily in conflict with theology, he said. 'But, as between Agnosticism and Ecclesiasticism, or, as our neighbours across the Channel call it, Clericalism, there can be neither peace nor truce.'[39] And he saw his agnostic crusade as shaped by his Protestant heritage: it was rooted, he said, in 'that conviction of the supremacy of private judgement . . . which is the foundation of the Protestant Reformation, and which was the doctrine accepted by the vast majority of the Anglicans of my youth'.[40] He saw the Church of England as having been taken over by a neo-medieval Anglo-Catholicism; that is, the Oxford Movement. He wanted to be a – secular – Protestant advocate of pure Christian morality, of what he called 'the bright side of Christianity'.[41]

The term 'humanism' was also becoming more current and less tied to Comte's dogmatism. Largely thanks to the Renaissance historian Jacob Burckhardt (who more or less invented 'the Renaissance' in his book of 1860, *Die Kultur der Renaissance in Italien*), 'humanism' began to refer to the idea of the dignity of humanity, a dignity suppressed by medieval church teaching. It began to refer to both 'high culture' and 'secularism' – as well as to the more radical ideas of Feuerbach and Marx.

A literary humanist

The novelist George Eliot, originally Mary Ann Evans, painfully rejected the Evangelicalism of her youth and opted for a humanism that remained full of Christian morality. Indeed, few thinkers are better evidence of the Christian basis of humanist idealism. Her example is particularly relevant today, for much mainstream secular humanism has a literary aspect (largely because opinion-formers tend to have studied English Literature). She was a key founder of the idea that literature is a site of post-religious humanism. Of course, this idea is already present in various Romantics, but in a rather blustery, unsettled way. She calmed it with a feminine touch.

She was raised in a pious provincial home in the Midlands but spent much time with some freethinking family friends. When, in her early twenties, she decided to reject religion, it felt like a sort of calling to a purer moral purpose. 'I wish to be among the ranks of that glorious crusade that is seeking to set Truth's Holy Sepulchre free from a usurped domination,' she told a friend.[42] She wrote to her father – though they lived in the same house – that she admired the moral teaching of Jesus but considered 'the system of doctrines built upon the facts of his life and drawn as to its material from Jewish notions to be most dishonor-able to God and most pernicious in its influence on individual and social happiness'.[43] This suggests a deist belief in a pure moral God, dishonoured by particularity. Or maybe she was just mitigating her atheism for her father.

She moved from the provinces to London and worked for a highbrow radical magazine. Her first publications were translations of German works of liberal theology, or post-theology: David Strauss's sceptical *Life of Jesus* and also Feuerbach's *The Essence of Christianity*. Both books confirmed her deep, even evangelical conviction that human love was the divine force in the world. Christianity had enshrined this, but also mixed it up with error: now it must be expounded in merely human terms. She lapped up Feuerbach's notion that 'the essential idea of the Incarnation, though enveloped in the night of the religious consciousness, is love.' Our saviour is not 'God' but 'Love; for God as God has not saved us, but Love, which transcends the difference between the divine and human personality'.[44]

She gradually saw novel-writing as the supreme means of expressing this post-religious vision. Of course, there was already a strong tradition of celebrating moral idealism in the novel – this had been done with increasing psychological realism since Richardson's *Pamela*. The point was to show the possibility of moral virtue in the real world (as we saw, Rousseau's novels pioneered such an agenda). For example, Elizabeth Bennett, in Jane Austen's *Pride and Prejudice*, is morally exemplary (despite her initial moralistic misjudgement), yet also possessed of wit, irony and some hinted sexuality, making her wonderfully credible. Dickens of course continued in this moralistic vein, with greater social but less psychological realism (he created two-dimensional icons of female virtue). And Dickens was very clear about his creed: Christian-based humanism. The essence of religion, his novels imply, is moral action; ritual tradition and supernatural faith are dubious accretions to the moral message of Jesus. Any character in his books who uses distinctively religious language is likely to be a Calvinist bigot. The 'real' Christians are quiet Christ-imitators, most often sexless angelic women. One of his most developed characters, Arthur Clenham from *Little Dorrit*, influenced by one such angel, rejects his native Calvinism in favour of real moral Christianity.

Back to Eliot. She united Austen's psychological realism with Dickens's Christian-based humanism. Her first book of stories, *Scenes of Clerical Life*, presented various ministers of religion, assessing their beliefs and their moral conduct – the thing that really matters. Belief is fine, indeed admirable, if it makes people good humanists, ready to grow and suffer for the moral truth. As omniscient novelist she hovers over religion, loftily assessing its moral worth.

Her novels are vehicles for this message that moral nobility is the truly sacred thing, whether religious-motivated or not. *Adam Bede* features an earthy icon of such nobility in Adam himself, and a more dramatic one in the Methodist preacher Dinah. This became her speciality: creating powerful salvific women, icons of Mary or Mary modernized. Dorothea Brooke of *Middlemarch* is an icon of post-religious moral yearning, of wanting to devote oneself to the Good. As she explains to her admirer Will Ladislaw, her belief is:

> [t]hat by desiring what is perfectly good, even when we don't quite know what it is and cannot do what we would, we are part of the divine power against evil – widening the skirts of light and making the struggle with darkness narrower.

This, she goes on, 'is my life. I have found it out and cannot part with it. I have always been finding out my religion since I was a little girl. I used to pray so much – now I hardly ever pray.' Like Kant, Eliot locates true morality in pure willing of the perfect Good rather than in particular actions, which more mediocre souls might happen to do. (In a sense the medium of the novel is ideal for demonstrating Kant's theory, as it can show moral action to be rooted in the will.) The mention of prayer is a perfect illustration of Eliot's post-religiosity: the pure moral will is nurtured by traditional religious forms – but the necessity for these forms falls away.

Her message, like Mill's, is that we must be humanists with religious passion. It is a deeply attractive message when framed in beautifully told stories: it reassures people with some grounding in religion but who find it hard to believe, which is most of us, that religion's moral essence can survive the collapse of religious belief.

But is it true? Is it true that there is a coherent post-religious humanism that retains passion for the absolute, even to the point of self-sacrifice? In general, no. Post-religious humanism tends to be pragmatic rather than passionate and perfectionist. Many Eliot enthusiasts, I suggest, want to pretend otherwise, want to see heroic moral idealism as somehow built into post-religious humanism. And – even more questionably – they are apt to see literature as part of this moral heroism, for Eliot sometimes presents the novel as a key site of the new morality: 'If art does not enlarge men's sympathies, it does nothing morally', she wrote.

> The only effect I long to produce by my writings, is that those who read them should be better able to *imagine* and to *feel* the pains and the joys of those who differ from themselves in everything but the broad fact of being struggling erring human creatures.[45]

So people grow morally by extending their capacity for sympathy with others, and novels perform this – so novel-reading is a way of participating in the brave new post-religious morality.

But she missed religion and was never entirely confident that morality could flourish away from it. A friend recalls her showing some anxiety on the matter in 1873: earnestly reflecting on the three words 'God, Immortality, Duty', she noted 'how inconceivable was the first, how unbelievable the second, and yet how peremptory and absolute the third.'[46] This reveals her latent anxiety that the duty of moral perfectionism might struggle to survive the decline of religion.

The Victorian era is famously the era of religious transition, in which intellectuals moved from accepting religion to rejecting it. What is surprising when one looks closely at the period is the tentative, almost reluctant, nature of this move. There is not generally an air of liberation as captivity to superstition crumbles, nor of excitement at the prospect of building a saner humanist culture. There were surprisingly few confident, charismatic secular humanists. The average intellectual was wistfully nostalgic for belief. Convinced, upbeat atheists were rather marginal figures, such as Bradlaugh. Most famously, Darwin kept quiet about his loss of religious faith and seems to have been worried that his work might fuel atheism. Why didn't he *want* to fuel atheism? Why didn't secular humanism emerge with more confidence, more chutzpah, more sense of its right to take over culture? It's hard for us to keep in mind that post-religious culture was new and that secular humanist idealism was a creed still under construction. Accordingly, many intellectuals had a sense of venturing with trepidation into the unknown. That's why losing one's faith was so traumatic for so many earnest Victorians: they were conscious of the instability of post-religious humanism. (A generation or two later, secular humanism acquired an aura of axiomatic stability, and so losing one's faith became easy.)

Another factor, perhaps, is that the British Empire was approaching its height – this meant that religious tradition was built into a hugely confident, pomp-rich culture, beside which secular humanism looked thin. And, of course, this Empire was seen as promoting liberal values, standing up to tyrannies, rooting slavery out of Africa, promoting civilization. Even liberals, aware of the bloodier reality, were reluctant to give up on these ideals.

It was only around 1890 that secular humanism acquired a new confident spring in its step. This was partly through Huxley's preaching of evolution over the preceding decades and partly through the new confident culture of municipal socialism. This produced figures such as the Webbs and then George Bernard Shaw, who became the figurehead of a new sort of secular humanism – jocular, at ease with itself (he imported some Tory style to the Whig tradition). In the United States at this time, a similar spirit emerged in the gentle scepticism of Mark Twain and in that of Robert Ingersoll, a journalist and popular speaker who called himself an agnostic rather than an atheist. He drew huge crowds with jokey lectures defending Darwinism (yet he warned against social Darwinism, which justified hyper-capitalism). Such thinkers helped to forge a reasonably coherent 'secular humanist' identity in the West. But just as secular humanism was acquiring this new confidence, the dark genius of the age was pulling the rug from under its feet.

Nietzsche

We have seen how deeply modern thought is determined by Christianity: even when it hotly rejects it, it is echoing Christian-based assumptions about universal moral progress and so on. Nietzsche saw this dynamic and resolved to buck it.

His eccentric vision reached back to the Romantic idealization of Greek culture: Goethe and others had announced that there was another vision of human flourishing here, an alternative to Christian assumptions. A mild, diluted version of this was commonplace: post-Christian humanism saw the ancient Greeks as a rich stream of influence. Nietzsche undiluted it. As a young classical scholar he argued that imitation of ancient Greece enabled a *total* detachment from Christian assumptions. Here was a truly alternative ethos, if one dared to see it.

Why should one want to see it? What drove his antipathy to Christian-based culture? He was drawn to the strain of Romanticism that bemoaned the weakening of social bonds through individualism. This led many to socialism but Nietzsche thought that cure worse than the disease. He was influenced by the philosopher Schopenhauer, whom he read in the late 1860s, to see all moral thinking as weak beside instinct, vital desire, will. Around the same time he discovered Wagner's grand vision of a new sort of art that could oppose materialistic individualism. Of course, Christianity claimed to oppose materialistic individualism, but *it simply didn't work*, Nietzsche said. It failed to turn its mythology into a powerful binding force; its adherents were going through the motions for old time's sake. He argued that we must return to Greek tragedy as the model for authentic religious culture, for tragedy was originally religious, rooted in Dionysian festivals. This showed that art, in its highest sense, was rooted in collective ecstasy, in a primal communion. This ideal of organic unity had to be asserted against liberal individualism.

In *The Birth of Tragedy*, published in 1872, Nietzsche excitedly announced this possible rebirth of true culture. But how does an organic, unified culture work? The core myth must be 'tragedy', which means honesty about the violence inherent in life and culture. This has a political aspect, to put it mildly. Democratic idealism must be utterly rejected and inequality, and even slavery, seen as natural phenomena. War too must be affirmed as a source of cultural health. Only such realism can produce cultural unity. By contrast, democratic ideology is divisive: its core narrative is the pursuit of social justice, which can never be decisively achieved, so in practice culture will be dominated by factional complaints about social injustice, inequality – in short, by the whinges of disadvantaged people. Unity can only come through a sort of violent realism: we must affirm unfairness as the natural order of things through performing myths about noble heroism – through an unashamedly elitist ethos.

The Birth of Tragedy voiced an insight that had been in the air for a couple of decades (Carlyle had grasped at it), and would intensify in decades to come: liberal Christian civilization is weakening, collapsing. By promoting equality and democracy it is doomed to lose centripetal force. The triumph of fragmented individualism will lead to a sort of post-civilization. Democracy, Nietzsche later said, is 'the *decaying form* of the state'.[47]

So we need a new core myth. But Nietzsche soon lost faith that it could come through Wagner's art or any existing artistic culture. A new way of thinking was needed, a reinvention of philosophy. So he developed a grand story about the regrettable rise of rational morality, launched by Socrates and Plato – 'the *decadents* of Hellenism'[48] – and magnified by Christianity. The notion of 'Truth', in which reason and perfect morality are combined, is a consoling illusion. The real truth is that 'truth' is culturally constructed, that it is the ideology of some powerful cultural tradition. The honest response to this is to affirm the most natural form of culture, in which human strength honestly dominates. Is this nihilistic? No, he says, what is really nihilistic is clinging to a myth that contravenes the natural order of things.

His great insight, for our purposes, was that conventional atheist and agnostic humanism remained semi-Christian, for it echoed the Christian dislike of natural human strength. Of course, he was influenced by Darwin's unveiling of the animality of humanity – let us reinvent culture around an *honest* assessment of what humanity is.

His determination to be a new sort of philosopher-prophet, showing how meaning and culture could be reinvented, sent him mad in 1889. Before that he tirelessly explained that 'good' and 'evil' were inauthentic categories; they should be replaced by 'noble' and 'base', for aristocratic strength defines what is good. At root he was arguing for a primitive form of morality, or pre-morality. Only this 'revaluation of values' could produce a new cultural honesty and vitality.

Nietzsche relentlessly attacked Christianity as the prime source of this corruption of values. He launched a new sort of atheism that emphasized not Christianity's falsity, as the rationalists did, but its celebration of the wrong values. Those rational-humanists who attack it as false fail to see that they are standing in its shadow, continuing its pathos, for they have no strong alternative vision, they are an offshoot of Christianity; they are serving Christian morality without God (George Eliot typified for him this failure to break with the religious past). The implication is that Christianity can only be countered by an alternative form of religion – neopaganism. The further implication is that all of human culture and meaning is at root 'religious'. The key question is what values it celebrates. Thus he scorned the idea of art for art's sake, for in reality art serves some cultural ideal: 'what does all art do? does it not praise? does it not glorify? does it not select? does it not highlight? By doing all this it *strengthens* or *weakens* certain valuations.'[49] It follows that secularism, in the sense of the desire for a post-religious culture, is illusory, for all cultures have values, and values never escape the pathos of religion (Nietzsche's thought might be termed 'post-secular', in that it refutes the idea of secular rational progress).

So this is a new form of atheism; it has amazingly little in common with that of D'Holbach, Shelley or Marx. It is shockingly amoral – and yet does not lead to a despairing shrug but to a bracing vision. Because there is no Truth, natural strength is the truth. It is shockingly simple.

Strange to say, this new form of atheism is one from which Christianity comes out rather well in the long run. It encourages a new conception of all of human culture as inescapably religious; it presents post-religious humanism as lacking in self-awareness. And the stark choice that it sets out is ultimately rather beneficial to Christianity. Either one celebrates the honest violence of early ancient Greece as one's ideal, or one belongs to Christian culture, whether explicitly or, like secular humanists, implicitly. Of course, secular humanists have been very unwilling to hear this ultimatum and have sought to interpret Nietzsche in ways that suit them. But that is his ultimatum. And, after Hitler, even to flirt with taking Nietzsche's side, in some donnish thought-experiment way, is intolerably offensive. So in a funny way Nietzsche emerges from the storm of the twentieth century as unwittingly useful to Christian apologetics.

Why so slow?

Let's recap a bit. The emergence of secular humanism as the dominant ideology of the West was surprisingly gradual: something like secular humanism was put forward by Spinoza in the late seventeenth century, but this thing did not really solidify, stabilize, for over two centuries.

Why was secular humanism so slow to cohere, to become a reasonably stable cause? One reason is the failure of deism. For over a century it seemed that an objective rational morality would be the new creed of Europe, replacing traditional religion. But divine rationalism lost its allure for the intelligentsia: a more emotive creed was needed, indeed a more quasi-religious one (it lost its credibility as well as its allure due to the scepticism of Hume and later the discoveries of Darwin). Secular humanism had to seek a new, post-deist base, and there were naturally different versions of this, drawing on different aspects of religion: for example, Marx reached back into the Judeo-Christian tradition in a new way, pulling out the radical eschatological vision that had been largely dormant for centuries.

Another reason is simply politics. The idea of universal human rights was hardly likely to catch on in Britain when this was the slogan of its enemies France and America. Something very new was emerging – the idea that society's core values could be detached from religion – but it was almost impossible to articulate this without seeming to attack the status quo, in an age when Parliament, the crown, the law and so much else had a religious dimension.

And we have recently seen another reason, that post-religious culture was scarily unchartered territory, and so the average intellectual, though he had ceased to believe, was seriously uncertain that humanism could survive without religion. One walks into a pitch-dark room with pigeon steps.

5

The secular century

Secular humanism is newer and frailer than we think. We've seen that it was surprisingly slow to cohere and that many Victorian thinkers were curiously coy and ambivalent about it. In the early twentieth century it remained a deeply uncertain thing; it seemed too weak to resist more extreme ideologies, most obviously communism and fascism. By mid century, when European fascism was defeated, it at last gained solidity as the creed of the West – the UN Declaration of Human Rights of 1948 launches this era. Also, it had by this time spread beyond the West. But such success was haunted by deep doubts about its coherence and resilience, as we shall see in Chapter 6.

Around 1900, political secularism was on the march in various places. Britain of course resisted explicit secularism but gradually softened its establishment (the admission of Bradlaugh to Parliament in 1886 was an example of this). France was renewing the explicit secularism of its revolution after a long attempt to return to Catholic-based order. In 1905 a law announced the principle of *laicité*, meaning an explicit separation of Church and state. Some other historically Catholic countries, in Latin America as well as Europe, were moving in this direction.

In the USA, despite the constitution's separation of Church and state, the cultural establishment of Protestantism was still taken for granted at the turn of the century. Catholics and atheists were often denied 'free expression'. The situation had been strained by the arrival of huge numbers of Catholic and Jewish immigrants in the late nineteenth century. Fearing that these newcomers would damage social cohesion, many called for Protestantism to be officially privileged – these calls intensified when Catholics began lobbying for state-funded faith schools. In response, a more logically consistent secularism began to be espoused by an alliance of liberal Christians, secular Jews and non-believers (secular Jews played a particularly important role in legal reform). A new consensus gradually emerged, at least on the East coast:

that the separation of Church and state should be more boldly affirmed and that only by highlighting this aspect of the constitution could the nation find unity in its new radical pluralism.

But this separation of Church and state was very different from that of France, which involved the promulgation of an explicitly non-religious state ideology. The French model of secularism claimed to be *neutral* towards religion, but in practice an explicitly secular state is very likely to give off the message that religion is rather a nuisance, that it gets in the way of civic harmony. And it is perhaps tempted to make a quasi-religion of the national creed, as had originally happened in revolutionary France. This is what soon happened in Russia: the Bolsheviks claimed to be following France's line on religion. Their Decree on the Separation of Church and State of 1918 was full of enlightened-sounding rhetoric about the freedom to believe what one wants, but the state soon treated religion as an intolerable rival to its authority. It's a bit unfair to say that this exposes the true logic of French secularism, but the overlap is surely noteworthy. A state that declares itself cleanly post-religious can hardly avoid telling a story in which religion belongs to the past, holds us back. Also, a European state that does this is simplistically denying the role of religion in the emergence of its modern ideology. On the other hand, the British solution, of formally retaining an official religion, is hardly ideal, as it fails to celebrate secular pluralism. The USA's more muted muddle is, I think, the least-worst option: its constitution enshrines the notion that liberty has religious roots (but at the cost of enshrining the dubious sub-religion of deism – it's complicated).

So various Western states were becoming more secular, in their different ways, in the first decade or two of the century. And intellectuals were beginning to take fuller leave of God (compare George Eliot's hurt love for Christianity with Virginia Woolf's brisk disdain for it). But there was no smooth transition to a new ideology called secular humanism. In the previous chapter we saw that secular humanism's slowness to emerge was partly due to the reticence of intellectuals, their perception that breaking with the religious past was an incredibly big deal. That sense of nervous awe now faded. A new generation of the intelligentsia felt at ease in the new landscape, but still the emergence of secular humanism was highly uncertain. Why? Because this new generation felt the need for something *stronger*. If we are really making an epochal break with religious tradition, it was felt, let us opt for a new creed that is positive, robust. There was an appetite for 'scientific' forms of secular humanism that strike us today as highly dubious. Many saw revolutionary socialism as the full expression of humanism, despite its taste for the violent regeneration of humanity. And many others were drawn to another sort of dogmatic belief in progress: social Darwinism.

To many people the theory of natural selection was not just a stunning new facet of biology; it was a source of hope. Humanity could be improved, physically, mentally, morally. It could take control of its own evolution through natural selection, by pursuing material progress more boldly and consciously and also by defending the purity of the 'fitter' races. H. G. Wells exemplified this overlap of whiggish humanism and social Darwinism. His extreme belief in progress was influenced by his mother's Calvinism and more explicitly by the social Darwinism of T. H. Huxley, who greatly influenced him in the 1880s. In 1901 he predicted the emergence of a superior breed of human being, a master race, unsentimentally aware of its superiority. He coolly explained that the demands of progress trumped any humanitarian concern for equality between the races, for 'the world is not a charitable institution'.[1] Such rhetoric had an aura of modish dash. Eugenics, or 'racial hygiene', was a fast-spreading new form of progressive idealism. Francis Galton, influenced by Darwin (who was his cousin), had taught that 'lesser' races bred faster and that the advance of civilization demanded that superior races take care to maintain the purity of their stock – this was 'positive eugenics'; 'negative eugenics' meant sterilizing those with any sort of perceived defect. Such ideas spread particularly fast in the USA in the first years of the century: in 1907 various US states adopted policies of sterilizing people deemed defective. In Germany and Scandinavia such ideas blurred with a cult of physical fitness and Nordic nationalism. We naturally see such ideas in the light of the rise of fascism a couple of decades later but this slightly obscures the surprisingly mainstream aura they originally had. It was almost axiomatic that a truly idealistic humanism would work at improving the core material of civilization, the physical human being.

So secular humanism was at this time vulnerable to two creeds that claimed a scientific account of progress: socialism and social Darwinism. These options attracted intellectuals and artists, who hungered for a clear and fulsome creed, capable of replacing religious tradition. Without this supposedly scientific edge, secular humanism seemed weak and shapeless. There was a huge assumption that a *strong* new creed was needed, one as fully satisfying as religion. A vague belief that humans should be as free as possible, and nice to each other, just seemed too empty. Indeed, there was a widespread fear of modern life descending into a safe banality. What about the passionate concern for shared truth that once shaped civilization?

Some thinkers were wary of this appetite for a strong new creed: we must wean ourselves off such meaty unifying systems. According to the great German thinker Max Weber, science has 'disenchanted' the world ('de-magicked' is closer to the original German term), and so we must choose for ourselves how to find meaning in life. A related case was made by the American thinker William James: religion no longer unites society by telling us life's meaning, so we must construct that meaning for ourselves, drawing on all the wisdom of the past, maybe recycling religion for our needs. Both thinkers insisted that scepticism and relativism defined the new landscape. The meaning of life is for each individual to decide: no answer comes from science (they both rejected pseudo-scientific moral visions). This is basically the cautious, agnostic secular humanism we take for granted. But to understand the early twentieth century, we must grasp how repellently vapid this attitude seemed to so many intellectuals – it seemed a recipe for meaningless individualism, indeed the end of civilization as a corporate endeavour. Human beings simply need a fuller creed than this, they said.

So the key argument within secular humanism was between a 'scientific' humanism explaining all of human life in terms of progress, and a sceptical humanism warning against such total explanations but offering no very positive vision. The latter view found a sort of scientific backing in the message of Sigmund Freud. He was a deeply Enlightenment figure, but instead of saying that rationalism can liberate us, create a better civilization, he said that all civilization is constricting of our animal natures. The true humanism, he said, is not a perfectionist idealism but a rational account of why we should be moral enough, civilized. He gave scientific authority to the sceptical, relativistic form of secular humanism.

The foremost creative minds of the day wanted something more engaging, more thrilling than this. Many were attracted to Nietzsche's neopagan rejection of secular humanism. Primitivism boomed, often in the form of a new intense aestheticism. One of its prime representatives was the poet W. B. Yeats, who developed a quasi-religious faith in the renewal of Ireland's pre-Christian mythological heritage. There was a huge vogue for such exotic aestheticism around 1910: it balanced mainstream notions of rational progress. It helped post-religious people to feel they had not become soulless. This neopagan flirtation was not as harmless as it seemed: after the trauma of the First World War, such irrationalist reaction became an ingredient of fascism.

In the 1910s a new Nietzsche fan emerged: the novelist D. H. Lawrence. He rejected his Protestant upbringing and yet saw the main alternative, rational progress, as thin, life-denying. He became an apostle of the natural vitality of humanity. We need a new, spiritually authentic humanism, he said; it must reject traditional moralism and affirm our animality, including our sexual urges. He generally presented Christianity as a barrier to such authenticity but it gradually became evident that the incarnational aspect of Christianity was a key positive inspiration (he often spoke of the *resurrection* of fully human life). It's a muddled vision, but there's something admirable about its stubbornly honest, earnest appraisal of the deepest human desires – to belong, to have meaning, to be fully alive. (There's an echo of Rousseau in the demand to see humanity's full potential realized – and again the idea of 'full potential' draws on Christian tradition.)

For Yeats and Lawrence, secular humanism was thin gruel, even in its 'harder' forms of socialism and social Darwinism: we must demand more meaning, fuller social belonging, more *life*.

The horrors of the First World War boosted dissatisfaction with liberal progress, leading many to seek a fuller creed. Many of course found it in communism, which in 1917 became a fact of historical life; others turned to Roman Catholicism; others developed an aesthetic scepticism. But the most influential reaction was rightwards: angular reactionary voices gained new authority – voices warning against the soulless fragmentation of liberalism, the rise of a banal technocracy. Didn't civilization need a bigger vision? The question was posed by Oswald Spengler in his book of 1917, *The Decline of the West*; he argued that the definition of 'civilization' had changed: it no longer implied unifying cultural values – it had become a matter of mere material security, devoid of higher meaning. Such reactionary voices began to eclipse the advocates of liberal progress, who now seemed falsely opti-mistic, stuck in a pre-war mentality. A related development occurred in Protestant theology: in the early 1920s the Swiss theologian Karl

Barth made a name for himself as an iconoclast of liberal Protestant assumptions, a prophet of the absolute otherness of God from all human systems. His message went down well in the new Weimar Republic, a secular state that struck many Germans as vapid, tinny, rootless. Those who found Barth too religious could find a similar energy in the philosophy of Martin Heidegger. He essentially secularized some Protestant themes, announcing with mystic force that the individual is 'called' to authentic 'being', and so on.

Another important reaction against secular humanism was made by an American poet and critic living in London, T. S. Eliot. He was influenced by right-wing Catholic thought that attacked liberal individualism as corrosive of traditional unity (and that partly blamed Judaism for this). Such thinking was not a million miles away from the new political movement that brought Mussolini to power in 1922. Eliot was at first sympathetic; but he soon decided that such politics was dangerous unless it had a very firm Christian basis.

Why did so many prominent figures disdain secular humanism? Again, it just didn't seem enough. It seemed to be a surrender to the idea that life had no meaning, beside the satisfaction of material desires. But isn't there a grand idealism in the hope for universal liberation and harmony? Those drawn to such idealism were drawn to its 'scientific' expression, communism.

In retrospect it seems obvious that liberal democracy had to be strengthened in the face of communism and fascism. But it wasn't clear at the time that it *could* be, that there was a positive ideology here. The recent horror of mass slaughter seemed to prove that benign hopes for human progress were just too weak. A good example of the uncertainty comes from Bertrand Russell. He was essentially a whiggish rationalist but he admitted that there was no philosophical basis for this creed. Consequently, immediately after the First World War, he was drawn to the revolutionary left:

> The war has left throughout Europe a mood of disillusionment and despair which calls aloud for a new religion, as the only force capable of giving men the energy to live vigorously. Bolshevism has supplied the new religion. It promises glorious things . . .[2]

A visit to Russia, and a meeting with Lenin, led Russell to rethink. He returned to seeking a stronger basis for rational humanism but found himself drifting in a sceptical direction. Writing in 1935, he argued that no form of morality had any rational basis. Echoing Weber's thesis, he insisted that science cannot tell us what values to affirm; therefore there is no disproving Nietzsche's world view: values are a matter of subjective preference. We can only try to spread our own emotional attachment to the values we consider benign. He retained a faith that the right values would gradually triumph, as it's in our nature to affirm them:

It is . . . not by ethical theory, but by the cultivation of large and generous desires through intelligence, happiness, and freedom from fear, that men can be brought to act more than they do at present in a manner that is consistent with the general happiness of mankind.[3]

This exemplifies the weakness of secular humanism at this time: it inherited a vague faith in moral progress but admitted that there were no secure grounds for such faith (in fact this remains our situation).

In the USA, confidence in liberal progress was relatively unshaken by the First World War, so it gained new pre-eminence as the centre of liberal idealism, with Woodrow Wilson's determination to 'make the world safe for democracy' and his trumpeting of the principle of national self-determination. The nation seemed confident in its ideology of Christian-based liberalism.

And Britain, just in time, gained its own confidence. In the 1930s its intellectuals began to affirm liberal democracy with the appropriate enthusiasm at last. This creed might be vague but it would have to be affirmed. Some, such as George Orwell, did so from a secular left-wing perspective; others from a liberal Christian perspective. Others espoused a vague international humanitarianism, a position somewhat aware of its frailty. This is captured by the narrator of Christopher Isherwood's novel *Prater Violet*:

I knew what I was supposed to feel, what it was fashionable for my generation to feel. We cared about everything: fascism in Germany and Italy, the seizure of Manchuria, Indian nationalism, the Irish question, the Workers, the Negroes, the Jews. We had spread our feelings over the whole world; and I knew that mine were spread very thin. I cared – oh yes, I certainly cared – about the Austrian socialists. But did I care as much as I said I did? No, not nearly as much.[4]

So the Second World War produced a degree of ideological unity: the Western allies were fighting in defence of democracy and 'Christian civilization', as Winston Churchill put it. Some intellectuals and artists, such as W. H. Auden, rediscovered their Christian faith in the face of the new political and moral extremity. George Orwell did not follow suit but he did draw fresh attention to the essential role of Christian morality in the national character. During the war he argued that the core moral and political attitudes of the English people were shaped by Christian moral teaching, especially the teaching that 'might is not right'.[5] And he sometimes worried, in a very Victorian way, that such morality would not long survive the decline of belief in heaven and hell but would be replaced by dissatisfied hedonism: 'The real problem is how to restore the religious attitude while accepting death as final. Men can only be happy when they do not assume that the object of life is happiness.'[6]

In some respects it seemed that the core ideology of the West, so hard to affirm in peacetime, was at last coming into clear view. In Britain, a new social democratic spirit produced the welfare state, which was widely understood as an expression of applied Christian morality. So there were some hopeful signs in mid century that the West was learning to defend its core ideology with pride, to see its Christian-based humanism as a coherent enough creed.

Human rights

This overlap of Christian and humanist idealism blossomed in the concept that rather suddenly came to the fore during the Second World War: human rights.

We tend to assume that human rights is an essentially post-religious thing but in fact it is rooted in the medieval natural law tradition, which insisted that there are certain God-ordained moral laws – and therefore rights: if murder is against the natural moral law, I have the natural right not to be murdered. So the concept of rights is logically rooted in the idea of an objective, timeless moral law, which every actual law code should reflect.

This rather vague tradition was transformed by modern constitutionalism and the idea of the citizen's rights that emerged around the time of Locke. Such thinkers adapted the religious tradition of natural law, emphasizing its rational aspect. It is natural and rational that people should be free to own property, choose how to worship and so on. The concept of natural law had faded: citizens' rights were now framed in *deist* terms, seen as flowing from the concept of divine rationality.

When citizens' rights were sharpened up in the revolutions of the late eighteenth century, the notion of universality was emphasized: these rights are not the arbitrary invention of this state but an objective fact; because all human beings are created equal, this nation has these laws. So 'universal human rights' was the rhetorical flourish that preceded a particular nation's statement of the rights of the citizen. In the case of America there was an almost funny ignoring of this universalism: because all men are equal, all citizens have the right to own slaves. As we saw, it was primarily zealous Christians who pointed out the contradiction and demanded that universalism be taken seriously – the right of the African not to be enslaved trumps our supposed right to own him. Those seeking justice for slaves had to reject a narrow legal conception of rights as what the constitution allows, and speak of our universal humanity, beyond national boundaries. But in fact abolitionists did not often speak of the slave's 'rights', knowing that this language was most at home in practical constitutional law, which was not on their side.

So there is an ambiguity in 'human rights': it refers to the actual rights of the citizen as enshrined in law, *and* to the ideal of all human beings being treated as equal citizens of an imagined ideal world-state. Both aspects of this are Christian-based. It was in (Protestant) Christian lands that individual liberty was gradually enshrined in law; and in modern Christendom generally, people began to say (inconsistently) that all humans should be treated as world-citizens. It is important to notice that this universal idealism is fully rooted in the Judeo-Christian vision of God bringing his kingdom. The problem with 'universal human rights' is that it discourages us from noticing this: it presents this supremely idealistic notion as obvious, natural, common sense. (This reflects the affinity of universal rights with deism.)

In the nineteenth century, talk of rights was strongly determined by liberal nationalism: the notion of international human rights was rather nebulous. The philosopher Hegel set the tone, explaining that it is through state power that liberty is spread. When campaigns for the rights of religious minorities, and of women, gained force, the national political context was taken for granted: the essential right was the right to participate in national politics. Yet technological advances soon enabled the rise of 'internationalism' in political campaigning – most obviously socialism claimed to transcend national boundaries. But this did not at first lead to a substantial notion of international human rights. For example, that grand humanitarian Gladstone did not think in terms of universal rights; rather in terms of spreading civilization, meaning spreading political liberty. As he saw it, an emphasis on the rights of native peoples was meaningless because they did not have an understanding of what was in their best interest. It is politically correct to condemn this, but surely there is some truth in the notion that the right of a cannibal to express himself is not an absolute good.

It was in the 1930s that the notion of human rights gained some currency. This was prompted by the Nazis' contempt for universalism (in 1933, Goebbels proclaimed that 'the year 1789 is hereby eradicated from history').[7] It was that supremely internationalist organization, the Catholic Church, that most acutely responded to this, speaking of the God-given human rights that no state can legitimately abrogate. In 1937 Pope Pius XI said, in his Nazi-critiquing encyclical *With Great Sorrow*: 'Man possesses rights that he holds from God and which must remain, with regard to the collectivity, beyond the reach of anything that would tend to deny them, to abolish them, or to neglect them.' He added in the following year: 'Christian teaching alone gives full meaning to the demands of human rights and liberty because it alone gives worth and dignity to human personality.'[8] Although this pope's practical response to Nazism was terribly inadequate, his theoretical response was profoundly important: it helped to create a new internationalism.

During the carnage of the war, the concept suddenly became central to the West's vision of a new peaceful order. In particular it took off in the United States, where it was largely espoused by religious groups; above all, the French Catholic thinker Jacques Maritain promoted it among American Catholics. And the phrase began to appear in Roosevelt's internationalist rhetoric. It was central to the launch of the United Nations in 1945, and then more fully expounded in the Universal Declaration of Human Rights in 1948. Most of the architects of the Declaration were Protestants, including the movement's figurehead, Eleanor Roosevelt. According to one historian, 'in different ways, Christianity primarily defined the world views of all three of the main framers of the Universal Declaration: John Humphrey, Charles Malik, and Roosevelt herself'.[9] Charles Malik, a Lebanese Christian, was particularly influenced by Maritain's concept of the 'human person'.

The Preamble to the Universal Declaration of Human Rights is a little different from the preambles to the revolutionary documents of the eighteenth century. It begins by recognizing 'the inherent dignity and the equal and inalienable rights of all members of the human family' as 'the foundation of freedom, justice and peace in the world', and goes on to talk about the 'faith' that the signatories have in 'the dignity and worth of the human person and in the equal rights of men and women'. Even before 'faith' is mentioned, there is a religious reference in the terms 'dignity' and 'worth' – as the Professor of Human Rights, Conor Gearty, explains:

> The universal application of these terms in pre-Declaration days had been largely associated with progressive elements within religious movements: the Dominican Bartolomé de Las Casas, for example, with his famous 16th-century defence of Native Americans. The Declaration appropriated this language, dispensed with its religious roots and sought to turn it to long-lasting secular effect.[10]

There was of course very little international agreement about the meaning of human rights: the Soviet Union, insisting that 'social rights' should have priority over individual rights, abstained from the ratification of the Declaration. The UK and France were wary of the concept fuelling decolonization, and as the Cold War intensified, US thinkers decided it was a distraction from the fight against communism. But in Western Europe human rights flourished: it was central to a hopeful new spirit of cooperation, culminating in the European Convention on Human Rights of 1950. For European politicians it had a very strong association with both anticommunism and Christianity; West German politicians were especially keen on it. In effect it was a way of reaffirming (Christian-based) liberal democracy as a project that transcended national boundaries – and it was in Western Europe that this felt particularly urgent. It was only later, as we shall see, that human rights became a progressive secular ideology that challenged national sovereignty. For now it was an essentially conservative or liberal-conservative force.

The Declaration reflected a seismic shift: the recognition of the wrongness of racism. It was a slow development: as we saw, the abolitionism of the nineteenth century was not neatly anti-racist (some abolitionists advocated segregation). Britain liked to sound righteously anti-slavery, but of course racial inequality was built into its empire. Its incursions into Africa in the 1880s were justified as battles against the slave trade, but there was little pretence that Africans were to be treated as equals. Things improved a bit around 1900, when international opinion denounced King Leopold of Belgium's brutal enslavement of the natives of the Congo. But even liberals could barely imagine moving beyond racial discrimination; it seemed a fact of life. In 1919 the League of Nations had considered condemning racism but lost its nerve. The rise of fascism finally clarified minds, showing the moral evil of theories of racial superiority. The habitual racism and anti-Semitism of the Western ruling class was now seen in a new light. Old attitudes did not magically disappear but there was a clear new recognition of their wrongness and danger. This new consensus contributed to a revival of humanist idealism – it simply became more possible to believe in human unity. Previously the pervasiveness of racist assumptions had weakened this ideal: talk of global human equality seemed unrealistic due to the seemingly inevitable inequality of the races; most Europeans struggled to imagine that those with darker skins could ever be considered their equals.

How important was Christianity in the slow erosion of racism? It is difficult to say. But it is clear that many of the pioneering advocates of racial equality were churchmen. Missionaries led the way – indeed, this was the case ever since Spain's conquest of Brazil, as noted by Gearty above. The case still had to be made in the late nineteenth century: for example, Bishop Colenso of Natal baffled his compatriots by showing profound interest in Zulu cultures he encountered in the 1860s, and protesting at the mass killing of Zulus the following decade. Such figures were the first to articulate modern liberal attitudes.

By the 1920s, European Christians were probably aware that the main churches were beginning to condemn 'colour prejudice', but it was difficult to take this seriously while empire was so strong. There is an interesting glimpse of this in a letter of T. S. Eliot from 1928. He discusses a Jewish friend:

> the nicest type of Jew . . . Up to a point, there is no better companion on earth. But my Christianity is always running up against this question of inferior races: of course a Jew of that sort or of any sort is superior to most Indians or .... (passage deleted by Censor) ....[11]

Even though he is conscious that Christian teaching condemns such discrimination, he cannot take that teaching fully seriously, instead feeling drawn to an 'honesty' that admits the truth of racial hierarchy (and that poses as daring, as if risking the ire of some censor). But it's worth noting that he did acknowledge racism as counter to Christian teaching.

The emergence of the UN and the rise of human rights was not popular with one growing sector of Christians: American Fundamentalists (not yet called Evangelicals). Since the start of the century this movement had attacked the liberal belief in progress as a denial of the imminent Second Coming. After the First World War, fundamentalism merged with intense right-wing anxiety about the rise of international socialism (the League of Nations was suspected of paving the way for the rule of the Antichrist foretold in the book of Revelation). It feared federal power and particularly hated the progressive schemes of Roosevelt, and began to speak of 'secular humanism' as a great godless conspiracy, refusing to see that it might have any Christian basis.

In fact the term 'secular humanism' has been mostly used in this negative way: spat out by disgusted American conservatives in the culture war (to which we'll return in the next chapter).

Beyond the West

We must backtrack a bit in order to consider an important twentieth-century development: the spread of secular humanism beyond traditionally Christian lands. An extensive survey is impossible here, so I will, after a brief run-up, focus on India.

European imperialism was always surrounded by humanitarian and missionary intentions. From around 1850 the British Empire put huge emphasis on opposing the slave trade – thus did it justify its incursions into Africa from the 1870s. A few Arab leaders were pressured into acknowledging this agenda, paying lip service to it, such as Ismael Pasha, the Khedive of Egypt, who authorized General Gordon's anti-slavery missions to Sudan.

Despite the rhetoric of the three Cs (Commerce, Christianity and Civilization), it was widely felt that the natives could not be educated until they were 'pacified'. For the time being their subjugation was seen as the most humane option. A good snapshot is Rider Haggard's 1885 adventure story *King Solomon's Mines*. While seeking ancient treasure, the hero, Allan Quartermain, assists in a modernizing tribal coup in unexplored Zulu territory; the natives he slays are enemies of progress and peddlers of dark primitive superstition, with a hint of sexual perversion; the rebels he installs in power are hungry to learn Western ways. (It's even suggested that the tribe's false gods are the very ones attacked by Old Testament prophets.) The story reflects the view that other cultures could learn Western values but only after a period of apprenticeship, during which it was appropriate to think of them as 'half devil and half child' (to anticipate Kipling's phrase). And of course this narrative was compatible with the belief that they might never quite be ready, and so their subjection would be eternally justified.

To condemn such attitudes is on one level simplistic. The fact is that Western imperialism did gradually introduce the intertwined traditions of individualism and the state to India, Africa and elsewhere, eroding, or partly eroding, tribalism, patriarchy, caste. It planted the idea of all people as individuals, equal before a common law. Yes, planting this idea coexisted with all sorts of inexcusable violence, but it was planted. Non-European peoples imbibed the idea that they should follow the Western model of politics; or rather they were forced to follow this model, having been uprooted from their traditional ways.

Despite historic antipathy to Christian invaders, the Ottoman Empire, centred in modern-day Turkey, could not help being impressed by Western modernity. A Western-friendly ruling class introduced fuller toleration for minorities and secular education reforms. Conservative religious opposition to such moves was at this time surprisingly muted, partly explained by the fact that the empire was not purely Muslim: the sultan ruled huge numbers of Christians – they made up around 35 per cent of the empire. Some Muslims felt that modernity would favour the Christian minority unless Islam caught up. The reforming Muslim scholar al-Afghani announced the need for an Islamic reformation, to ensure that Muslims were not left behind: 'The true spirit of the Koran is in perfect accordance with modern liberties', he said in 1891; 'A learned Mussulman well acquainted with the liberal principles of Europe, can easily convey them to his people with the authority of the Koran, without the difficulties which surrounded Luther.'[12] The comment points to an assumption that these liberal principles are essentially independent of religion; they are seen as rational philosophical truths that all religions should be equally capable of accommodating.

Such thought gathered force over the next two decades and came to the fore after the First World War with the fall of the Ottoman Empire and its division by the West into a set of new states. Kemal Atatürk, the founder of the new state of Turkey, had much in common with anticlerical liberal nation-founders such as Bolivar and Garibaldi. But he sensibly made a muted affirmation of Islam, which was declared the official religion of the new secular state (an Englishman can hardly scorn this as contradictory). During the 1920s the ancient caliphate was dismantled and Western-style secular democracy established. In the early 1930s women were given the vote. Atatürk often stressed the need to join universal modern civilization; the alternative was to be 'crushed' by the West.[13] The founding of Turkey was perhaps the most dramatic spread of Western values beyond the West – but the price, mounting Islamic resentment in the surrounding regions, has been high.

Another dramatic Westernization had already occurred in Japan, which had not been directly colonized. In the 1870s its exposure to Western economic power created a determination to pursue rapid reforms, and in 1885 the writer Fukuzawa Yukichi summed up the attitude of the ruling elite: Japan should 'escape Asia' and join 'the civilized nations of the West'.[14] This culminated in 1889 when Japan adopted a Western-style constitution, despite retaining its 'divine' emperor (a vague copy of Britain's compromise with political modernity). In the next decade it began to imitate Western colonialism, seizing Chinese territory – which suggests that social Darwinism was the prime gospel it had adapted to its ends. On the other hand, liberal political ideas also spread, often thanks to converts to Christianity such as Nagai Ryutaro, who championed universal suffrage and women's rights but also promoted pan-Asian consciousness. A tense balance began, of affirming Western ideas and condemning the cynical aggression the West had shown in Asia, with the legacy of Britain's Opium War still smarting and its abiding presence in India resented. The Chinese reformer Liang Qichao also sought to affirm aspects of Western liberalism while criticizing Enlightenment materialism.

In Japan and China, as in the Ottoman Empire, a desire to copy the West was accompanied by an indignant rejection of the notion that the West had the moral high ground. On the one hand this entailed an impulse to see liberal ideas in rational, functional terms, rather than stemming from religious tradition; on the other there was a desire to reject Western rationality in favour of Eastern religion. The same complex response was perhaps even more pronounced in India, where European claims to the moral high ground rang especially hollow and where an alternative spiritual ideal was asserted against the colonists.

Indian secularism

The British ruled over a patchwork of tribes and small feudal princedoms. Due to the emergence of an educated elite of natives, around the 1890s the theoretical possibility of independence arose. India could hardly have been less likely soil for a modern state, with the intensely hierarchical traditions of Hinduism so powerful and Islam providing a contrary model of social unity. But the influence of Western nationalism was unstoppable. A key problem for the independence movement was that most members of the native elite were too Westernized, too detached from Indian traditions to forge a viable new national identity. Mohandas Gandhi was different: he saw the need for a religious-based movement towards independence. As a lawyer in South Africa, he was influenced by Tolstoy's book *The Kingdom of God is Within You* – one of the Russian sage's radical Christian humanist tracts. His method in opposing racial discrimination against Indians in South Africa, he said in 1896, was 'to conquer this hatred by love'.[15] When he turned his reforming attention to his homeland, his big thesis was that Indian unity depended on a new spirit of religious toleration. So he affirmed Islam and Christianity (and Buddhism) as largely valid reformist responses to aspects of his own Hindu tradition, most obviously the caste system. Through showcasing toleration, the Indian people could become spiritually worthy of independence. This entailed resisting the lure of Western rationalism and materialism. A broadly similar case was also being made by the Bengali poet Rabindranath Tagore; indeed, he went further in primitivist opposition to material progress and modern European political models. He was one of the 'Asian intellectuals defining Western modes of politics, economics, science and culture as inhumanly utilitarian'.[16]

Jawaharlal Nehru was more fully Westernized (he was educated at Harrow). He saw the need to combine Gandhi's mystical toleration with hard-headed secularism. He himself was a sceptic who saw traditional religion as 'the enemy of clear thought'.[17] Crucially the two managed to work together: the independence movement, which gathered force in the 1920s, was simultaneously secular and religious in a new broad sense of 'religious'. Gandhi tried hard to stretch this broad sense to include Islam, the religion of about 25 per cent of India. This only partly worked, but Nehru's rigid secularism would have worked less well: the nation needed to think of itself as a modern state *with a religious basis*. Gandhi's genius was to echo the Western – especially Anglo-Saxon – narrative, in which liberal values flow from a religious basis rather than constituting a rupture with the past.

As independence loomed, partly thanks to the disruption of the Second World War, Nehru emphasized that his vision was not merely imitative of modern Western nationalism: India, he claimed, had a superior track record of making religious pluralism work.

> The whole history of India was witness to the toleration and even encouragement of minorities and of different racial groups. There is nothing in Indian history to compare with the bitter religious feuds and persecutions that prevailed in Europe. So we did not have to go abroad for ideas of religious and cultural toleration; these were inherent in Indian life.[18]

There was some truth in this: the Buddhist ruler Ashoka promoted tolerance in the mid third century BC. But had this tradition really survived to the extent that it could be revived? And Nehru claimed that the Second World War exposed a pervasive moral malaise in the West. It was simplistic to think that the Western allies were free of fascist tendencies: instead, fascism flows from 'empire and racial discrimination'; Britain had at first appeased fascism 'because of a certain ideological sympathy with it'.[19] He was therefore claiming that India could more purely express the ideals that it had been taught by its hypocritical colonizer. It could be a more humane democracy, incorporating aspects of socialism (a creed the West overanxiously rejected, he said). He even claimed that 'humanism, which coloured the outlook of Europe for so long, is a vanishing tradition there'.[20]

In spite of such comments there was no hiding his essentially Western mindset: he looked with horror on the desire of Muslims to form a separate state. The desire for a religious-based state is a 'reversion to some medieval conception which cannot be fitted into the modern world'.[21] It confirmed his view that organized religion 'tends to close and limit the mind of man, and to produce a temper of a dependent, unfree person'. But on the other hand, he had a Romantic-influenced aversion to Western materialism (epitomized by the United States). In the West 'we eat ersatz foods produced with the help of ersatz fertilizers; we indulge in ersatz emotions and our human relations seldom go beyond the superficial plane'.[22]

To a significant extent, Nehru had to downplay the Westernness of the new nation and exaggerate his antipathy to 'semi-fascist' Britain and 'vulgar' America. Only so could the arrival of liberal democracy in India feel authentically Indian.

A careful student of the West, Nehru put a sophisticated form of secularism at the heart of the constitution. As he explained, the word 'secular' does not 'mean a state where religion as such is discouraged. It means freedom of religion and conscience, including freedom for those who may have no religion.'[23] More explicitly than the American constitution, which enshrines Christian deism, it says that no religious tradition has special status. And it avoids the French implication that religion is a nuisance from the past. But does this secularism have sufficiently strong roots in national tradition and the dominant religious traditions? Or is the secularism an import from the West that remains frail? The unofficial survival of ancient caste traditions, and the resurgence of Hindu nationalism in recent years, have kept the question open.

When Nehru died in 1964 the ideal of secular democracy seemed firmly in place. The democracy aspect seemed more fragile than the secular aspect, due to the strength of Marxism. But in the 1980s the Hindu majority grew resentful at the government's perceived favouritism towards other groups – and nervous at the rise of Islamic fundamentalism. Religious tension grew, and Congress failed to protect minorities from violence. The BJP became a major force; its creed of 'Hindutva' mixed Hinduism and race. Its growing popularity suggested a widespread hunger for national identity that the nation's official secularism could not address. The BJP attacked secularism as a foreign imposition and, influenced by Western communitarian thinking, as a dated relic of the Enlightenment.

India is largely defined by its antipathy to Islamic theocracy – but it is torn as to whether secularism is a strong enough antidote, or whether a rival form of religious unity is needed. The key question is whether the majority religion, Hinduism, has a deep affinity with the principle of secularism or whether it feels it to be alien.

Islam in flux

The fledgling new states of the Arab world, many fresh-minted in 1919, gravitated to autocracy. Some were influenced by European fascism (which inspired the Baath Socialist movement and the Pan-Arab movement). And these secular autocracies provoked an opposition movement: Islamic fundamentalism. It rejected the very notion of the state as Western, and aimed to restore Islam as a coherent civilization in which politics and religion were united, as in the pre-1924 caliphate. It resented the West for forcing the Islamic world to imitate it, to become a bunch of modern states in which political and religious authority are severed from each other. Islamic fundamentalism is a massive yearning for *reunity*, for the reuniting of religion and politics. This movement was also influenced by aspects of Western political extremism, in its ideal of anti-liberal revolution. The Egyptian thinker Sayyid Qutb was influenced by Western models in his rhetoric of liberation and equality:

> [Islam] is really a universal declaration of the freedom of man from servitude to other men and from servitude to his own desires, which is also a form of human servitude; it is a declaration that sovereignty belongs to God alone . . . [Islam] is for all human beings, whether they be rulers or ruled, black or white, rich or poor, ignorant or learned. Its law is uniform for all, and all human beings are equally responsible with it. In all other systems, human beings obey other human beings and follow man-made laws.[24]

As we saw in Chapter 2, Islam was at inception an explosively egalitarian force (within certain limits). This was now revived, in rivalry to Western universalism, seen as entirely materialistic:

> Humanity is bankrupt in the realm of 'values', those values which foster true human progress and development. This is abundantly clear in the Western World, for the West can no longer provide the values necessary for [the flourishing of] humanity.[25]

The West has spread a false universalism, defined by materialism. Islam must match its power and ambition, presenting itself as the *comprehensive* alternative.

But the West hardly even noticed the emergence of Muslim fundamentalism in the 1950s and 60s: it assumed that nasty dictators such as Nasser would soon give way to nice democratic governments. Maybe the new nation of Israel would inspire change in the region, once Arab opposition to it subsided. Few imagined that Arab dictators were keeping the lid on a far more threatening force.

It would be rash to draw firm conclusions from this very brief foray into postcolonial history, but it's probably safe to say two things. First, political liberalism did dramatically spread beyond historically Christian lands in the early twentieth century. Second, the recipients of this influence were understandably resentful at the notion of Western moral superiority. They chose to heighten the amoral functionalism of Western values in order to heighten the necessity of native morality and religion. This narrative, in a mild form, provided the impulse for Indian independence. It was a mild form, because the virtue of Western secularism could be admitted. But the same narrative, in a fuller form, contributed to the rise of Islamic fundamentalism. It took the critique to the logical extreme: if Western values are merely materialistic, all the trappings of Western politics must be rejected.

6

In our time

We saw that the rise of secular humanism was intensely uncertain in the early twentieth century, with many seeing it as insubstantial, too vague for words; and that the Second World War brought it new solidity. The West was in the end able to stand up for freedom, liberal democracy, human rights; it fought for them at huge cost. To call this 'Christian civilization' was antiquated, for this civilization plainly protected people's right to espouse other religions or no religion – in contrast to the secular theocracies of fascism and communism. But what else to call it? In practice this creed was secular, in the sense of promoting freedom to choose about religion, but 'secularism' was seen as anti-religious and divisive. It was safer to trumpet the religion-neutral terms 'freedom', 'democracy', 'human rights' and to assume there was a coherent ideology here.

But a bit of prodding revealed a worrying hollowness. What exactly was this creed? A hugely idealistic vision, of liberty and justice for all? Or was it the mere practice of liberal democracy, which is clearly compatible with cynical capitalist individualism and the slow erosion of communal purpose? The question is still with us. The creed of the West is Janus-faced in this sense: it involves a grand universal moral ideal of freedom and justice for all but it also half-denies this ideal – it allows the grandness (indeed the absoluteness, the perfectionism) to be ignored, shrugged aside. It allows itself to be conceived in non-idealistic terms, as simply the world view that comes naturally to civilized rational people and one that is compatible with scepticism and self-interest. It fails to be distinct from the thin-gruel ideology of liberal capitalism, which puts the emphasis on the right to get rich. So this is the maddening complexity of secular humanism: it is simultaneously a belief in liberty and justice for all, and a system that legitimizes self-interested individualism. In a sense Marxism is right to stamp its foot and cry foul at this; in a sense it is a more honest form of secular thought, for it faces up to the absoluteness of the universalist moral ideal and says that it is not compatible with an ethos of selfish individualism. Let us decide whether or not we have a coherent ideology, rooted in some absolute value, it cries.

In the years after the Second World War, secular humanism gradually attained the axiomatic aura with which we are familiar. It became the default position of the civilized Westerner – before long she was rather eccentric if she saw religion as an important matter. And yet it did not gain in coherence. It's worth noting the strangeness of this. Secular humanism became the basic creed of the West, in effect replacing Christianity, but it did not gain solidity – partly because it did not achieve a clear break with the religious past. In fact instead of gaining solidity, it gradually became less coherent, more contested, especially among intellectuals.

Post-war

As well as showing the need for idealism about human rights, the Second World War had also strengthened an anti-idealistic mood, a new scepticism. A post-religious pessimism seemed an apt reaction to the full horrors of the Holocaust and the new threat of nuclear Armageddon. The French novelist André Malraux summed up the mood in 1946 when he said that only a 'tragic humanism' remained possible.[1] The stylish despair of writers and artists such as Samuel Beckett and Francis Bacon did very well.

In France, Jean-Paul Sartre tried to redefine humanism. The full rejection of religion entails the rejection of any idea of the essence of humanity, and any preordained moral purpose, he said. The new sort of humanism confronts the raw chaotic experience of existence (thus 'existentialism'): 'This is humanism, because we remind man that there is no legislator but himself; that he himself, thus abandoned, must decide for himself.'[2] Sartre largely followed Nietzsche: humans create all systems of 'truth'. And yet a sort of optimism remained, in the idea that we are free to create our own values rather than impelled to follow Nietzsche in power worship. Sartre used his own freedom to commit himself to communism. Why communism? It seems that the desire for absolute freedom is attracted to the absoluteness of communism, its apocalyptic abolishing of ordinary reality with its final utopia. There is something anticlimactic about announcing one's heroic freedom and plumping for the normal compromises of secular humanism. But Albert

Camus advocated this course, calling Sartre's political solution an escape from freedom: one should construct a humble humanism, aware of its rational ungroundedness or 'absurdity'. In his novel *The Plague*, Dr Rieux's altruism is not rooted in religious belief – rather the opposite: he explains to a friend 'that if he believed in an all-powerful God he would cease curing the sick and leave that to Him'. Then he ventures the paradox: 'mightn't it be better for God if we refuse to believe in Him and struggle with all our might against death, without raising our eyes toward the heaven where He sits in silence?' The fleetingness of our victories over death is 'no reason for giving up the struggle'.[3] This sort of humanism, despite its atheism, is transparently indebted to the Christian assumption that moral action has intrinsic authority and that (Job-like) defiance of theistic orthodoxy might be spiritually heroic.

In the United Kingdom such earnest post-religious thinking seemed rather foreign. The wartime fusion of religion and humanism was still strong in some ways. The Church of England had played a role in the post-war modernization of the state, contributing to the new social democratic landscape. Of course, it also had a nostalgic side, grandly displayed in the Queen's coronation in 1953, but it continued to play a role in progressive reform in the 1950s: the Church mostly backed the Wolfenden Report, which called for a de-puritanization of the law, and also backed decolonization. Indeed, Anglicans led the international opposition to South African apartheid, through the novelist Alan Paton and priests including Trevor Huddleston. As in the anti-slave trade campaign and abolitionism, Christian-based humanitarian zeal was largely expressed in secular terms.

In the United States the separation of Church and state was becoming sharper: shortly before the war the Supreme Court had begun enforcing the First Amendment's ban on 'establishment of religion' on a state level, pushing changes such as the secularization of public schools, which became law in 1948. To balance this, a reassertion of the nation's religious character emerged. The Cold War demanded this: to face down the meaty ideology of communism, the USA had to show that it believed in more than individualism. It believed in universal freedom: the Truman Doctrine committed the USA 'to support free peoples who are resisting attempted subjugation by armed minorities or by outside pressures'.[4] There was a will to present this liberty-defending ideology as religious-based, despite the clearer separation of religion from public life. We are still fundamentally religious, the nation said (this was increasingly expressed in general monotheistic terms rather than specifically Christian ones, to encompass Jews and also vague, deist-type Christians). This movement put its mark on national symbolism in the 1950s: 'In God we trust' found its way on to the currency and 'One nation under God' was declared the national motto. President Eisenhower expressed this national-religious impulse most acutely: 'Our form of government makes no sense unless it is founded in a deeply felt religious faith, and I don't care what it is.'

So as the USA became more technically secular in the sense of separating Church and state more fully, it also renewed its claim to be a fundamentally religious nation. This balancing act was maintained into the Kennedy era: Kennedy himself was a strong advocate of the separation of Church and state (he wanted to assure people that his Catholicism was a private matter), yet he was also an icon of Christian patriotism, a religious Cold Warrior. And the chief opinion-formers were still advocates of Christian-based democracy, such as Reinhold Niebuhr. This vision, of a Christian-based nation pursuing liberal reforms at home and defending liberty abroad, more or less united the nation; then it was sharpened in a way that divided it.

The prophet

The Cold War ensured that 'Christian democracy' was widely affirmed in the 1950s, but in tones of realism rather than idealism: the emphasis was on the indispensability of US strength.

Then someone came along who expressed the core Western ideology with new intensity and fullness. Martin Luther King was its most powerful voice since . . . Well, hyperbolic though it sounds, maybe he exceeds any predecessor in his fusion of humanist idealism and the Christian source of such idealism. Though he was not an original thinker and some of his rhetoric was simplistic, he was perhaps the most focused and forceful articulator of the Christian-based secular humanist vision.

His thought was obviously formed by the Bible – or the African-American reading of it – and by American history: the liberal founding vision, which became more fully expressed after the Civil War yet remained stymied by racism. It was also formed by the liberal Protestant theology he studied, with its emphasis on the compatibility of religion and humanism. And his vision was also formed by the huge shift that followed the Second World War: decolonization. It was this that led him to see the struggle for civil rights as a more-than-American issue – as a monumental event in world history – and so led him to dare to perform a Moses-like role.

He emerged in the mid 1950s as a charismatic young Baptist pastor in Montgomery, Alabama, a key organizer of the bus boycott of 1955–6. It's worth noting that the government had, after the war, acknowledged racial inequality as a problem – chiefly because it gave the USA's communist critics such strong ammunition. In 1954 the Supreme Court finally rejected the 'separate but equal' doctrine that had underpinned segregation since the 1890s: this put the wheels of racial equality in motion, though there was little will to prioritize the process. This is significant because it enabled King to affirm the basic good intentions of the government, to give it the benefit of the doubt, without looking completely naive.

Right from the start he related civil rights to the international situation; this tendency increased after he attended Ghana's independence ceremony in 1957. In that year he co-founded the Southern Christian Leadership Conference, with the motto 'To save the soul of America'. The idea that black liberation could restore or redeem the original American vision was not new – it was a feature of Civil War abolitionist rhetoric and reaffirmed by W. E. Du Bois around 1900. 'There are today no truer exponents of the pure human spirit of the Declaration of Independence than the American Negroes,' he said.[5] But only now, with King, was this claim made with appropriate confidence, indeed in a tone of authority echoing the founders.

As a preacher King naturally rooted humanist idealism, especially the ideal of the equality of all races, in Christianity. The emergence of postcolonial nations shows that the era of slavery is over: 'And that seems to be the long story of history. There seems to be a throbbing desire, there seems to be an internal desire for freedom within the soul of every man.'[6] It is a holy desire, for 'to take from [a man] his freedom is to take from him something of God's image'. Though liberation might entail pain and sacrifice, 'Ghana tells us that the forces of the universe are on the side of justice.'[7] He concludes with the prayer 'that it will come in this generation: the day when all men will recognize the fatherhood of God and the brotherhood of man'.[8] This bold simple fusion of humanist urgency and Christian evangelism reaches back to the era of abolitionism and the era of America's founding. His genius was to defy the tired complexity surrounding this message and simply restate it freshly. In a sense, he dared to say that the emperor is *not* naked, that the core idealism of the West *works*: there is a big vision that coheres. We don't need a new vision: we need to face up to the radicalism of the vision we have inherited.

Though he affirmed the separation of Church and state, he was unafraid of using strongly religious language in the public square. Christianity should announce itself as the source of our humanism. In 1961 he wrote a brief letter to a critic who had sensed theocratic danger in his rhetoric:

> When I referred to America becoming a Christian nation, I was not referring to Christianity as an organized institutional religion. I was referring more to the principles of Christ, which I think are sound and valid for any nation and civilization.[9]

He soon affirmed the key secularizing measure of the day, the law against prayer in schools (this law helped to rouse the religious right into existence, though in reality desegregation was at least as hateful to it).

In 1963 King gained the attention of the nation. First his campaigning and arrest in Birmingham, Alabama prodded many of the churches into a more activist approach; then his famous speech in Washington brought his oratorical gifts to a hugely wider audience. A key aspect of his rhetoric was affirmation of the USA's founding principles: those who protested at lunch counters:

> were in reality standing up for what is best in the American dream and for the most sacred values in our Judeo-Christian heritage, thereby bring-ing our nation back to those great wells of democracy which were dug deep by the founding fathers in their formulation of the Constitution and the Declaration of Independence.[10]

On one level there was nothing very original about invoking the moral and Christian basis of the constitution – but his particular context gave such an invocation unique power.

As the civil rights movement gained strength, he continued to relate it to postcolonial struggles; and he continued to relate both things to Christianity:

> The fact that we are living in a world of revolution is in large measure attributable to the preaching of the Gospel, and the work of missionaries

around the world . . . It was Christian preaching that first spread the idea of the Brotherhood of mankind throughout the world.[11]

Again, what is striking is the sheer confidence with which he declares that there is a true universalism. It is not quite confined to Christianity: it originates in the Hebrew prophets ('it has been their concepts of justice and equality which have become ideals for all races and civilisations'[12]), and its greatest recent exponent, he says, has been a non-Christian, Gandhi (he even calls him 'the greatest Christian of the modern world'[13]).

When civil rights legislation was passed, King turned his focus to poverty and peace. In 1967, explaining his opposition to the war in Vietnam, he spoke of the ideal of human unity. This:

> call . . . that lifts neighborly concern beyond one's tribe, race, class and nation is in reality a call for an all-embracing and unconditional love for all men. This oft misunderstood and misinterpreted concept – so readily dismissed by the Nietzsches of this world as a weak and cowardly force – has now become an absolute necessity for the survival of man.[14]

This ideal is the essence of all the great religions, he says, though he elsewhere claims that Christianity expresses it most completely. In other words, the true universalism is a religious phenomenon; it is not a rational theory. Its goal can be expressed in secular terms, yet it must be understood as flowing from a religious vision.

Perhaps because he was a political leader who was not a politician, King was uniquely able to express the moral and religious basis of progressive politics. *He expressed the ideology of the West as a unified theopolitical vision.* This had not really been done with any passion in living memory, not even under the threat of Nazism. Churchill's wartime speeches were uniquely effective in steeling a nation's resolve, but King's had a deeper purpose: reviving a sacred vision.

The vision fragments

Surely King's vision could unite the nation through bringing its humanist and religious idealism together? Alas, no. Instead, opposition to racial integration fused with the force that we noted earlier: the Fundamentalism, now called Evangelicalism, that denounced the liberal reformism of the federal government. It aggressively claimed the religious high ground, identifying progressive politics with 'secular humanism' and 'liberalism', which it presented as akin to atheistic communism. It therefore rejected the – rather delicate – traditional idea that the nation was simultaneously Christian and secular, in the sense of separating Church and state so as to defend liberty of conscience. This traditional idea lived on (what else could unite the nation?), but in a battered, demoralized way. And the whole issue of the ideology of the United States, in relation to religion, became harder to speak about. It became harder to affirm the old paradox: that this nation was based in a Christian vision of liberty, entailing secularism; because now a powerful religious lobby poured scorn on this narrative.

And in turn secular humanism became warier of religion. This was boosted by the war in Vietnam, which made progressives more suspicious of all traditional authority, and by the sexual revolution, which made religious morality seem dated. The new landscape of 'culture war' damaged the coherence of Western ideology. It became more difficult to speak about its Christian roots when the most vocal Christians were anxiously opposed to secular humanism. The old notion that the West was simultaneously religious and secular was under attack. Simplistic ideologues on both sides demanded that it choose. (Choosing between religion and secularism is the essential Western heresy.)

Over in the UK, things were more muted: religious culture war was not its style. A strong culture of conciliation and compromise ruled, due to the lower-temperature religious culture and the established Church. As religious observance declined from the mid 1960s, it became axiomatic that liberal values were detached from any religious basis that they might once have had. The assumption grew that religion was pretty irrelevant to politics, except in the eyes of traditionalists who wanted a more morally conservative culture. And it began to seem obvious that 'liberal values' was simply normality, neutrality, the default position, and religion a voluntary extra. So whereas in the USA, secular humanism was almost too contentious to be discussed, in the UK it was almost too uncontentious to merit discussion; it scarcely occurred to anyone to bother affirming something that was so completely taken for granted by all.

On one level, secular humanism was smoothly triumphing in Western Europe by the 1970s. (Liberal democracy replaced autocracy in Portugal, Greece and Spain in this decade.) But it still had an air of vagueness; intellectuals were more likely to disparage it, usually from a Marxist perspective, than to affirm it. 'Liberalism' was the preferred term in academic discussions. Its main advocacy was downbeat, pragmatic. For example, Isaiah Berlin, the famous sage of Oxford, said that the state should defend 'negative liberty'; it should leave individuals alone to do what they want, to pursue various ends; it should acknowledge the 'plurality of human values'. He warned against 'positive liberty' – a strong vision of human liberation, of the common good; this could lead to a new state oppression. He was part of a wide movement that criticized the excessive confidence of Enlightenment rationalism: liberalism must be more humble and realistic, rather than claim to provide life's meaning. This semi-sceptical approach, though an understandable reaction to totalitarianism, was too limited. It implied that the West had no coherent positive ideology, that it just created space in which people could pursue their various notions of 'the good life'. (There was an echo here of the Bloomsbury Group's idea that the private sphere, and 'personal relations', trumped political commitments.)

In the United States, a fuller vision was attempted by John Rawls in his book of 1971, *A Theory of Justice*. At the heart of political liberalism, he said, was the rational pursuit of universal justice (a revival of Kant's confident assumption). Let us assume that all rational individuals naturally desire the good of all, and let us develop a system to promote this process, to show how individual liberty must be balanced by the general good. In effect he offered a systematic version of secular humanism in which all tribalism and religious affiliation is put aside so that equality may prevail. In a subsequent book he further defended the secularism of the liberal state: it must be the neutral space in which various 'comprehensive' beliefs – ones that deal in the whole meaning of life – coexist.

Rawls was articulating the vague creed of the West – but seeking to remove the vagueness, pin it down. And that meant ignoring the other side of the coin, that secular humanist idealism coexisted with older affiliations – religion, nationalism, class – that could not be airbrushed out of political thought. (And some pointed out that his own approach was really a particular ideological commitment disguised as mere neutrality.) His work was widely seen as a throwback to the Enlightenment tradition of rational humanist progress. A more realistic, 'communitarian' approach gained force, especially among conservatives. But this overlapped with a wider intellectual movement that straddled left and right: 'postmodernism' announced that all the big theories of human purpose that had dominated modern times, all the 'grand narratives', were now lacking in credibility. It was largely a repackaging of Nietzschean scepticism, a critique of all Enlightenment-derived ideologies. Many tried to combine this insight with left-wing radicalism, but wasn't Marxism a product of the Enlightenment? It was also combined with the new identity politics, the assertion of the rights of minorities. So even as liberalism became harder to defend in abstract terms, a practical belief in human rights intensified.

It was now, in the 1970s, that human rights became a major international phenomenon. This was largely due to the rise of one campaigning group, Amnesty International. It had been founded in 1961 by Peter Berenson and Eric Baker, both very committed Christians. They launched it with an earnest message: they aimed to rally 'the idealists of the world', 'to absorb the latent enthusiasm of great numbers of such idealists, who have, since the eclipse of Socialism, become increasingly frustrated; similarly it is geared to the young searching for an ideal.'[15] This group pioneered the semi-religious aura of campaigning – lighting candles, celebrating martyrs – that gradually took off. As Samuel Moyn says, it was instrumental in the 'explosion of human rights in the mid-1970s when so many were to search for a substitute utopia.'[16] Although most human rights campaigns protested at communist regimes, the groups learned to seem apolitical, above the Cold War fray (it helped that there were also plenty of victims of right-wing dictatorships to champion). Fairly suddenly, human rights had an air of objective moral authority (this was perhaps aided by the USA's loss of moral authority due to Vietnam and Nixon). At his inauguration in January 1977, Jimmy Carter expressed his Christian idealism in these terms: 'Our commitment to human rights must be absolute.'[17]

Despite the new interest in human rights, liberal idealism generally felt rather contested, incoherent – especially in academic circles. But one form of liberalism was in rude health: economic liberalism, which began to dominate politics in the USA and the UK from around 1980. Its success intensified the old problem, that the ideology of the West seemed little more than capitalist individualism. Governments seemed to endorse the message of the 1987 film *Wall Street* – 'greed is good'.[18] When communism collapsed, the more idealistic side of Western politics came to the fore: the triumph of liberal democracy was heralded. But there was also a growing cynicism: wasn't liberal democracy just the necessary ideology masking capitalism? Could one really *believe* in the prospect of heightened consumerism, a branch of McDonald's in every city in the world?

In his book *The End of History and the Last Man* (1992), Francis Fukuyama offered a defiantly simple message: it is good news that liberal democracy has emerged as the stable ideology of the West and now has an air of finality. In the early twentieth century it was seriously contested – no longer. Almost every serious person agrees that it '[can]not be improved on'.[19]

But what exactly is it? In a rather dry way Fukuyama explains that it is the fusion of liberalism, which emphasizes the individual's right to be free from government control, and democracy, which is essentially a further right, to participate in politics. He then argues that its core engine has been 'modern natural science' and the economic development it has enabled. He therefore offers an economic-determinist account: science-based capitalism generally leads to political liberalism. Like a Marxist, he sees noble ideas about liberty and justice as secondary to economic processes. And he echoes the old Enlightenment rhetoric of the *rationality* of this system: 'now, outside the Islamic world, there appears to be a general consensus that accepts liberal democracy's claims to be the most rational form of government'.[20]

Fukuyama briefly considers whether religion played a role in the rise of this creed. Echoing Hegel, he suggests that the energy of liberalism came from the urge to secularize the Christian teaching of equality, to translate it into this-worldly terms. But this shouldn't be overstated: though 'a great majority of today's democracies have Christian religious heritages', religion can't be seen as a major cause of this, for:

> Christianity in a certain sense had to abolish itself through a secularization of its goals before liberalism could emerge. The generally accepted agent of this secularization in the West was Protestantism. By making religion a private matter between the Christian and his God, Protestantism eliminated the need for a separate class of priests, and religious intervention into politics more generally.

He concludes that religion is on balance 'a cultural obstacle to democracy'.[21]

This ignores, or is ignorant of, what we saw in Chapter 3 – that liberal politics arose from a religious desire to move beyond theocracy. Was Cromwell or Milton, for example, *abolishing* Christianity by arguing that it calls for liberty? It is a convenient secularist simplification to say that Christianity abolishes itself when it promotes political liberty and humanitarian zeal. In reality, it is expressing itself in a new post-theocratic way – and as it does so it also creates a semi-oppositional tradition: secular humanism.

Nevertheless, Fukuyama offers an acute analysis of the course of liberal democracy. The principle of equality has triumphed, he says, but it seems to be human nature to kick against this. Though we have rejected communism and fascism, some of us half-resent the constraints of democracy and are attracted to a more exciting form of politics: 'those who remain dissatisfied will always have the potential to restart history'.[22] Also, the triumph of equality as a principle does not produce stable satisfaction but leads to 'a hyperintensified demand for the recognition of equal rights' that threatens social cohesion.[23] This reflects a deep-lying uncertainty in the ideology of the West: 'while modern societies have evolved toward democracy, modern thought has arrived at an impasse, unable to come to a consensus on what constitutes man and his special dignity, and consequently unable to define the rights of man'.[24]

As Fukuyama noted, a large part of the world was particularly resistant to liberal democracy's gradual victory: the Muslim part. In 1989 the affair over Salman Rushdie's book *The Satanic Verses* showed the potential of Islamic fundamentalism to disconcert the West. The United Kingdom's response to Iran's fatwa on the novelist was mixed: though Rushdie was protected and his right to free speech affirmed, the broader response was to seek to minimize offence to British Muslims; to affirm pluralism and multiculturalism rather than be clear about the sheer incompatibility of radical Islam and liberal values. It emerged that there was little sense of a common public creed uniting the nation. What did unite Britons? The old answer was too minimal (acceptance of the authority of the Crown in Parliament and perhaps nominal acceptance of other institutions, including the established Church), but no new answer had emerged. But this did not yet greatly matter.

Later in the decade, the British entered a phase of rather febrile yearning for a re-moralizing of politics: much faith was placed in Tony Blair's neo-socialism in 1997. Even while things seemed to be going well, there was a sense of frailty in New Labour's claim to be repairing a lost moral consensus. Further evidence of the UK's ideological insecurity came with Princess Diana's death, the cultish excess of the mourning and its edge of anger. If the monarchy is what binds us together, then we demand a morally and emotionally satisfying monarchy, people seemed to be saying.

As the millennium approached, big thinking about the nature of the West seemed rather redundant. But one thinker issued a stern warning against complacency. In 1996, Samuel P. Huntington's *The Clash of Civilizations and the Remaking of the World Order* urged the West to see itself as a particular civilization, rather than the bearer of universal moral values. We should beware of thinking that liberal democracy is 'universally valid', Huntington argued, for that tempts us into moral crusading, causing needless tensions.[25] And there is a subtler danger: by affirming the abstract equality of all, the West will dilute its traditions through aiming to be more inclusive, multicultural; it will give space to other civilizational habits: 'The survival of the West depends on ... Westerners accepting their civilization as unique not universal and uniting to renew and preserve it against challenges from non-Western societies.'[26] The West is defined by shared history, Huntington argued; it is 'what used to be called Western Christendom'.[27] Its other characteristics include 'the Classical legacy', 'European languages' and 'individualism'.

So in effect he warned against secular humanism as I've defined it – such moral universalism is a dubious ideal that weakens the West. Let us affirm our historical identity, preserve its boundaries, consolidate it. Let us respect – and also stand firm against – the otherness of civilizations that do not share our assumptions, most obviously Islam. Let us be who we are – and not suppose that everyone is meant to be like us. But this attempt to separate the West from moral universalism feels brittle, for Christendom, which he calls the primary basis of the West, entailed the spreading of a universalist religious idea. Why should universalism have ceased to be central to the West?

Another view, close to my argument, was put forward by Larry Siedentop in 2000 in his *Democracy in Europe*. He argued that the European Union was dominated by a narrowly economic idea of Western values. Theorists of 'ever closer union', the ideal that had triumphed in the 1990s, assumed that liberal values would follow in the wake of global capitalism, he said; they were not properly reflecting on the *moral* vision that underlies the liberal state:

> The idea of the state carries within it a 'deep' value which has not been shared by all human societies – far from it. The state carries within it a

value which developed in the West and became the fulcrum of that modernity which the West has exported to other parts of the world. That value is equality, belief in the equal moral worth of humans.[28]

In many parts of the world, he explained, the state is only superficially established; such places lack the 'deeper habits and attitudes which sustain capitalism or a market economy . . . clannishness and clientism continue to operate behind legal superstructures'.[29] The West has forgotten that liberal politics does not come naturally but emerges from a long tradition in which Christian moral teaching has been central. Christianity spread the idea of the equal worth of all humans, irrespective of their social position; and in modernity this idea finds gradual political expression. If the West does not admit the very particular, traditional nature of its foundational belief in equality, said Siedentop, then it fails to affirm it:

> It is unfortunate and even dangerous that the West is so little conscious of the connection [between Christianity and liberalism]. For it cuts Western culture off from its roots, and sometimes weakens both its ability and its inclination to defend its own values.[30]

This century

The terrorist attacks of 9/11 *ought to have* clarified thinking about the basic creed of the West. They carried an accusation: the godless West believes in nothing beyond its own power, which it uses to destabilize the Muslim world.

But the event that necessitated fresh thinking about Western values also prevented it, for careful reflection was eclipsed by partisan responses to the rush of events. The question of the West's core creed was elbowed aside by questions relating to the new landscape: Why do some Muslims hate us so? Can they learn our values? Is there a clash of civilizations? How can we win it? This was inevitable yet rather regrettable, for there was also a need to ask with new care: What exactly is our ideology? The strongest voices were reluctant to spend too much time with this question: they saw the task as asserting our values against this violent opposition, not navel-gazing. These virile voices, known as neoconservative, quickly dominated talk of 'the West' and its creed.

Huntington's thesis of five years earlier was popular with those who felt that the USA was being held back by excessive concern for universal liberal values. The idea that US foreign policy should be determined by respect for the human rights of every inhabitant of the planet was draining the nation of vitality, they said. The USA should serve the cause of freedom by putting itself first a bit more, seeing itself as special. It should be wary of pooling its power in international treaties. Such thinking dominated George W. Bush's administration, elected in 2000. Plans were sketched for aggressively consolidating US power in the Middle East, whatever the UN might say. After 9/11, such thinking gained new urgency: Bush and his advisors quickly showed that they were putting the national interest first and treating liberal universalism as a distraction, even a source of weakness. And yet the matter is not clear-cut: US nationalism is never clearly distinct from the rhetoric of liberal universalism. Bush justified the invasion of Iraq with idealistic rhetoric about the USA's role in a universal project. Spreading God's gift of freedom to all nations is the country's mission 'across the generations' and 'the calling of our time', he declared in his Second Inaugural Address.

So discussion about Western values was deeply coloured by US foreign policy, by the claim that the free world had to be defended by US power, even if that power ruffled liberal universalist feathers. Leftist intellectuals were wary of defending liberal democracy, or secular humanism, and seeming to be apologists for US power. Discussion of the meaning of the West was largely left to the neoconservatives.

A more traditional conservative view was stated in 2002, soon after 9/11, by the British Tory thinker Roger Scruton in *The West and the Rest*. The West, he argues, is defined by the nation state, in which ancient tribal loyalties cede to the idea of 'territorial jurisdiction', which involves respect for secular law. Only on such a basis does the idea of 'social contract' and democracy make sense. Christianity was an important ingredient in this, he says, but its universalism should not be translated into political terms. Like Huntington, whose thesis he closely echoes, Scruton warns that universalism can detract from national unity: universalism 'is not the aim of citizenship. Citizens remain bound to a particular temporal community . . . [which] they defend in war, and which they build in peace through charitable works and public spirit'.[31] This raises an interesting question about loyalty. Do we, citizens of Western nations, have a primary loyalty to the nation or to the universalist idea of secular humanism? The reality for most of us, I suggest, is that national allegiance has become inextricable from allegiance to the universal moral creed of secular humanism. The nation deserves allegiance because it expresses, or mediates, this wider creed. One can imagine rejecting one's nation if an aggressively nationalistic regime took it over; it is harder to imagine rejecting one's belief in secular humanism. To put it differently: national loyalty is nowadays conditional on the sense that the nation serves secular humanism. Scruton therefore undervalues the positive ideology of the West, an ideology that transcends national borders. Yes, nation states remain crucial expressions of this, but the allegiance they command is dependent on this wider allegiance.

It was all but impossible to affirm the moral universalism of the West at a time of US belligerence. Rather, the climate was favourable to thinkers who criticized liberal assumptions in sweeping terms. One of these was the British philosopher John Gray, who had for years criticized liberal political theory and the complacent certainties of the Enlightenment (in common with plenty of other postmodernists). After 9/11 he stepped up his critique, warning that the USA's desire to export liberal values by force was hubristic and intensely dangerous. And this hubris reflected the true face of liberalism itself, he argued. The proper response, he said, is not to affirm a moderate, cautious secular humanism but to reject modern humanism altogether as an erroneous belief in the power of reason. It is 'the faith that through science humankind can know the truth – and so be free'.[32] The illusion originates with Socrates and Plato, and then Christianity adds universalism and historical *telos*: 'The Christian origins of secular humanism are rarely understood'; 'Humanism is a secular religion thrown together from decaying scraps of Christian myth.'[33] He explained that this composite creed is unsustainable, incoherent, and leads to arrogant attempts to transform the world that end in tears. We should renounce all such grand visions of life's historical meaning and just live, humbly accepting our finitude.

Following the invasion of Iraq, Gray intensified his critique:

During the past twenty years western governments, led by America, have tried to export a version of liberal values to the world . . . The attempt to remake the international system has had effects similar to those of previous Utopias. The disaster that continues to unfold in Iraq is the result of an entire way of thinking, and it is this that must be abandoned.[34]

Liberalism has been as utopian as other philosophies in positing a kind of ultimate harmony as an achievable goal. The vision of a world where human rights are universally respected . . . is a daydream, which obscures the conflicts among rights and the many sources of human violence.[35]

In a later book, he repeated the claim that humanism is a belief in rationality: it holds that 'history is a story of human advance, with rationality increasing over time'.[36] Because this ideal of rational progress does not cohere, secular humanism is an offensive lie that must be pulled down. As I see it, this focus on rationality is a major red herring. In reality, secular humanism is not tied to rationalism in the way Gray suggests. It is above all a tradition of moral idealism, of hope for the good of all. It is a *desire* for the general good of humanity, not a logical theory. Of course, Gray has a point that, in the hands of a superpower, this ideology can inspire disastrous foreign policy adventures. But in such cases liberal idealism is probably subordinate to the 'realist' desire to be a feared world power: the two things are hard to untangle. For example, the war in Vietnam began with Kennedy's pledge to 'bear any burden' for global freedom; Johnson stepped up the war in order to show that such pledges needed to be seen through; Nixon prolonged the war in order that the USA should not seem weak. George W. Bush invaded Iraq for the same reason, subsequently adding liberal universalist motives.

The wider reality is that almost all of us – maybe including John Gray if he is honest – deeply value a cultural tradition in which the equality of humans is affirmed and in which the hope of universal justice is taken seriously. By exaggerating the role of rationalism, Gray defines secular humanism in a way that is easy to reject so that he can pose as a daring sceptic, more daring than Nietzsche even. I consider him a major poseur, muddying the waters of reflection.

But Gray's thesis does at least engage with the big question of what we in the West suppose we believe. It directly discusses 'secular humanism', which is more basic than liberal democracy. (Liberal democracy is a political system; secular humanism is a belief system, a creed.) This deeper ideology found surprisingly few intelligent advocates in the years after 9/11, largely due to the fear of sounding like a neoconservative, applauding the USA's attempt to impose liberal democracy on Iraq.

One thinker who dissented from the trend was the French philosopher Bernard-Henri Lévy, writing in 2008. We must get over the urge to denounce US power, he said, and reaffirm liberal universalism. In particular, the French left should abandon its old Marxist suspicion of liberalism. It should rediscover the simple truth of human universalism. To do so is not arrogant or imperialist: human rights may have emerged in Europe but they spread beyond,

> to that new Europe being invented in America; and then to the lands Europe colonized, by those nationalists inspired by Enlightenment ideals who used them as a weapon against their oppressors – and I don't see why their origins ought to keep them, today, from taking root in those non-European countries where neoprogressivism is trying to block their path.[37]

True universalism is anti-imperialist; it entails 'the idea that humanity is a single family'. Huntington's idea of distinct civilizations must be opposed: human rights must be replanted 'in the soils of civilizations that might not necessarily have thought of them'.[38] This universalism should be seen as a sort of faith. The democratic idea is 'a wager . . . on defining humans in such a way that we can not only assign them rights but claim that those rights are universal, inalienable, identical for everyone'.[39] And then he pondered the question of where this universalism comes from, which raises:

> the real final question, and probably the most difficult one of all, which is the question of the foundation of this reestablished Universal: In whose name, at the end of the day? Human universality, fine; humanity as a family, okay; the solidarity of the weak, all right; but family implies fraternity; fraternity means, in some way, paternity; and so what is a Universal doing which, in claiming that 'God is dead', would purposely skip over the question of the Father?[40]

The question cannot be answered but must be acknowledged, he says; it must be admitted that progressive universalism is a religion-rooted phenomenon. (He has subsequently said: 'I'm certain that there would be no human rights without the highly audacious Christian hypothesis of man as a creature in God's likeness and therefore inviolable.'[41])

Also in 2008, a new affirmation of liberal idealism seized the world's attention: the presidential campaign of Barack Obama. He presented the other side of the American ideology, which had been denigrated by neoconservative realism: democratic idealism, and in particular the ideal of equality. Here, in real life, was the textbook American idealism that had been showcased in the recent TV drama *The West Wing*.

Obama's appeal was partly his promise to reconnect secular liberal idealism with its religious roots. In his autobiography he had explained that his politics was formed by the civil rights movement, with its religious-based vision of justice and its non-violent activism. He told, slightly cagily, of having come to Christian faith through his involvement in political campaigning inspired by that movement.

His speeches often echoed Martin Luther King's claim that the true national ideology was the universal creed of human equality. When he addressed an immense crowd in Berlin, he explained that the true American vision is not narrow tribalism but universal humanism:

> What has always united us – what has always driven our people . . . – is a set of ideals that speaks to aspirations shared by all people: that we can live free from fear and free from want; that we can speak our minds and assemble with whomever we choose and worship as we please.

And he finished in a sort of ecstasy of humanist hyperbole:

> People of Berlin – and people of the world – the scale of our challenge is great. The road ahead will be long. But I come before you to say that we are heirs to a struggle for freedom. We are a people of improbable hope. With an eye toward the future, with resolve in our hearts, let us remember this history and answer our destiny and remake the world once again.[42]

He was expressing, with rare directness, the latent ideology of the West (for of course, 'the West' is really the 'people' he is addressing here). We are united by a big idea, he is saying, by a form of faith. Is it true? It is certainly easy to sneer at this as naive and to say that what really unites us is merely capitalism (and more local forms of identity). But there is a sort of cynical naivety in this response itself, a failure to accept that such idealism is also a real phenomenon, a real force in the world.

Obama's rhetoric was like the rare surfacing of a sacred whale (no wonder everyone got so excited). Why so rare? If it is 'our' creed, why does it not find countless impressive advocates? It seems that a strong, earnest expression of secular humanism requires very particular political circumstances and of course a charismatic performer. But it's still there, under the surface, even when no charismatic performer is around to voice it.

Was he arguing that liberal politics needs a religious basis? He sometimes came close to such a position. In a speech of 2006 he had warned against making a clear distinction between religious and political discourse:

> If we scrub [political] language of all religious content, we forfeit the imagery and terminology through which millions of Americans understand both their personal morality and social justice. Imagine Lincoln's Second Inaugural Address without reference to 'the judgements of the Lord'. Or King's I Have a Dream speech without references to 'all of God's children'. Their summoning of a higher truth helped inspire what had seemed impossible, and move the nation to embrace a common destiny.[43]

He was therefore claiming to speak for a unified tradition, saying that liberal-humanist idealism should not be fully severed from its religious roots. Yes, it can be affirmed in non-religious terms, and on one level it *must* be affirmed in non-religious terms, so that it can be inclusive of all; but there is nevertheless a religious basis to this tradition.

In a sense Obama was a lonely reviver of liberal idealism. His idealism excited progressives throughout the West but they didn't know how to echo it, build on it. And almost at once the moment passed: the economic crash of 2008 rudely ushered such high idealism offstage, and Obama began to be seen as a virtuoso rhetorician, unrooted in any substantial cultural movement.

As soon as the liberal euphoria at his election faded, a reaction grew. The vitriolic response to Obama's presidency, which first took the form of the Tea Party movement, was an echo of the 1960s, when the advance of civil rights led to the rise of the religious right, and to Nixon. The American psyche again showed a sort of schizophrenia in relation to its own ideology of Christian-based secular humanism. When it is powerfully expressed, a large sector of the nation howls in anguish, fearing reforms imposed by an overweening federal government. It's not quite right to call this the 'religious right', fearing the advance of secularism, for the motivation is more cultural than religious – hatred of meddling cosmopolitan liberals (the movement surrounding Donald Trump's 2016 presidential campaign was primarily secular).

For Europeans, the question of Western ideology continued to be dominated by the problem of integrating substantial Muslim minorities, a significant proportion of whom flirted with radicalism. Of course, such flirting was hard to distinguish from mainstream conservative Islam, which had always criticized Western decadence.

The picture was complicated by the rise in the UK of a strident secularism, a demand that religion of all stripes be kept out of public life. A complicated debate about 'religion in public life' was attempted. In previous decades the landscape had been softened by a liberal established Church, showing religion and secular humanism to be compatible. Now, however, secularists insisted that religion was a threat to liberal values. Though they mainly had Islam in mind, they preferred to be more general, arguing against all forms of religion with sociopolitical power (in particular they attacked the recent rise in faith schools, which were nearly all Christian). The Church of England had to argue against such general secularism, which involved coming to the defence of British Muslims, renewing the 'multicultural' idea that religious minorities should be allowed to be a bit different, rather than pressured into conformity with liberal norms. The Archbishop of Canterbury, Rowan Williams, often defended Muslims from suggestions of disloyalty, and famously said that the British legal system should accommodate aspects of sharia law. Such a response was perhaps necessary, amid a strident new secularist mood; but this mood overlapped with a valid desire to see the country's basic public creed defined more clearly in a new era of religious extremism. And the Church seemed to disparage this concern by launching a bullish defence of the legitimacy of faith communities. The old landscape, in which the national Church was closely allied with 'liberalism' in a broad sense, had largely gone. Religion and 'secular liberalism' now seemed somewhat at odds, rather like in the USA. The Church of England was in a pretty impossible position, but nevertheless could have done more to help the nation reflect on the changed landscape. (Ideally, it should have promoted awareness of the nation's underlying creed, which is Christian-based secular humanism.)

Pope Benedict also warned against secularism but was less careful to sound inclusive of Muslims. Europe must rediscover its core Christian identity, which, he argued, is the true foundation of healthy liberal politics. He therefore suggested that both secularism and Islam were alien to Europe's true culture. (He strongly opposed the EU's decision to leave God out of its constitution.)

In the UK the centre ground shifted a bit as many liberals argued that the nation should be prouder of the positive values people have in common – meaning, in effect, the national version of secular humanism. It became acceptable to criticize multiculturalism and to say that Muslims should be better integrated. But integrated into what unifying national idea? Discussing this has proved intensely difficult. How can the debate avoid the Scylla of intolerance and the Charybdis of oversensitivity to minority grievance? And how can secularism be discussed without the atheist agenda taking over?

On the thorny question of secularism, Rowan Williams proposed a distinction between 'procedural secularism' and 'programmatic secularism'. Procedural secularism is the belief that various perspectives should coexist in the public square, with none claiming special authority. Programmatic secularism is the belief that an explicitly secular state should keep religion out of the public square. Williams affirms the first and warns against the second in very strong terms, sometimes linking it to totalitarianism. The good secularism respects the traditional overlap of religious and civic idealism:

> Rather than trying to build civic loyalty from nothing, a sympathetic state will build on the experience of co-operation and passionate concern for the common good that is nurtured in particular communities, especially by a religiously formed ethic of self-giving, so that this ... can carry across into the wider political realm.[44]

This is a useful warning against simplistic secularist reform but it overlooks the fact that liberal states have to marginalize those forms of religion that seek power on the old theocratic lines, and that this involves proclaiming secularism, in one sense, as positively central to national identity. The task is to ensure that this secularism is broad and respectful of religion. Ideally it will have some understanding of its own religious origin. This is what makes the USA's official secularism looser than France's: its language remembers its debt to religion. The constitution invokes God and sees 'liberty of conscience' as a God-given right.

Should the UK update and clarify its theopolitics? Its retention of an established Church is problematic, for *in principle* establishment endorses theocracy and denigrates secularism. But in its awkward way the status quo tells the truth that secular humanist culture is rooted in Christian tradition. Clumsy modernization would falsely proclaim the nation's detachment from religious tradition and establish the idea, as in France, that citizenship is cleanly post-religious. In theory I favour non-clumsy modernization, in which establishment loses its last few teeth, but this should be balanced by some acknowledgement of where our values come from. Maybe a new UK constitution should say something like this: 'We affirm secular humanism, which developed from our Christian tradition.'

'But this is unlikely to placate conservative Muslims', you might say. 'Surely they are still left out of a national creed defined as "Christian-based secular humanism"'? Well, fear of offending religious conservatives – of all sorts, not just Muslims – must not deter us. We should not be ashamed of affirming secular humanism, though it clashes with the desire of some to see one religion dominating society. Our tradition rejects theocracy and we must say so clearly. It is loose, accommodating, it tolerates dissent to a large extent. It can give some space to theocratically inclined religions, trusting that sunlight will soften them, but not carte blanche. It must treat them with respect and not tread on their toes; but it must tread with confidence, not tiptoe around them.

This might sound overprescriptive and lose me a few friendly readers, but I think it is appropriate to ask all Muslims living in the West the following question: Does your understanding of Islam clearly reject the traditional theocratic interpretation of that religion? Are you Still-Theocratic (ST) or Post-Theocratic (PT)? These little acronyms could, I think, serve to focus the whole tricky debate on the real heart of the matter. 'How dare you pick on Muslims in this way', it might be said. 'Why not put the same question to all religious believers, for until very recently, Christians have failed to distance themselves from theocracy.' Fine, let it be put to all. I'm PT.

It was hoped that Islamic extremism would decline with the eventual ending of the wars in Iraq and Afghanistan. In 2011 a series of uprisings in Arab lands briefly seemed hopeful, but the Arab Spring soon turned depressing. In Egypt the ousting of a dictator led to the election of an Islamist party; it failed to unite the country and was replaced by a new dictator. As in Iraq, it seemed that liberal democracy could not be hastily installed: it needed deep roots. Libya soon proved the same point: popular rejoicing at the fall of a dictator led only to chaos, in which jihadis prospered. And in Syria the attempt to oust a dictator led to a horrific civil war that's still dragging on at the time of writing. In part of Syria and part of Iraq, a new extreme form of Islamism established itself, calling itself the new caliphate, or Islamic State (IS). This new order was – and still is – a savage theocracy, glorying in its primitive violence.

Up to a point, IS clarified Western minds: *that* is exactly what we are *not*. But this negative sense of self-knowledge was hardly enough. Alarmingly, it emerged that hundreds of European Muslims were travelling to Syria to join the regime, over 2,000 just from the UK and France by 2015. In 2015, fears that such traffic made Europe more vulnerable to terrorism seemed well founded: in Paris Islamists murdered satirists who had published a cartoon of Muhammad; and there were further attacks in Paris and in Brussels. But the even bigger story of 2015 was the mass migration from war-torn Syria into Europe.

There was already a mounting problem of African migrants crossing the Mediterranean, often dying at sea – anarchy in Libya hugely increased the traffic. Many of these were refugees from war and tyranny but most were economic migrants – and the distinction began to look flimsy. But now far greater numbers were arriving from Syria. Surely Europe was obliged to welcome these authentic refugees, according to the UN's 1951 charter on refugees and asylum? The numbers were so great, however, that much of Europe was deeply reluctant; and there was a humanitarian case for such caution: welcoming them would increase the flow of economic migrants, leading to more drownings. It might also increase the likelihood of Islamist terrorism in Europe.

The situation seemed designed to expose the limits of Western humanist idealism. In theory, all humans are of equal worth, and those in dire need must be treated with urgent compassion. But in practice national self-interest must come first. And if popular resistance to mass immigration is ignored, nationalist politics is bound to rise. It had already been on the rise for a decade in Europe, with a slightly sanitized far right dominating French politics. Now even liberal Sweden was erecting borders. The European Union seemed in danger of fragmenting.

Quite apart from this crisis, the West was still suffering the after-effects of the crash of 2008. Capitalism was failing to spread wealth; instead of trickling down it was getting stuck at the top. It used to be felt that social democracy could step in and change this, but in the UK and elsewhere such confidence was low. It now seemed that wealth was a god beyond the control of governments: try to bend it to the service of the national good and it will turn its back on you altogether. It has become harder to believe that democratic governments can do things. Rising immigration has contributed to this sense: working-class solidarity becomes impossible when there is a strong influx of low-wage workers from Eastern Europe.

The crash showed the financial system to be dangerously determined by the herd mentality. All notions of rational and morally responsible behaviour were exposed, as mere matters of convention, conformity. This raises the possibility that secular morality in general is like this: our idea of the good is fully determined by what passes for 'the good'. If so, what might we drift towards?

Also, the old 1990s' confidence that, after communism, all nations were moving towards liberal democracy had been eroded by China. It had calmly gained superpower status by pursuing capitalism without liberal democracy. The West began to mute its criticism of China's human rights abuses, fearing trade would suffer. China's success at half-humbling the West emboldened Vladimir Putin to take Russia in a semi-fascist direction: he suppressed democracy and whipped up nationalism by seizing Crimea from Ukraine in 2014. He presented Western values as inimical to Russia's traditions, using gay rights as proof that the West had succumbed to decadent individualism. There was a nasty resemblance to the 1930s, when liberal-scorning fascist leaders cut a dash. It has become apparent that reactionary autocratic nationalism is surprisingly resilient, that it can master capitalism, sever it from liberal democracy and human rights.

Human rights and utilitarianism, again

When secular humanists do occasionally try to reflect on their core ideology, they often tend to do so in the form of human rights. As we saw, human rights was a half-ignored concept for 30 years, then took off in the 1970s as a radical form of secular humanism with religious trappings. It played a huge role in the fall of communism in 1989 and the fall of apartheid in South Africa a few years later. In the 1990s, partly in response to the Rwandan genocide, human rights became central to Western foreign policy, and the dilemma of intervention in failing states. It is perhaps the primary way secular humanism has tried to reach beyond its Western heartlands.

In domestic politics human rights became more prominent and more problematic. On one level its work was done in the West – the principle of equality was not fundamentally contested. But insoluble culture-war arguments were conducted in these terms, leading many to weary of the concept. As various thinkers pointed out, competing rights claims cannot be settled when there is no agreed vision of human dignity and purpose. The liberal left has often used rights to press for a more equal society, after the traditional means, socialism, seems to have run out of steam. In a sense the desire is for a more *compassionate* society in which the full worth of minority groups is acknowledged – but pushing morality through law tends to create resentment.

The arguments became yet more heated after 9/11, with new assertions of the right to criticize religion and of the right of believers not to be subject to religious hate-speech. And the same happened in relation to homosexuality, conservative believers claiming the right to condemn homosexuality and homosexuals the right not to be hated. The whole thing soon stepped up a gear with the claim that homosexual marriage was a right.

Despite these dead-end battles, human rights remained central to secular humanism's self-understanding. As we saw, some Christian thinkers have denigrated the concept but most have tried to highlight its debt to religion, to show that it points beyond itself to a wider, thicker world view. Rowan Williams put this case boldly:

> the language of the Universal Declaration is unthinkable without the kind of moral universalism that religious ethics safeguards. The presupposition of the Declaration is that there is a level of respect owed to human beings *irrespective of their nationality, status, gender, age, or achievement.*[45]

Religious people are not the only ones to believe this but, Williams adds, they 'will argue that they alone have a secure "doctrinal" basis for believing it, because they hold that every human subject is related to God independently of their relation to other subjects or to earthly political and social systems'. Also, religion ties rights to a universal moral obligation to treat others with compassion. From a purely secular point of view, rights are less meaningful: on the one hand they are only real when politically enforced, on the other they refer to an aspiration that is not grounded in anything beyond itself. Some religious believers want to reject the whole concept as an unhelpful muddle (Williams mentions Alasdair MacIntyre), but this is a mistake:

> It is important for the language of rights *not* to lose its anchorage in a universalist religious ethic – and just as important for religious believers not to back away from the territory and treat rights language as an

essentially secular matter, potentially at odds with the morality and spirituality of believers.[46]

Believers must 'not allow the language of rights to wander too far from its roots in an acknowledgement of the sacred'.[47] At the risk of trying to recruit Williams to my cause, here he is effectively endorsing secular humanism as a tradition that translates Christian universalism into thinner terms. The task is not to reject this thinning as illegitimate but to point back to the original thickness.

As already mentioned, the migrant crisis of 2015–16 led to much secular humanist soul-searching. Indeed, the contradiction within human rights – its reference to actual citizenship and to a utopian aspiration – is most acutely raised by migration and asylum. For the arrival of an asylum seeker poses the urgent question of whether our privileged notion of rights should be extended to this outsider. Should the ideal that everyone in the world has rights be converted into political reality – even at the risk of weakening our own social cohesion?

If we turn away these suffering Syrians, said many liberals, then our professed belief in universal human rights is a sham. But, said others, if Europe opened itself to all migrants, it would surely be overwhelmed by many millions of impoverished people from Africa and the Middle East. The liberal mind struggled to balance compassion and realism. This is worth illustrating in relation to two newspaper columnists.

The Guardian columnist Zoe Williams reflected that putting compassion in the foreground might mean admitting an element of hypocrisy:

> Compassion is such a rich part of the human experience and yet such a shaming thing to express, because you will always fall short of what your own words demand from you. You will never do enough. It makes you wonder how the concept of human rights was ever born. How did anybody ever overcome the knowledge of their own failings for long enough to establish universal principles that they knew they would probably never do enough to propagate?[48]

This is an important insight into our public moral creed, to which we normally pay so little attention. It is incredibly morally demanding – indeed, it goes against human nature. There is an intensity, an absoluteness, a perfectionism here, lurking under the surface. Normally secular liberals such as Williams imply that secular humanist morality is *just normal*, the default position of enlightened people who have not been prejudiced by religion or greed. The migrant crisis jolted her into – briefly – seeing secular humanism's basis in an impossible moral duty.

Another columnist, Matthew Parris, was similarly jolted. We simply do not know what our moral obligations are in relation to these people who try to cross the Mediterranean and often drown on the way. Should we love our neighbours as ourselves and rush off to help them? How can we reconcile our universal humanism with the need to prioritize the welfare of our own tribe? Isn't Western morality just too demanding? Its excessive demands on us leave us without a sensible, moderate sense of our moral duty, and so we are impotently guilty. And he puts the blame on 'our Christian religion':

> I say 'our' Christian religion because, though an atheist, I accept that my morality – and to a considerable degree what we call western morality – is anchored in a Christian culture. Whether or not we ourselves believe in God, we've all soaked up the ethical teachings.[49]

And this inheritance leaves us stranded due to the extreme idealism fused with practical vagueness, he adds: 'If, as I believe, the main difficulty that faces us in deciding moral duty is the difficulty of prioritizing, then Christianity is profoundly unhelpful.' It is great to see a secular humanist admit his debt to Christianity – even if he is complaining about the difficulty of the inheritance! The real issue is that secular humanism, and human rights, inherits the absoluteness and perfectionism of Christianity, which of course cannot be limited into a set of moral rules or 'priorities'.

As well as human rights, utilitarianism is an approach that secular humanism regularly tries to use to bolster itself. There is a vague consensus that this is how secular ethics works. But on close inspection this tradition is not so attractive: it involves a pretentious claim to adjudicate between different sorts of good on a single scale and it separates morality from particular communal traditions and from the notion of character. Also, it fails to ponder the primary question of *why* we should assume the greatest good of the greatest number to be worth pursuing – it treats this perfectionist ideal as mere common sense.

These faults are repeated by the principal utilitarian of recent years, Peter Singer, an Australian secular Jew. Very like Richard Dawkins, he has stridently revived a dated dogmatic perspective, and like Dawkins he dismisses religion as insufficiently moral. In his book *Practical Ethics* he argues that morality, or ethics, is a natural human faculty. A form of it is observable in primates, which shows that we have evolved to be moral – but this is a blunt, fallible impulse until reason steps in: 'We have inherited a set of moral intuitions from our ancestors. Now we need to work out which of them should be changed.'[50] Since ancient times, he says, 'philosophers and moralists have expressed the idea that ethical conduct is acceptable from a point of view that is somehow *universal*.'[51] He mentions Moses and the Roman Stoics before jumping to Enlightenment thought. A strong consensus, he claims, agrees that 'ethics takes a universal point of view'.[52] To be ethical is to see that all sentient beings are worthy of consideration and that individual egotism must be subordinated to this. It's a very skimpy account of moral universalism. In reality, as we've seen, the moral universalist impulse of ancient times is a shaky nebulous aspiration – only in Christian and post-Christian tradition does it develop the power to break with tribal habits and aristocratic assumptions. To treat a radical form of universalism as axiomatic, as the natural impulse of civilized rational people, is to deny the importance of tradition – and to be unconscious that one inhabits a particular tradition rather than being a free-floating rationalist. He finds the question of *why* one should act morally 'perplexing' – it's a 'question about something normally presupposed'.[53] But the authority of secular humanism is not 'presupposed' in any grand philosophical sense – it is just taken for granted (in the West). In other words, Singer reheats the old Enlightenment assumption that it comes naturally to seek the good of all humanity – we just need to knock a few irrational ideas out of our heads before we can get going.

The same evasion plagues a recent rehash of utilitarianism, restyled 'effective altruism'. William MacAskill's book of 2015, *Doing Good Better*, bypasses all the theoretical complications and urges us to be practical utilitarians through donating money and time to those most in need. One should be coldly rational in assessing which causes to help, he says, not swayed by sentimental personal attachments, such as being friends with the people one is helping.

> Effective altruism . . . takes a scientific approach to doing good. Just as science consists of the honest and impartial attempt to work out what's true, and a commitment to believe the truth whatever that turns out to

be, effective altruism consists of the honest attempt to work out what's best for the world, and a commitment to do what's best, whatever that turns out to be.[54]

This suggests that MacAskill has an idea of 'doing good' as a special activity, separable from the rest of life. According to this theory, one should not visit one's lonely grandmother if one could be making money as a banker that could be sent to distant victims of disease. Such a view seems unacquainted with what human life is, utterly tone-deaf to the way particular traditions and affiliations mould our conception of the good. Utilitarians resemble robots who have read about human beings in an air-conditioned library somewhere, and find their dilemmas utterly fascinating.

Some writhings of the left

Traditionally, the left sees secular humanism as too vague, too broad: socialism must give it teeth. In recent times the British left rethought this, then reacted against the rethink. First it moved away from socialism and more or less adopted the vagueness of secular humanism as its philosophy. Then, after the financial crash of 2008, it reacted against such a dilution, seeking new clarity in the old way.

But meanwhile some intellectuals on the left were seeking to open up the question of the universalism at the heart of Western thought, to reconsider the origin of the vision of justice for all. In Chapter 1 we noted Terry Eagleton's response to the new atheists: he was prodded to reflect on the Judeo-Christian basis of all progressive Western thought, including Marxism. And we saw above that Bernard-Henri Lévy moved towards a similar idea. They were joining a wider drift: radical leftist philosophers had been flirting with faith, of a shadowy sort, for a decade or so, perhaps beginning with Jacques Derrida in the 1990s. After 9/11 the German semi-Marxist Jürgen Habermas joined the drift, noting that the ideals of liberty and equality had a religious basis. And the concept of revolution was presented in semi-religious terms by the latest obscure French sage, Alain Badiou. He pointed to St Paul as the originator of revolution, on account of his belief in an 'Event' that utterly overturned existing structures of meaning. In this view, revolution is an act of faith – one must defy the common-sense assumptions of one's day (meaning regular secular humanism). We must pursue 'the possibility of the impossible'. This approach was influenced by the psychoanalytical thinker Jacques Lacan, who had taught that one must follow one's 'desire' in defiance of social rationality. It also drew on Martin Heidegger and Søren Kierkegaard: it put a secularized fideism at the heart of radical thought (we saw a similar move in Sartre, a linking of revolution with the individual's radical decision). Such thought was popularized by the trendy Slovenian thinker Slavoj Žižek – like Eagleton, he sometimes presented Christianity as the purest revolutionary praxis that remains misunderstood. In his 2012 book *Faith of the Faithless*, Simon Critchley pulled some of these trends together, arguing that radical leftist thought was rooted in 'utopianism' and that this should be understood in broadly religious terms, as it exceeds normal secular categories. David Marquand, a more pragmatically English thinker, came to a broadly similar conclusion in 2014 in *Mammon's Kingdom*: the left has failed to challenge capitalist individualism; to do so it needs a fuller idea of humanism, in which 'the public good' is idealized and seen as overriding individualism. This idealism cannot emerge from 'the diminished liberalism of our time'.[55] Though an agnostic, he concludes that this 'richer discourse' must largely draw from religious traditions.[56]

This warming to religion was not reflected in the left-wing press or in the Labour Party, which took a leftward turn after its defeat in 2010 and then another, stronger one after its defeat in 2015. It was trying to go back to basics in its habitual secular way, tapping into the mood of anti-establishment anger. But there were signs that political idealism had become more amorphous, more unsettled, stranger.

One aspect of this was expressed by the comedian and celebrity Russell Brand, in his 2014 book *Revolution*. Some might wonder whether this personality merits consideration in the rarefied intellectual context of this book, but I think his book is worth pondering – especially for its determination to include religion, or spirituality, in a political vision.

In a frank, 'authentic' style, Brand announces that we must overthrow global capitalism, which is a conspiracy that dehumanizes us. He draws on the Romantic-primitivist idea that modern culture makes us selfish robots, cut off from each other; that we need to recover grand purpose, common cause (sometimes there are flashes of D. H. Lawrence in his earnest, unembarrassable, poetic ramblings). One must make a break with fatalist normality and have pure-hearted belief in a totally good alternative. There must be a dramatic turnaround, in which we move from allowing injustice and planetary destruction to solving these things. But he explicitly rejects the Marxist idea of revolution on account of its violence, and calls instead for a spiritual idea of revolution. The basis of this is the belief in a 'higher power' that is taught to recovering addicts, mixed with some yoga and Christianity. We need to reunite around a big new version of religion, he says; we need a new *myth* (he has read the myth theorist Joseph Campbell, and Jung):

> When you get Richard Dawkins yapping menopausally at some poor hamstrung old archbishop, while we dismantle our environment due to the materialistic, pessimistic principles that the atheistic tyranny of the day is tacitly sponsoring, it is time to look for a new story.[57]

This is Lawrentian, this yearning for a rousing new creed. To turn things around we need more than new economic policies: we need *faith* in the possibility of a world of love and peace and freedom.

So the concept of 'revolution' is semi-spiritualized. It's not a matter of guillotines and gulags but of 'a powerful but gentle process where we align to a new frequency'.[58] So is anyone who believes in God on the side of the light? No, it seems that there must be a fusion of spiritual and political idealism, and no existing ideology yet grasps it. No religion is sufficiently focused on practical change. And normal politics lacks visionary bite. One must dissent from normal politics and refuse to vote – only so can one signal the otherness, the absoluteness of one's idealism, one's desire for apocalyptic reversal.

What does his idealism amount to? In effect it is secular humanism minus the normal shrugging vagueness and fatalism. He wants freedom and justice for all, on a planet saved from destruction. The old way of toughening up humanism (Marxism) is discredited but he still needs the idea of revolution (otherwise he's just a regular secular humanist). So it must be spiritualized. The revolution means 'the assertion of spirituality, of whatever form, to the heart of our social structures'.[59] Politics alone can't solve our deepest issues, 'it doesn't have the language. Religion does'.[60] But which one? Wrong question. 'When people get all worked up about which religion is superior, that is not religion, that is individualistic, materialistic, territorial ideology asserted through the language of religion.'[61]

It is easy to dismiss Brand's desire to unite spirituality with political radicalism as incoherent (and arrogant in its prophetic posturing). But it is in a sense more honest than conventional left-wing writing, for it acknowledges the absoluteness of the secular humanist vision and grasps that this absoluteness must be understood in some sort of spiritual terms, if the old option of violent revolution is renounced.

Why can't this vision be understood in merely pragmatic terms? It can be, but such pragmatism entails an evasion of its absoluteness, and the appetite to admit such absoluteness is awkwardly and sporadically surfacing in our time.

What about theology?

Some readers might wonder how Christian theology has responded to secular humanism in recent times. Has it, at least in part, tried to show that the core moral universalism of the West is rooted in Christianity? In other words, is my argument consonant with recent theology? To a surprising extent, no. Theology has generally not been concerned to make this sort of argument for a generation or more – though, as we shall see, there are some signs of change. The reason for this is that Christian theology has for many decades been in the grip of a strong anti-liberal reaction. The most influential theologians have been warning against an alliance of theology and liberalism. This was an understandable reaction to a flawed form of liberal Protestant theology that dominated since the Enlightenment – to the deism that we have discussed, and its offshoots.

In the early twentieth century, theology was dominated by a complacent confidence in a smooth synthesis of Christianity and liberal culture. This confidence was attacked by the Swiss theologian Karl Barth in the 1920s; he spoke like a reformer about the need to separate God from rational humanism, and the idolatry of progress. For a few decades he seemed an eccentric throwback, and humanist-friendly theology still got more attention – for example that of Reinhold Niebuhr and Paul Tillich, the last big American liberal theologians. Such liberal theology was supportive of secular humanism, liberal values, democracy, but it made the mistake of seeking a synthesis of Christianity and secular humanism; it affirmed the idea of a liberal Christian culture in which religious thought was highly accommodating of rational humanism. It inherited the liberal Protestant assumption that doctrine should be 'demythologized' and that ritual was a questionable secondary aspect of religion. At root it still followed Hegel's plot, of Christianity transforming itself into sensible modern liberalism.

In the 1960s, liberal theology still seemed dominant, but this was superficial: the sharpest theologians had begun questioning all Enlightenment assumptions and reaffirming the particularity of Christian tradition. Barth's approach began to dominate, and neoconservative Catholic theology also rose to prominence. This was largely due to the decline of mainstream church allegiance: theology began to assume counter-cultural form. Theology's divorce from humanism was largely a good thing: rational-humanist assumptions had blunted it for centuries. Theology needed to recover confidence in its particular language, to rediscover the primacy of faith and ritual. (Ludwig Wittgenstein's philosophy of language played a big role in this emphasis on Christianity as a particular cultural tradition.)

But this massive reaction against 'liberalism' entailed a failure of nuance. Theologians failed to affirm political liberalism and the idea of secular humanism as a necessary public creed; instead they tended to agree with the harshest critics of the entire tradition. (This began with Barth, who failed to affirm the frail Weimar Republic with clarity.) The rise of postmodernism boosted this shift. In the 1980s the communitarian thinker Alasdair MacIntyre influentially dismissed the whole tradition of liberal thought as vacuous. Human rights have no more existence than unicorns, he announced. Christians should be countercultural, defying liberalism just as St Benedict defied barbarian culture when he established his monastic order. We should affirm the particular culture of the Church and puncture the arrogance of secularism and liberalism. Theologians such as Stanley Hauerwas, a tough-talking Texan, followed suit. In the 1990s and after, this bullish approach dominated academic theology, partly thanks to the Anglican thinker John Milbank (and in fact Rowan Williams' thought, though less assertive, was part of this neoconservative postmodernist movement). This new consensus was hard to contest: sympathy with liberalism, of any sort, marked one as a theological 'wet' (to borrow from Thatcherism). Milbank set the tone in his 1990 book *Theology and Social Theory: Beyond Secular Reason*. He presented 'secular reason' as the enemy ideology that had destroyed the old unity of religion, politics and culture. Christian culture must dare to reject it and assert its own social vision – a postmodern reassertion of the organic medieval ideal. As he put it a bit later, 'the universality of the Church' must robustly oppose 'the universality of enlightenment', which is defined by 'mere non-interference with the liberties of others'.[62] In other words, there is no health in secular humanism; it is a temptation to be rejected. Of course, this was consonant with Roman Catholic teaching – which was now being assertively presented by Joseph Ratzinger, soon to be Pope Benedict.

This approach therefore rejected the vague assumption that secular humanism is a good thing, that theology should endorse it. In a sense it was right to do so: the vague assumption had to be thrown out before clear new thought was possible. This neoconservatism was, perhaps, a necessary transitionary phase.

Let's put it like this: the tendency of recent theology has been to dismiss secular humanism as superficial, incoherent, an illegitimate adaptation or corruption of Christianity, and to assert actual authentic Christian culture against it. The true task is subtly different: simultaneously to criticize secular humanism as derivative from Christianity and incoherent when it tries to stand alone, *and* to affirm it as the right public ideology. A non-religious universalism is providential: Christians must affirm it, without anxiety that they are betraying their tradition. This means that secular humanism must be affirmed in its otherness (or semi-otherness): the temptation to fuse with it, to construct a humanist version of Christianity, must indeed be carefully resisted.

After 9/11, the bullish post-liberal mood intensified and spread from the academy to public life, influencing the Church of England, as we have seen. Just as Islamic extremism had sharpened the need for articulation of Western values, theology was still dominated by its post-liberal reaction.

Over the last decade some frail signs of change have emerged. A few thinkers have begun, tentatively, to emphasize the positive connections between Christianity and secular humanism. Prodded by 9/11 and deepening turmoil in the Middle East, a new sense has emerged that the West must reaffirm its moral universalism and that such universalism has religious roots.

This perhaps began with the Canadian Roman Catholic thinker Charles Taylor. His large 2007 study of modernity, *A Secular Age*, analysed the shift from a religion-dominated world to a secular one. Though it does not put forward any strong simple argument, it does insist that secular modernity arose on Christian soil, that humanism was an expression of Christian impulses. It traces the way medieval Christianity develops the humanist potential within Christianity, and so gives rise to the 'exclusive humanism' of the Renaissance and after, which sees human flourishing as the sole sure good. It shows that Protestant zeal against superstition was inherited by the deists; their rationalism was evangelical. It rejects the normal secular account of modernity as a false 'subtraction story': according to this story, once the error of religion is taken away, human reason is liberated. In reality, as I have tried to show (somewhat influenced by Taylor), our idea of human liberation is *shaped* by religion. Taylor then shows how, after Romanticism, the moral universalism of the Enlightenment is contested by anti-universalist thinkers, most obviously Nietzsche, and how this tension defines recent Western thought.

Frustratingly, Taylor does not move towards a clear argument, rather he revels in abstruse complications and jargon-ridden sub-complications (he invents a large handful of jargon in the course of the book). But towards the end he briefly becomes comparatively clear. He says that we now inhabit a three-way struggle between religious believers, secular humanists and Nietzschean anti-humanists. Then he suggests that there are actually four parties, since believers are divided:

> Some think that the whole move to secular humanism was just a mistake, which needs to be undone. We need to return to an earlier view of things. Others, in which I place myself, think that the practical primacy of life has been a great gain for human kind, and that there is some truth in the self-narrative of the Enlightenment: this gain was unlikely to come about without some breach with established religion. (We might even be tempted to say that modern unbelief is providential, but that might be too provocative a way of putting it.)[63]

Oddly, Taylor raises this huge crucial issue of religion's attitude to secular humanism, only to let it drop immediately. He hints that secular humanism might be part of God's cunning plan *in a parenthesis* – and turns away. Perhaps he has so internalized the dominant theological orthodoxy that he cannot quite see this as an avenue worth exploring. Perhaps his great erudition and his academic reputation deter him from such a course, seen by most of his peers as dated error.

And yet his insistence on the Christian basis of modern humanism had some influence on other writers, including Terry Eagleton, whose response to the new atheists we considered in Chapter 1. In a sense Taylor gave others the permission to revisit such territory.

We have already referred to the historian of ideas Larry Siedentop: first, in Chapter 2, in relation to the transition from ancient to Christian morality; then, earlier in this chapter, we noted his book of 2000 in which he accused the European Union of overvaluing economics and lacking an understanding of the religious roots of liberal democracy. In 2014 he expanded on that thesis in *Inventing the Individual: The Origins of Western Liberalism*. He begins by noting that the concept of 'the West' is in doubt: we Westerners seem to have lost our 'moral bearings', for we 'no longer have a persuasive story to tell ourselves about our origins and development'.[64] We must retell such a story, about the emergence of liberalism or 'liberal secularism', which must be asserted as a positive creed, rescued from its image of 'indifference and permissiveness'.[65] This involves confronting its Christian origins. He proceeds to give an account of the origins of modernity, first showing that primitive morality was dominated by the family. In ancient Greece this tribal loyalty expanded into allegiance to the state, which preserved the inequality of the family unit: no serious notion of equality could emerge, no break with hierarchy was possible. Until Christianity: 'For Paul, the Christ is a God-given challenge to humans to transform their conception of themselves and reach for moral equality.'[66] Nor was there a serious notion of secularism before Christianity, despite the assumptions of modern secularists: 'instead of an antiquity free of religion, priesthood and superstition – a "secular" inspiration for modern Europe – we find on closer examination that the family, tribe and city were each a kind of church'.[67]

The rest of the book shows how this principle of moral equality is gradually realized in medieval Christendom. Siedentop argues that most accounts of the rise of modern liberalism overstate the Renaissance, failing to see that the emphasis on the individual is already established in the theology of the preceding era. And there, rather abruptly, the story ends – the rise of secular humanism in the Protestant era is not described.

Siedentop concludes that we must rediscover 'the idea that liberalism and secularism have religious roots'; this has been obscured by the separation of Church and state and by a 'civil war' in which 'religious belief and "godless" secularism are understood as irreconcilable opposites'.[68] In reality, 'secularism is Christianity's gift to the world'.[69] We must rediscover liberal secularism as a positive moral thing, a shared vision. This awareness is, in theory, built into the United States' constitution – though in practice this is threatened by fundamentalists' aversion to secularism.[70] Europe on the other hand is still stuck with dated notions of liberty being intrinsically anticlerical. This must change if Europeans are to meet the challenge of Islam and:

> counter the argument that European secularism is a form of non-belief or indifference. Their self-understanding is at stake. If Europeans understand 'secularism' in the terms favoured by its critics – as mere consumerism, materialism and amorality – they lose touch with their own moral intuitions. They forget why they value freedom.[71]

This is very close to what I have been arguing: no other author of recent years is as erudite, urgent and bold. And yet there is an important difference (though it might seem oversubtle to some). Siedentop implies that Christianity and 'liberal secularism' can be reunited, that the 'civil war' can be ended and the Western vision reunified. This comes too close to conferring a general blessing on secular humanism as the fulfilment of Christianity (in keeping with post-Hegelian liberal Protestant theology). As long as the secular humanist knows that his creed has Christian roots, Siedentop implies, then he is the true bearer of the Western vision. This ignores the dialectical theme I have tried to emphasize throughout: the inevitability of tension between Christianity and its offshoot universalism. If this is not emphasized, the argument gravitates to affirming a nebulous synthesis of religion and secular humanism – in which actual religion will always be marginalized as something that used to be crucial but is now mainly decorative. As I have tried to explain, Christianity is the continuing awkward engine of secular humanism. And Christians must not simply affirm secular humanism but must *dialectically* affirm it – they must see it as inadequate, its universalism as thin, but necessarily so.

I also suggest that Siedentop's terminology is confusing. The title's emphasis on 'the individual' seems unfortunate because individualism is associated with the negative side of 'liberal secularism'; 'equality', which is also central to his thesis, is more positive. But none of these terms quite prioritizes the vision of universal human flourishing that I suggest is at the core of this tradition – the term 'humanism', despite its various ambiguities, does so best. It hints at the utopian perfectionism that underlies this whole vision. But these cavils should not detract from Siedentop's achievement in putting this supremely unfashionable subject back on the academic table.

Another straw in the wind came from the intersection of religious studies and political science. In 2012 Robert Woodberry published an academic article making a deeply unfashionable case. Entitled 'The Missionary Roots of Liberal Democracy', it argued that nineteenth-century missionaries, especially Protestant ones, had educated women and the poor, promoted widespread printing, led nationalist movements that empowered ordinary citizens and fuelled other key elements of democracy. In Woodberry's summary:

> Areas where Protestant missionaries had a significant presence in the past are on average more economically developed today, with comparatively better health, lower infant mortality, lower corruption, greater literacy, higher educational attainment (especially for women), and more robust membership in nongovernmental associations.[72]

This argument would not have turned a hair in the mid twentieth century, but the secularization of academic culture and demonization of colonialism had made it intensely controversial. Woodberry had started work on the thesis in 2002 and had at first struggled to secure the interest of academics. The huge interest his research received ten years later might suggest a shift in the landscape, a willingness to return to issues relating to Christianity and liberal values that had recently seemed dated and dull.

Over the last decade, then, a positive account of liberalism, or secular humanism, has gradually become more theologically respectable. A few smaller fry authors deserve a mention, including, in fact, me! I was provoked by the post-9/11 religion debate to try to tell a more positive story about Christianity and liberalism, without reverting to the errors of liberal Protestantism. I first argued for the Christian roots of liberal politics in relation to the thought of John Milton in my 2008 *Milton's Vision: The Birth of Christian Liberty*. Subsequently I widened the canvas in *Reinventing Liberal Christianity* of 2013, arguing that a good form of liberal theology (that affirms political liberalism) should be distinguished from a bad sort (the rational-humanist, deist sort that rejects the cultic basis of Christianity).

Nick Spencer, research director of the Christian think tank Theos, has drawn on both Taylor and Siedentop to make the case for 'Christian humanism'. A 2014 report on the issue, written with Angus Ritchie, argues that the term 'humanism' should not be ceded to non-believers.[73] It shows in detail that there is substantial overlap between Christianity and humanism as defined by the 2002 Amsterdam Declaration of the International Humanist and Ethical Union, a document affirmed by the British Humanist Association. It rightly contends that Renaissance and Enlightenment humanism are deeply steeped in Christianity, and so the fairly recent anti-religious slippage of the term should be contested. It points out that the secular notion of human dignity that underpins human rights is in effect baseless, a mere assertion. As Rowan Williams says in his Foreword to the report: 'There is ... room for a good and significant conversation in our society about where exactly our convictions of human dignity or equality or liberty come from and how they are to be defended, in theory and practice.' Spencer covered similar ground in his own book of 2014, *Atheists: The Evolution of the Species*, drawing attention to the para-religious motivation of so many of the main atheists of the Enlightenment.

In 2016 Dominic Erdozain has made a similar argument in *The Soul of Doubt: The Religious Roots of Unbelief from Luther to Marx*. He argues that the most influential secularists were motivated by an essentially Christian moral agenda:

> A visceral sense of right and wrong, rather than a scientific or historical suspicion of supernatural truth claims, has served as the primary solvent of orthodoxy in the West ... modernity has been characterized by the internalization of religious ideas, not their disintegration.[74]

He shows how Spinoza, Pierre Bayle, Voltaire and others were steeped in reformist Protestantism: 'The "reason" with which the Enlightenment assailed a persecuting religious culture was neither secular nor primarily intellectual. It was the direct heir to the "inner light" of spiritualist Christianity.'[75] The anticlericalism and anti-Calvinism of such thinkers was more Christian than non-religious, even if they rejected the Christian label.

This cluster of writers is rethinking recent theology's blanket rejection of the old flawed alliance with Enlightenment liberalism. The real task is subtler: to reject what was flawed in that alliance – which was admittedly a great deal – and yet reclaim modern humanism for Christianity. I hope in this book to have raised the stakes, or widened the canvas, or struck a new ambitious note, so that this uncertain movement gains some force.

Stop press: events of 2016

While I was completing this book, Britain voted to leave the EU: in part an expression of resurgent nationalism, fuelled by the migrant crisis of the previous two years. Then, while the book was being edited, Donald Trump was elected president of the USA. This was a far clearer blow to assumptions about Western political culture. For his campaigning rhetoric went beyond the normal right-wing disparagement of 'liberalism', and was not balanced by the normal cross-party idealism about liberal democracy and America's duty to spread it. He motivated his core supporters by defying some of the norms of secular humanist discourse, by flirting with racism, Islamophobia, sexism. And he spoke against various aspects of liberal internationalism: free trade, the need to sanction illiberal regimes, the need to tackle climate change.

So does his election plunge my basic thesis into doubt – my claim that 'we in the West' basically affirm secular humanism? Not quite. His victory showed that a huge sector of Americans, almost a third (turnout was under sixty per cent, and he won less than half of the popular vote), have a strong antipathy to a liberal order that they feel has not benefited them. But even this antipathy to 'liberalism' is ambiguous. Its target is not liberal values in a broad sense, but the particular expression of such values in progressive politics. So we should distinguish between a broad, vague belief in equality, human rights and the rule of law, which we might call 'basic liberalism' (or indeed 'secular humanism'), and liberalism as a concrete political programme, which we might call 'sharp liberalism'. It says that liberal values must find expression in certain particular policies – and the issues it focuses on often have a tribal, urban-elitist flavour. This angers a huge sector of the population so much that they vote for a crude clear alternative, even if it seems to go against the tenets of 'basic liberalism', even if it seems illiberal.

Liberal or 'progressive' politicians will, one hopes, respond by re-grounding their message in the 'basic liberalism' that we have in common. And affirming the religious basis of this basic liberalism might not be a bad idea; it counters the impression that progressive politics is dominated by cosmopolitan elitist secularism. (The religiosity of his rhetoric surely helped Obama to energize voters in 2008, in a way that Hillary Clinton failed to.)

Preliminary conclusion

It seems that it embarrasses us, this matter of our basic common creed in the West. It is too vague to be worth focusing on, say hard-headed people of the world. Left-wingers say it is too vague to inspire the fight for social justice. Right-wingers say it is too vague, too weak to deliver meaning or to underpin deep social bonds. But the real embarrassment is that it raises the very largest moral questions. If we are to affirm the ideal of universal human flourishing, we risk being asked: 'Why? What *is* this tradition that seeks the good of all, the rights of all? Where does it come from?'

I have tried to expound the paradox: secular humanism cannot be understood in purely secular terms. It is not cleanly post-religious. If we are to affirm this moral tradition, celebrate it, be proud of it, we must acknowledge that our public creed is not simply secular humanism but *Christian-based secular humanism*. Only so can we strongly affirm it. We garble and falsify our ideology if we do not acknowledge its religious basis. Only if we acknowledge its debt to religion can we have a sense of this tradition's groundedness, its depth.

But admitting its debt to religion is not straightforward, for it is *secular* humanism that we proclaim as our public creed. Politics needs a universalism that is secular, not religious. But this secular universalism is like a sheet of pastry rolled too thin: it breaks up. So we must re-root it in its source. Roll it out, root it back. This unstable movement is necessary. We must admit the instability of this creed that is secular yet religion-rooted. A smooth synthesis of these elements is not possible. Modern theology and post-theology tried to forge a stable universalism; it failed. And theology remains in a state of defensive hurt, vowing not to be let down again.

We can best affirm secular humanism if we see it as the necessarily thin aspect of a thick vision. It is my strange claim that Christians are particularly able to affirm this creed, for they also affirm something else: the base on which secular humanism rests, the thick undercoat of this superficial – in a sense – creed. Ironically, it is secularists who find secular humanism too flimsy and yearn for something solider.

What's my agenda in putting this case? I suppose it's twofold. I want to see a more confident, robust and self-aware secular humanism. Only with a renewed sense of its ideological purpose can the West stand up to threats coming from the Middle East, China, Russia. We must become prouder of our ideology: moral universalism, human rights. And this means becoming proud of the *story* of this ideology: the story of Christian universalism learning to reject theocracy and express itself in inclusive, even post-religious terms. This story is difficult, paradoxical. (It is with a heavy heart that one dusts down the word 'dialectical'.) But without this story we do not quite know who we are.

Also, my agenda is 'apologetical': by highlighting its influence on our public morality I am trying to persuade people to take this religion a bit more seriously than they are accustomed to. Am I suggesting that if you like secular humanism, 'you might also like' its basis, Christianity? Maybe I am.

The reader might reply: 'Hmmm, maybe it's true that secular humanism has Christian roots, but so what? Surely I can prefer the fruit of a tree to its roots. And surely post-Christian secular humanism is an improvement on Christianity – for surely it purges the tradition of its irrational and authoritarian elements? Why can't we have the sensible modern fruit without the traditional mythology and ritual and so on? Why not just believe in the good of all, in the sacredness of universal human rights? Why not stick with *secular* humanism?'

I suppose I want to suggest that there is something small-minded, pinched, intellectually dishonest about such a response. For what do secular humanists actually believe? (I do apologise for this accusatory tone.) They believe in the good of all humanity, but only within reason, only in as far as it seems normal. They are always looking over their shoulders, seeing how far such idealism is deemed normal, rational. If one thinks for oneself, one might notice that the good of all humanity is an *absolute* ideal, a utopian perfectionism; it entails a narrative of paradise regained. Secular humanism wriggles away from this absoluteness; it does not really believe in its own idealism. It turns this ideal into a vague aspiration, most commonly expressed in negative form – in the insistence that certain actions and attitudes are wrong because they impede the rights of others. But authentic humanism is positive and absolute; its desire for human flourishing is unlimited. Secular humanism lacks a mechanism that fixes it to absoluteness (though the

Marxist belief in revolutionary transformation is a stab at this). It is parasitic on the absolutism that it comes from and scorns.

Am I saying that Christians desire the good more completely than secular humanists? Well, that's a hard thing to measure, but it is surely the case that they see 'the good' in more intense, absolute terms: as a call to moral perfection – an impossible demand that one cannot fulfil but must struggle to; as a demand that exposes one's inadequacy, one's inner division between obedience and sin (to slip into religious speech). Christians can face up to the absoluteness of this moral ideal because they have a story that makes sense of our failure to live up to it. The secular humanist, by contrast, thinks in more realistic terms – of being morally good enough by affirming the rights of others. 'Of course no one is perfect,' she says, 'so let's put aside the unhelpful notion of moral perfection and instead uphold realistic rules of conduct, a moral law – it is enough to be among the morally civilized people, who affirm equality.' But this is a brittle, somewhat dishonest position, for all humanism, religious or not, is half-hypocritical. All are equal, we say, but we'd rather hang out with an interesting attractive person than a poor, uneducated, smelly one. In other words, morality entails a tension between idealism and our selfishness, and secular humanism lacks a language for pondering this and so evades it. We all have a duty to be moral, it says, and it assumes that this civilized moral way is straightforwardly possible. But morality, in this tradition, cannot be confined to such sensible rule-based pragmatism. It is about the perfectionist good of all, and we betray that vision with every dirty little thought we have. (Not just sex-thoughts, of course, but Augustine was right that sex is a good summary of the fact that natural desire is embarrassingly limited to the orbit of the ego. Consequently secular humanism is very evasive about sex, or rather about the dramatic moral tension that surrounds sexual desire.)

I am claiming that Christianity is the pure humanism, the ur-humanism. 'Well, we'd rather have humanism in a more developed, evolved, form,' you might say, 'purged of its irrationality.' But that's a dilution. Full-blooded humanism is absolutist, perfectionist; it needs this mythical and ritual context. It needs to inhabit the paradox that we must exceed our human nature, defy sin, rely on the miracle of God's grace. It needs these rationally indefensible concepts and phrases, which belong to a ritual tradition. Why? Because otherwise the absoluteness slips away – one moves to a sensible moderate version of humanism in which this ideal is thought to be normal, our default position. To put it differently: Christianity is a primitive form of humanism. But this primitivity can't be rationalized, progressed on from. This is primitivity that can't be improved on, like dance.

So Christianity should affirm secular humanism and remind it of the half-forgotten absoluteness of its idealism. But it must *also* call secular humanism inadequate. 'Yes, this is the right *public* ideology,' it must say, 'but we must also look beneath the surface and nurture its roots.' It is not enough to advocate this good public ideology, with its necessary agnosticism. It is also necessary to nurture a more comprehensive narrative of meaning, to affirm and perform the good myth, from which secular humanism derives. What an impossibly contradictory agenda! Christianity must both affirm *and dissent from* the dominant ideology around it.

The agnostic might agree, or half-agree, that there is a mythic coherence, or fullness, to Christianity that secular humanism lacks, a more comprehensive account of meaning. 'But I think I'll stick with *this* incoherence,' he might reply, 'rather than trade it in for the more extreme and conspicuous incoherence of believing in God and Jesus and so on. How can the Christian accuse the secular humanist of incoherence when he believes in things that are directly at odds with modern rationality?'

Good question. In fact it's one I feel obliged to answer at length. I have in this book offered a sort of apologetics, showing how Christianity deserves to be taken seriously due to its pivotal role in modern moral thought. But this is incomplete without an explanation of how I suppose that affirming an ancient myth, dripping with irrationality, is possible. So I am, at this late stage, going to change apologetic tack and look at the question of religious belief. How does anyone with any intelligence find Christianity credible?

7

So what? How is
Christianity credible?

I have been arguing in favour of Christianity on the grounds that it underlies our basic moral and political creed. If we are to affirm the latter, then the former is surely to be taken seriously, respected. Many readers will say: 'I do respect Christianity on such grounds. But that's as far as I can go; I feel decisively cut off from Christian faith by virtue of being a modern sceptical person. I could no more revert to believing in Father Christmas.'

I'm not sure that apologetics can do more than what I have attempted: highlighting the Christian basis of our moral assumptions. In fact I think other approaches are largely counterproductive: they tend to imply the compatibility of faith and reason. Not only does this fail to persuade the agnostic; in my view it falsifies the nature of faith.

So how can the agnostic be prodded to a revaluation of faith? Well, printed words probably can't do very much. People only 'get' religion if they have hung out with it for a bit, let it get under their skin. But for some people, the skin must be initially punctured by a jolting new idea of faith, which writing might mediate. It might sound absurdly unappealing at first, yet quietly needle.

In two minds?

Just consider for a moment what Christians believe, or say they believe. There once lived a man who was divine, who was the incarnation of the one God, who created all things. This man performed various miracles and came back to life when executed. He will come again in glory, and through him God will put everything right, cancel history's horror, defeat suffering and death.

How can anyone believe all this? No wonder people want to deny or downplay secular humanism's Christian basis, for this religion strikes the average modern mind as simply incredible. 'The atheist attack on religion might be simplistic,' thinks the average intelligent person, 'but what sort of rebuttal is possible? Those religious folk simply seem to believe in the unbelievable, bless them.'

I think that we Christians must attempt a fresh approach to the subject – one that begins with a surprising admission: 'Yes, it is incredible, the Christian myth – well spotted. All its claims merit extreme scepticism.' So how is belief possible? It is possible because it can coexist with scepticism, in an endless internal argument.

For example: do I really believe that God created the world? Only with one part of my mind – a part that is deeply attached to the idea (the myth, the image) of God as creator, which partly consists of Sunday-school pictures of Adam and Eve in the Garden of Eden. The same applies to my belief in God in general. Is it not a childish or primitive part of me that believes in him, that thinks praying to him makes any sort of sense? Do I believe that Jesus rose from the dead? Well, I affirm it, with ritual-based phrases from the liturgy and the Bible ('He is risen indeed', 'Death, where is thy sting?'), and I also think of old paintings of the risen Jesus holding that red and white flag, an image that has a sort of authority for me. But I also think: 'What *really* happened to that historical corpse?' Putting aside my sentimental attachment to these ritual phrases and traditions, let's be honest: dead people stay dead, don't they? You might assume that this voice wins out, for surely my attachment to scientific reason is stronger than my attachment to certain ritual phrases and images. But no, neither voice entirely wins out: I affirm the resurrection *and* I continue to be conscious of its rational impossibility, which makes me wonder if I really can believe in it. And the resurrection's not the end of it: can I also believe that Jesus will return and somehow redeem the cosmos, make all well, unleash utopian love and peace? My rationality, amazed at these absurdities, patiently reiterates the case for cold-eyed atheism.

It might sound as though I'm a believer who struggles with 'doubt'. *No* – this utterly misrepresents things, implies that belief is meant to be full and stable. According to my understanding, Christian belief is *meant to be* unstable, in tension with scepticism, for it is not a normal belief or opinion like believing in socialism or the scientific case for climate change. Instead this belief is inseparable from a special, 'other' way of using language – at root a *ritual* way of using language. To express belief in God is at root a ritual act or speech-act. And ritual is other, set apart from the rest of life. One cannot constantly and completely inhabit this otherness but must also stand outside of it.

So instead of attempting arguments in defence of certain Christian beliefs, I want to problematize 'belief'. Christianity is about participation in a ritual tradition. What the Christian 'believes' is a messy mix of this tradition and his or her more normal patterns of thought.

This is how Christian faith works, I suggest. It rejects smooth synthesis in favour of *internal dialogue*, a clash between two different voices. The content is too impossible, too extreme for any sort of calm stable belief. And it is in this impossibility and extremity that we know that we are talking about *God*.

Am I trying to make a virtue of my shaky faith, or is this a legitimate, well-attested approach to Christian faith? It is admittedly far more common to present faith as a stable coherent position, and an essentially reasonable one in some higher sense of 'reasonable' – this unites the philosophy of Thomas Aquinas with the apologetics of C. S. Lewis. Most contemporary apologists continue in this vein, explaining that faith is really just a form of trust and that trust is involved in all forms of human knowledge, so let's not overstate the difference of what's going on in faith. Perhaps such an approach inevitably dominates, for putting oneself at odds with reason is uncomfortable. But some of us favour another approach, one we see as more awkwardly honest. For us, the tradition of faith becomes inhabitable when we admit that we cannot straightforwardly, wholemindedly believe in Christianity.

Am I saying that one need only *half*-believe? Sort of. I am saying that Christian faith is a matter of accepting a ritual tradition, an inherited pattern of worship-speech; but one cannot fully inhabit this ritual tradition; one keeps one foot in normal thought and speech. Faith therefore involves surprising open-mindedness: it allows one to hold on to one's scepticism; indeed it positively requires this.

In other religious traditions it is doubtless possible to combine belief and scepticism, but Christianity puts this tension in the foreground in a unique way. It develops and intensifies an ancient Jewish theme: that belief in God entails an internal argument, for it is through dialogue with scepticism that one perceives his miraculous otherness. In the rest of this chapter I want to sketch this account of faith in relation, first, to the Bible and then in relation to its great rediscoverer, Martin Luther. (It is good to see Luther receiving plenty of attention 500 years after his rise to fame – yet one suspects that his dialectical reinvention of faith is receiving less attention than other aspects of his career more amenable to slick journalistic use.)

Bible

At the heart of the Hebrew Bible is the collection of worship songs, or liturgical poems, the book of Psalms. Many of these express an individual's extreme disaffection, near-despair – and then his defiant decision to trust God. To express abandonment by God is in effect to voice doubt about the reality of God – but on an emotional or existential level rather than a theoretical one. In some cases, however, there is an explicit flirtation with scepticism. The speaker asks why the creator of the universe and the protector of Israel is not more clearly active *now*. Why does the world seem devoid of his justice, his authority? Why does the speaker experience failure, humiliation, a sense of complete abandonment by God? And how come other people get away with denying God's reality? These people prosper – which makes their perspective seem convincing. The wicked man literally gets away with murder, complains Psalm 10, and his scornful rejection of God goes unpunished – which makes the godless attitude look like disillusioned, grown-up realism. The speaker begs God to act, to disprove these disobedient voices. He has made the world, crushed the monster Leviathan, delivered Israel from her enemies, so why has he gone all quiet? Why does he allow his authority to seem unreal? In Psalm 73 the speaker recounts his near-seduction by the faithless attitude, his envy of the God-mockers: 'They say, "How would God know? Does the Most High know anything?".'[1] Then he attends worship and is assured that God will punish such pride.

In these psalms, faith entails facing the problem of God's seeming weakness or absence and calling for him to come out of hiding. This means that the expression of faith entails acknowledging the case for scepticism; unbelief must be represented, as a foil for the assertions of God's power. In a sense this is how a new assurance of God is conjured up. Despairing scepticism must be routed by the reassertion of faith. The believer questions his grounds for belief, then clings to the half-credible traditional poetic images of divine power and so revitalizes them.

The difference between this dynamic and a simple, stable 'belief in God' is obvious. Faith in *this* God entails this drama of yearning for his authority to become apparent, to become real – and pointing out that *as yet it is not*. Two perspectives are needed, two voices – a sceptical one as well as a trusting one. It is not enough to affirm God's greatness, his mighty deeds of the past, his promised salvation. This is empty rhetoric unless it is also admitted that God's authority is, at present, agonizingly absent. The psalms do a strange thing: they put this tension between trust and scepticism at the heart of ritual; they insist that these painfully honest reflections on God belong to the kosher tradition of worship.

The dynamic of the psalms is dramatized in that strange fairy tale for grown-ups, the book of Job. God allows Job to be brought down by Satan to test his trust. Job issues a huge eloquent complaint, demanding to know why God is treating him thus. He is visited by some theologically minded friends who insist that God is just and that no one ever has a valid case against him. Job's complaint against God is shockingly self-important, they say, and they seem to have a point. Job's response is nuanced: it is true that one should trust that God's justice will ultimately be manifested, but one should *also* tell the truth about the present absence of this justice; one should complain, protest, admit there is a crisis. In Job's case this chiefly means insisting that he has not deserved his fall from grace, though he sometimes also makes the wider complaint of the psalmist, that the wicked prosper.

God endorses Job's approach and rewards him by delivering a thrilling poem about the natural world (the ancient equivalent of a lovely nature film). The story insists that real living faith entails honesty. God wills us to face the absence of divine justice rather than pretend it is sort of present in some mysterious way. It is important that Job does not deny the core principle of his visitors: that God is just, that his justice will be revealed. He shows that authentic faith needs two voices: one to affirm God's justice, the other to ask 'Where is it then?'

Christianity originated as a mutation of Judaism in which this theme of trust in God's coming justice has absolute priority over the other tradition, of cultural stability, law.

Jesus announced the kingdom of God, a sharpening of the prophetic vision. God's saving action is not deferred to some future time, once the tumult of current affairs has died down: it begins *now*. He speaks as if Jeremiah's prophecy has come true and his hearers have new hearts or can choose to have new hearts, law-doing hearts.

Be perfect, as God is: don't even think about immoral actions but trust that God is remaking your mind.

But is this possible for us? Can we decide to be morally perfect, faultless instruments of the kingdom? Paul's letters, the earliest Christian documents, grapple with this question. He develops Jesus' idea of the imminent reign of God, but transforms it. The emphasis is now placed not on our morally perfect action but on our belief in a transformative act of God, coming soon (to a cosmos near you) – an apocalyptic event. God already supplies us with a taste of this transformation – his Spirit is among us, enabling us to exceed normal human behaviour. Sort of. The shift to a new way of being is not clear-cut, for as yet we only have sporadic glimpses of this transformation – we are also aware of inhabiting the old order. So as in the psalms, Christian faith has a powerful tension at its heart.

Writing to the fledgling church in Corinth, Paul excitedly presents faith as a sort of secret knowledge, at odds with existing assumptions about how God is known (the Jewish law, Greek wisdom). In its reliance on God's future action and its discontinuity with existing reality, faith is 'foolishness'. In another letter to the Corinthians he develops a paradoxical formula for what faith is: 'we fix our eyes not on what is seen, but on what is unseen'.[2] Christians go beyond normal seeing, which is associated with worldly realism, common sense: 'For we live by faith, not by sight.'[3] Faith is a new way of seeing, a new perspective. Does it entirely replace the old way of seeing? Crucially, no. It coexists with it. Faith does not stop us seeing the world in the old way – Christians are still human beings, living in the present age. They therefore have a *dual perspective*. They strive to see the world from the perspective of God's future action, but this cannot be a stable new position. There is inevitable tension or struggle between the two perspectives.

Paul's letter to the Roman Christians explains that we know God through faith rather than through the Jewish law. The law tells us how to be perfectly moral – but highlights the fact that we *can't be*. So Jews try to be moral but face an endless battle with sin – they can't overcome their human limitations. How does faith in Christ change this? It is the belief that God intervenes and gives us a new identity – he magically makes us perfect. He saves us from possession by sin, through the stronger possession by his Spirit. So Paul presents Christianity in terms of Spirit-possession: God takes us over, frees us from our fallen selves.

(We partly know him as an invading *voice*, rather as if we are his ventriloquist dummies.)

This is not a stable new world view, or identity! Instead, God gives us a glimpse of human nature transformed, but because we are still old-fashioned humans, this vision is strange, alien, other. And so when we affirm this vision, Paul explains, we should understand that this is the action of the Spirit in us. We should admit that we are not at home in this discourse; we do not know how to pray, but should let the Spirit take control. We don't really know what we're talking about.

Which means – unorthodox though it sounds – that this vision of humanity made new is beyond 'belief' in any normal sense. Can we, who are pre-new, really grasp it? We can have a sense of God's voice breaking into human history and announcing its transformation, and we can assert our allegiance to this new message, but such an allegiance is strange, at odds with human life, human knowing. Which means that faith is unimaginable away from a conflict between the old and new ways of seeing. There are two perspectives in dialogue – the eschatological extremity of faith makes this unavoidable.

To wield a rather broad brush for a moment: after Paul, theology sidelined this stormy tension and emphasized the overlap of Christianity and Greek philosophy. The idea of a tension at the heart of faith, corresponding to God's eschatological otherness, was effectively buried. (Or half-buried, for it shows through in Augustine's insistence that we are all always sinners, in need of grace.) In the later Middle Ages, theology's vague alliance with philosophy was tidied up. Using Aristotle's rationalism, which spread from Muslim to Christian universities, Thomas Aquinas created a theological structure that affirmed a rational understanding of God yet subordinated it to revelation. He reasserted what theology had implied since the third century: reason belongs to faith; it doesn't challenge faith's claims but backs them up. This new system provoked a slow-burning reaction, a will to rediscover the otherness of God from all human knowing. This first took the form of nominalism, a philosophical movement that distrusted abstract rationality and emphasized God's power, unpredictability, wildness.

Luther

Martin Luther was the key discoverer of faith's capacity for *honesty*. Instead of claiming to be pure and holy, we can and should be honest about our inability to be pure and holy, and even about our inability to believe in this religion in a stable way. Because the natural human mind resists God, faith is always a struggle, doubt is inevitable. And it's *only through this honesty* that we relate to God – for only so can we know him as other, as the saving power that we need.

Before Luther, theology gave out mixed messages on this crucial issue. It said that we are all sinners, incapable of Christ's divine goodness, but it also implied the opposite: that *real* Christians are set apart from the moral mediocrity of the world, that only heroic saints are fully assured of salvation and that one can best imitate them through the institutionalized rigour of the monastery. In other words, all Christians are equally sinful in relation to Christ, but some are less equal than others. One must strive to join a spiritual elite. What was the alternative? Advising people to relax in their sin? Luther, through obsessively seeking Paul's meaning, discovered that there was in fact an alternative, that the circle could narrowly be squared. He said that all Christians remain sinners, that there is no technique of lessening one's sinfulness, that there is no religious elite. And yet Christians can fully participate in God's salvation. How? Through faith? Yes, but this is open to misinterpretation. For *pure* faith is just as impossible as morally perfect action. He said that normal, flawed, struggling faith is enough – which means that one can be honest about the fact that one's psyche also contains doubt, fear, gloom. So the mark of true Christianity, all of a sudden, is *psychological honesty*. The true Christian says: 'Yes, I half-hate this impossibly demanding religion, which I can only partly believe in; yes, I'm still tempted to think and act badly.' Christianity doesn't just allow for this sort of honesty, it *demands* it. It calls such honesty the mark of authenticity. One is meant to be in two minds, in a state of internal division or dialogue.

Why? Isn't full and certain belief superior to such equivocation? No, says Luther, 'full and certain belief' cannot be belief in the true God, who is at odds with human imperfection, who is too strange and too *other* for wholehearted acceptance. 'Full and certain' belief treats God like your pet dog; it domesticates him. Let's put it like this: it is only through endless honesty about our failure to serve God, and even fully to believe in him, that we know we are talking about *God*, who demands perfection and lets us participate in it.

Luther was born in 1483 to a businessman of peasant stock who could just about afford to send him to school and university. He learned to trade on his working-class roots; he was the straight talker, unimpressed by urbane evasions. He became famous largely through his style, which involved polemical rudeness, scatological language and a taste for dramatic religious imagery, especially a willingness to talk about the Devil.

To his father's fury, he gave up studying law and joined a monastery. He wanted to be part of the pure, hard-core Christian culture. But life as a monk brought him little sense of assurance in salvation. Was he doing something wrong? Or was there something authentic and necessary about the inner turmoil he felt? The conventional view, echoed by his spiritual director John Staupitz, was that this self-division was an abnormal experience, a form of spiritual illness – or maybe in some cases a special revelation granted to mystics. 'No,' Luther gradually found the courage to say, 'it's *normal*.' This is a major clue to Luther's genius: he insisted that his seemingly eccentric and excessive psychological experience was what everyone is meant to feel. It's as if a young person these days suffered depression and was advised to take medication, and he or she forcefully replied, 'No! – my condition is not a malady but a proper response to the world, evaded by others.'

Luther's nagging question was this: how do we know that we're on track for salvation? Influenced by Augustine, he had established that salvation cannot be earned through doing pious things; salvation is fully God's gift. But how do we develop sufficient faith in this to feel assured of salvation? Conventional theology seemed to sideline this question and to recycle the dubious notion that one should busily undertake pious activities, cultic and moral, in order to put one's salvation beyond reasonable doubt. Well, he had tried this, for years now – he had assumed that immersion in monastic routine would steadily build up his trust in God. It didn't: the fear remained that he lacked the saving faith that Paul seemed to exhibit in his letters. He continued to tremble at the thought of God judging a struggling sinner like himself.

Then he had a breakthrough, a mystical sense of finding the key to the gospel. It's impossible to date this eureka moment exactly, but it probably coincided with his sudden ascent to fame, when in 1517 he picked a fight with the papacy over indulgences. 'If I am to be a star theologian,' he may have felt, 'I had better clarify my reading of Paul, hammer it into unity.'

The issue that had been obsessing him for a decade was this: how can we be Christian *and honest*? How can we believe that God saves us, that we participate in his perfection of the cosmos – *and also admit that we remain soaked in sin*? Re-reading Paul's letter to the Romans, Luther saw new significance in the idea that God 'justifies' or 'makes righteous' those with faith. He did not simply decide that all you need is faith, as opposed to legalistic 'works' – for years he had been thinking in this direction but coming up against the problem that total faith, which is surely what God requires, seems impossible. What suddenly occurred to him is that flawed, human faith – the *attempt* to have full faith – counted, because God treats our flawed faith as true righteous faith. It is not a matter of our having such strong faith that God sees we are righteous. Instead, God accepts our flawed faith, sees the half-empty cup as full enough. So suddenly Luther's sense of lacking full faith did not feel like a disqualification. Indeed, he saw that total faith was impossible because we remain human: struggling with doubt, depression and fear is inevitable. Faith *is* this struggle – in the real world no pure, unwavering form of faith is possible. To struggle to believe does not mean one is failing to be a Christian but that one is a Christian. In his new favourite phrase, the Christian is *simul justus et peccator* – simultaneously justified and a sinner. We don't know if our faith will save us, but we do know that frail, fallible faith is the only sort of faith there is; so we should trust that we are indeed in the running for salvation. This insight felt like an immense liberation; like entering the gates of paradise already, as he put it.

In a torrent of writing he performed his reinvention of faith, showing the necessary presence of doubt. True engagement with God's word entails battling with the perspective that scorns it. Scepticism is a necessary conversation partner or foil. We must perform our trust in God's word by acknowledging this tension, understood as a battle with Satan, who wants to rob us of our capacity to trust God's word and plunge us into uncertainty: he must be fought off. Prayer is the chief means of fighting him off but sometimes one must take a break and dispel him through having fun, drinking, playing music, marital love – actively affirming the goodness of creation and normal 'secular' life. He was a sort of humanist, insisting that we should enjoy God's gifts. And yet we should never trust in our own resources: as he puts it in one sermon, in an early anticipation of Freud perhaps: 'each one of us is himself a great and spacious sea, filled with reptiles and animals'.[4]

Luther's insistence on the imperfection of all human faith meant deconstructing the seemingly perfect faith set out in the New Testament.

Despite his seemingly unshakable confidence, Paul must have experienced doubt of his salvation: 'I don't think he could have believed as firmly as he spoke on that subject. I cannot myself as firmly believe as I speak and write about it.'[5] This is an important insight into how faith works: it involves an act, or pretence, of certainty. Faith must both perform certainty, in order to mediate God's word, and also admit that this is a performance, that human uncertainty remains.

Luther's theology took root in a few countries but it soon emerged that Calvin's version of reform was a sleeker product that lent itself more easily to widespread adaptation. On paper, Calvin's view of faith was very close to Luther's, but instead of performing the clash of faith and scepticism, he developed a new sort of smooth theological discourse in which faith is presented as an alternative, higher rationality. He presented faith as the systematic knowledge of God, gained through Scripture.

Though he technically agreed with Luther that all human faith is fallible and embattled, his systematic approach said the opposite – that faith is a lofty, orderly affair. Luther's radical honesty was as much a matter of style as content.

After Luther

Luther's dramatic idea of faith exerted great influence but in a rather scrappy, indirect way. I think it had huge influence on poetry, making internal dialogue central to the idea of poetic discourse. For example, it enabled the Anglican poet-priest George Herbert to rediscover the drama of the psalms. Many of his poems stage a conflict between trust in God and a gloomy scepticism. In his masterpiece 'The Collar', a voice of atheist rebellion is performed, a voice of energetic autonomy-seeking humanism. It's a little hymn to freedom but there's a febrile pride mixed in. Then God's voice intrudes: 'Me thought I heard one calling Child!' – and the whole edifice of rebellion collapses as the speaker simply responds, 'My Lord.' Sometimes God's voice is represented more directly, in a literal dialogue – most famously in 'Love (III), Love Bade Me Welcome'. And some of the poems represent militant faith, in which, in very Lutheran vein, the speaker addresses demonic forces that bother his psyche, exorcizing them with the help of the Word.

In many of Herbert's poems the existential scepticism is almost unrelieved. 'Almost', because the very act of calling out to God is an act of hope. The most compellingly grim poem of frustrated yearning is 'Denial', with its shockingly abrupt verse endings. Here's the opening:

> When my devotions could not pierce
> Thy silent ears;
> Then was my heart broken, as was my verse:
> My breast was full of fears
> And disorder . . .

There are five verses in the past tense: the reader expects that a happy resolution will finally be performed. But no: the final verse begs for this resolution, indicating that the crisis continues. It's hypnotically bleak.

The message of his poems is intensely Lutheran – we are not capable of stable, wholehearted faith. Our main faith experience is one of unresolved tension, necessitating continual appeals for God's help. He must intervene in order to rescue us from endless fruitless self-division. Faith entails honesty about the absence of any stable assurance. It therefore contains existential or emotional scepticism, a sense of God's ineffectiveness or distance. Herbert is not really concerned with rational scepticism, a sense of the rational absurdity of Christian teaching. Scepticism is always emotional rather than theoretical – it is felt as revolt, as despair, as abandonment.

In fact what the hell: let me speak personally here. Reading Herbert as an undergraduate, I saw that Christian faith was still a vital tradition, despite its antiquated, irrational, childish features. For I saw that this tradition was surprisingly open to self-criticism; there was scope for kicking against it, from within. There was room for honesty – about one's sense of angry dissatisfaction, of utter non-harmony, of near-despair. Before, the language of faith had seemed not quite available – something for more pious people who had a deep assurance of God. 'No,' said Herbert, 'it's for dodgy edgy types too.' For the rebellious voice of 'The Collar' is allowed expression rather than suppressed. Honesty lives here – an uncanny expanded sort of honesty that both affirms God and bitterly wonders where the hell he is. Two voices. And so, reluctantly in a sense (for dismissing religion is far more straightforward), I admitted that it felt possible to inhabit the antiquated, irrational, childish language of prayer – because one can dissent from it from within.

This 'dialogical' idea of faith sometimes surfaces in subsequent theology and in Christian literature – but has remained disappointingly marginal. We seem to desire a belief system to be unified; we find internal division chaotic, unsettling. But Christianity calls us to this complexity, I suggest. For its content doesn't fit in normal human thought-boxes. It splashes and spills.

Concluding conclusion

In this chapter I have tried to anticipate a basic objection to my argument. Even if humanist morality came from Christianity, this does not oblige us to believe in Christian teaching. It might encourage agnostics to respect this religion but it does not show them how it is inhabitable. So I've tried to sketch my understanding of faith as something that is *half*-inhabitable: as an endless internal argument between acceptance of this mythological and ritual tradition, and rational scepticism. Faith entails honesty about the fact that this tradition is not neatly inhabitable; that part of one's mind will put up resistance or sulk in the corner. Again, to call this 'doubt' is not quite right, for that implies that full belief is possible. It isn't: belief takes the form of participation in ritual speech-forms, and one can't stay in that odd water all the time.

I'm trying to get away from the assumption that belief is a stable and abstract thing. Instead it is tied to the language of prayer and praise – a language that is in tension with more prosaic parts of one's mind. Let's not overstate the instability of this. It's not as if one is a Christian on some days and an atheist on others, because rational scepticism is in the ascendant. It is a stable instability. Despite the inner tension, it is a stable form of belief and identity. One does believe, despite one's partial unbelief.

Of course, the atheist will be amazed at the open goal I seem to have offered up. 'Why not just admit that you don't really believe any of it?' he will ask. Aren't I admitting that faith is 'trying to make yourself believe what you know ain't so' (to cite Mark Twain)? Well, it can feel a bit like that – and yet the believer stubbornly sees authority in the cultic language of faith. He sees this language, and this myth, as the engine of life's meaning.

But why, oh why, bother at all with this business of half-believing in something, with setting up this internal argument in one's mind? Why not just reject mythological thinking? Or rather, why not see it as enlightened moderns tend to – as mere mythology, a decorative hinterland to healthy moral values? Why ascribe authority to a mythological idiom, and intense irrational speech-forms? Why keep even one foot in the realm of magical thinking?

Why? Because we believers believe that this is the realm of meaning, saving meaning. We are not ashamed to say that we need this primal force of meaning, this good plot in which all the pretty shards of culture can be gathered up. It enables a decisively healthy form of human culture – easily mistaken for a weak, wet and timid form – in which our vital urges to celebrate and create can be rightly loosed.

Yes, it is psychologically and intellectually difficult to move from secular normality to inhabiting or half-inhabiting this culture, but it's a difficulty one is grateful for, because despair-solving meaning is made right here. The burden is light.

Notes

1 The ideology in the room

1 R. Dawkins, *The Selfish Gene*. Oxford: Oxford University Press, 2006, p. 201.
2 R. Dawkins, *A Devil's Chaplain*. Boston: Houghton Mifflin, 2003, pp. 10–11.
3 Dawkins, *Devil's Chaplain*, p. 11.
4 Dawkins, *Devil's Chaplain*, p. 11.
5 Dawkins, 'The Great Convergence', in *Devil's Chaplain*, p. 149.
6 C. Darwin, *On the Origin of Species*. New York: Dover, 2006, p. 307.
7 R. J. Richards, 'Darwinian Enchantment', in *The Joy of Secularism: 11 Essays for How we Live Now*, ed. G. Levine. Princeton, NJ: Princeton University Press, 2011, p. 194.
8 Dawkins, 'Rejoicing in Multifarious Nature' (1978), in *Devil's Chaplain*, p. 199.
9 Dawkins, 'Light Will be Thrown' (2002), Foreword to a new student edition of Darwin's *The Descent of Man*, in *Devil's Chaplain*, p. 66.
10 R. Dawkins, *The God Delusion*. London: Random House, 2006, p. 263.
11 Dawkins, *God Delusion*, p. 270.
12 Dawkins, *God Delusion*, p. 271.
13 C. Hitchens, *God is Not Great: How Religion Poisons Everything*. New York: Twelve, 2007, p. 7.
14 Hitchens, *God is Not Great*, p. 175.
15 Hitchens, *God is Not Great*, p. 176.
16 Hitchens, *God is Not Great*, p. 192.
17 Hitchens, *God is Not Great*, pp. 213–4.
18 Hitchens, *God is Not Great*, p. 205.
19 A. C. Grayling, *The God Argument: The Case Against Religion and for Humanism*. New York: A. & C. Black, 2013, p. 7.
20 Grayling, *God Argument*, p. 138.
21 Grayling, *God Argument*, p. 140.
22 Grayling, *God Argument*, p. 141.
23 Grayling, *God Argument*, p. 141.
24 Grayling, *God Argument*, p. 144.
25 Grayling, *God Argument*, pp. 245–6.
26 Grayling, *God Argument*, p. 146.
27 Grayling, *God Argument*, p. 146.
28 J. F. Haught, *God and the New Atheism: A Critical Response to Dawkins, Harris, and Hitchens*. Louisville, KY: Westminster John Knox Press, 2008, p. 22.
29 J. Barnes, *Nothing to Be Frightened of*. New York: Knopf, 2008, p. 116.
30 Barnes, *Nothing to Be Frightened of*, p. 117.

31 Barnes, *Nothing to Be Frightened of*, p. 118.
32 Barnes, *Nothing to Be Frightened of*, p. 119.
33 T. Eagleton, *Reason, Faith and Revolution: Reflections on the God Debate*. New Haven, CT: Yale University Press, 2009, pp. 77–8.
34 Eagleton, *Reason, Faith and Revolution*, p. 68.
35 Eagleton, *Reason, Faith and Revolution*, p. 124.
36 Eagleton, *Reason, Faith and Revolution*, p. 127.
37 Eagleton, *Reason, Faith and Revolution*, p. 168.

2 Sowing the seeds

 1 Isa. 1.13, 17.
 2 Confucius, *Analects* 12:11, in K. Malik, *The Quest for a Moral Compass: A Global History of Ethics*. London: Atlantic, 2014, p. 99.
 3 *The Meditations of Marcus Aurelius*, trans. G. M. A. Grube. Indianapolis, IN: Hackett, 1983, p. 27.
 4 *Meditations of Marcus Aurelius*, p. 43.
 5 *Meditations of Marcus Aurelius*, p. 63.
 6 L. Siedentop, *Inventing the Individual: The Origins of Western Liberalism*. London: Allen Lane, 2014, p. 352.
 7 Mark 12.17.
 8 Augustine, *The City of God*, trans. H. Bettenson. London: Penguin, 1984, p. 842.
 9 R. Williams, 'Do Human Rights Exist?', in *Faith in the Public Square*. London: Bloomsbury, 2013, p. 151.
10 B. Lewis, *What Went Wrong? Western Impact and Middle Eastern Response*. London: Phoenix, 2002, p. 110.
11 S. Schama, *The Story of the Jews: Finding the Words 1000 BCE–1492 CE*. London: Bodley Head, 2013, p. 236.
12 Siedentop, *Inventing the Individual*, p. 152.
13 Siedentop, *Inventing the Individual*, p. 213.
14 Siedentop, *Inventing the Individual*, p. 207.
15 C. Taylor, *A Secular Age*. Cambridge, MA: Harvard University Press, 2007, p. 61.
16 E. Auerbach, *Dante: Poet of the Secular World*, trans. Ralph Manheim. New York: New York Review Books, 2001, p. 132.
17 A. N. Wilson, *Dante in Love*. New York: Farrar, Straus & Giroux, 2011, p. 114.
18 Quoted in L. E. Halkin, *Erasmus: A Critical Biography*. London: Blackwell, 1994, p. 117.
19 Halkin, *Erasmus*, p. 118.
20 Halkin, *Erasmus*, p. 287.
21 M. Montaigne, *The Autobiography of Michel de Montaigne*, trans. M. Lowenthal. Boston: Houghton Mifflin, 1935, p. 108.
22 Montaigne, *Autobiography*, p. 157.

23 Montaigne, *Autobiography*, p. 303.
24 Montaigne, *Autobiography*, p. 219.
25 Montaigne, *Autobiography*, p. 222.
26 Montaigne, *Autobiography*, p. 317.

3 Mutations of Protestantism

1 S. Castellio, *On the Art of Doubting*, quoted in H. R. Guggisberg, *Sebastian Castellio, 1515–1563: Humanist and Defender of Toleration in a Confessional Age*, trans. B. Gordon. Aldershot: Ashgate, 2003, pp. 220, 224–5.

2 B. Spinoza, *Tractatus Theologico-Politicus*, in N. Spencer, *Atheists: The Evolution of the Species*. London: Bloomsbury, 2014, p. 55.

3 D. Erdozain, *The Soul of Doubt: The Religious Roots of Unbelief from Luther to Marx*. Oxford: Oxford University Press, 2016, p. 108.

4 B. Spinoza, quoted in M. Gullan-Whur, *Within Reason: A Life of Spinoza*. New York: St Martin's Press, 1998, p. 96.

5 Gullan-Whur, *Within Reason*, p. 164

6 Gullan-Whur, *Within Reason*, p. 235.

7 J. Locke, J., *The Reasonableness of Christianity as Delivered in the Scriptures*, ed. J. C. Higgins-Biddle. Oxford: J. C. Clarendon Press, 1999, p. 153.

8 Voltaire, quoted in H. S. Commager, *The Empire of Reason: How Europe Imagined and America Realized the Enlightenment*. London: Phoenix, 1978, p. 43.

9 Erdozain, *Soul of Doubt*, p. 167.

10 D'Holbach, quoted in Spencer, *Atheists*, p. 107.

11 Spencer, *Atheists*, p. 115.

12 J. Rousseau, *Discourse on Inequality*, in *Rousseau's Political Writings*, ed. A. W. W. Ritter. New York: Norton, 1988, p. 9.

13 J. Rousseau, *On Social Contract*, in *Rousseau's Political Writings*, p. 172.

14 Quoted in L. Damrosch, *Jean-Jacques Rousseau: Restless Genius*. New York: Houghton Mifflin, 2005, p. 262.

15 In R. Pearson, *Voltaire Almighty: A Life in Pursuit of Freedom*. London: Bloomsbury, 2005, p. 360.

16 T. Jefferson, *Notes on the State of Virginia*, in G. Himmelfarb, *The Roads to Modernity: The British, French, and American Enlightenments*. New York: Knopf, 2004, p. 208.

17 In Himmelfarb, *Roads to Modernity*, p. 204.

18 Quoted in Himmelfarb, *Roads to Modernity*, p. 183.

19 I. Kant, *Groundwork for the Metaphysics of Morals*, ed. C. M. Korsgaard. Cambridge: Cambridge University Press, 2012, p. 25.

20 Kant, *Groundwork*, p. 59.

21 I. Kant, *Religion Within the Limits of Reason Alone*, trans. T. M. Greene and H. H. Hudson. New York: Harper, 1960, pp. 5–6, 79.

22 C. Taylor, *A Secular Age*. Cambridge, MA: Harvard University Press, 2007, p. 19.

4 Struggling to be born

1 Quoted in G. Himmelfarb, *The Roads to Modernity: The British, French, and American Enlightenments*. New York: Knopf, 2004, pp. 120–1.

2 Quoted in A. Hochschild, *Bury the Chains: Prophets and Rebels in the Fight to Free an Empire's Slaves*. New York: Houghton Mifflin, 2005, pp. 86–7.

3 Hochschild, *Bury the Chains*, p. 88.

4 Hochschild, *Bury the Chains*, p. 246.

5 Hochschild, *Bury the Chains*, p. 366.

6 G. W. F. Hegel, 'Christianity: The Consummate Religion' (1824), quoted in P. C. Hodgson (ed.), *G. W. F. Hegel: Theologian of the Spirit*. Minneapolis, MN: Augsburg Press, 1997, p. 259.

7 Hegel, 'Christianity', quoted in Hodgson (ed.), *Hegel* p. 259.

8 R. W. Emerson, 'Address to Harvard Divinity School', 14 May 1835, in W. H. Gilman (ed.), *Selected Writings of Ralph Waldo Emerson*. New York: Penguin, 2003, p. 262.

9 Emerson, 'Self-Reliance', in *Selected Writings*, p. 279.

10 L. Feuerbach, *The Essence of Christianity*, trans. M. Evans. New York: Calvin Blanchard, 1855, p. xv.

11 Feuerbach, *Essence of Christianity*, p. xviii.

12 Feuerbach, *Essence of Christianity*, p. xxi.

13 A. Desmond and J. Moore, *Darwin's Sacred Cause: How a Hatred of Slavery Shaped Darwin's Views on Human Evolution*. Boston: Houghton Mifflin Harcourt, 2009, p. 148.

14 Desmond and Moore, *Darwin's Sacred Cause*, p. 321.

15 In H. Mayer, *All on Fire: William Lloyd Garrison and the Abolition of Slavery*. New York: Norton, 1998, p. 176.

16 F. Douglass, *Narrative of the Life of Frederick Douglass, an American Slave*. London: Penguin, 1982, p. 157.

17 In J. Oakes, *The Radical and the Republican: Frederick Douglass, Abraham Lincoln and the Triumph of Antislavery*. New York: Norton, 2007, p. 145.

18 J. S. Mill, *Autobiography*, ed. J. Robson. London: Penguin, 1989, p. 50.

19 Mill, *Autobiography*, p. 52.

20 Mill, *Autobiography*, p. 68.

21 Mill, *Autobiography*, p. 54.

22 J. S. Mill, 'Utility of Religion' (1854), in J. S. Mill, *Three Essays on Religion*. New York: Henry Holt, 1874, p. 97.

23 Mill, 'Utility of Religion', p. 97.

24 Mill, 'Utility of Religion', p. 109.

25 Mill, 'Utility of Religion', p. 113.

26 In G. Himmelfarb, *The Moral Imagination: From Edmund Burke to Lionel Trilling*. Chicago: Ivan R. Dee, 2006, p. 98.

27 Mill, 'Theism' (1870), in *Three Essays on Religion*, p. 250.

28 Mill, 'Theism', p. 255.

29 Mill, 'Theism', p. 256.

30 Mill, 'Theism', p. 257.

31 In M. Burleigh, *Earthly Powers: Religion and Politics in Europe from the French Revolution to the Great War*. London: HarperCollins, 2005, p. 245.

32 Burleigh, *Earthly Powers*, p. 247.

33 Burleigh, *Earthly Powers*, p. 248.

34 K. Marx and F. Engels, *The Communist Manifesto*. London: Penguin, 1967, p. 247.

35 N. Spencer, *Atheists: The Evolution of the Species*. London: Bloomsbury, 2014, p. 152.

36 In J. Berlinerbauer, *How to Be Secular: A Call to Arms*. Boston: Houghton Mifflin Harcourt, 2012, p. 94.

37 Berlinerbauer, *How to Be Secular*, p. 96.

38 Mill, *Autobiography*, p. 210.

39 T. H. Huxley, in D. Erdozain, *The Soul of Doubt: The Religious Roots of Unbelief from Luther to Marx*. Oxford: Oxford University Press, 2016, p. 184.

40 Huxley, in Erdozain, *Soul of Doubt*, p. 186.

41 Huxley, in Erdozain, *Soul of Doubt*, p. 187.

42 In R. Mead, *My Life in Middlemarch*. London: Granta, 2014, p. 66.

43 Mead, *My Life in Middlemarch*, p. 67.

44 Feuerbach, *Essence of Christianity*, p. 53.

45 Feuerbach, *Essence of Christianity*, p. 70; emphasis in original.

46 In Burleigh, *Earthly Powers*, p. 256.

47 F. Nietzsche, *The Twilight of the Idols* and *The Anti-Christ*, trans. R. J. Hollingdale. London: Penguin, 1968, p. 103; emphasis in original.

48 Nietzsche, *Twilight of the Idols* and *Anti-Christ*, p. 118; emphasis in original.

49 Nietzsche, *Twilight of the Idols* and *Anti-Christ*, p. 91; emphasis in original.

5 The secular century

1 H. G. Wells, *Anticipations*, in M. Coren, *The Invisible Man: The Life and Liberties of H. G. Wells*. New York: Atheneum, 1993, p. 66.

2 M. Burleigh, *Sacred Causes: Religion and Politics from the European Dictators to Al Qaeda*, London: HarperCollins, 2006, p. 39.

3 B. Russell, *Religion and Science*. Oxford: Oxford University Press, 1997, p. 242.

4 C. Isherwood, *Prater Violet*. London: Methuen, 1946, pp. 83–4.

5 G. Orwell, 'The English People', in G. Orwell, *The Collected Essays, Journalism and Letters*, vol. 3, ed. S. Orwell and I. Angus. London: Penguin, 1968, p. 22.

6 Orwell, 'Arthur Koestler', in *Collected Essays, Journalism and Letters*, vol. 3, p. 281.

7 S. Moyn, *The Last Utopia: Human Rights in History*. Cambridge MA: Harvard University Press, 2010, p. 55.

8 Moyn, *Last Utopia*, p. 54.

9 Moyn, *Last Utopia*, pp. 64–5.

10 C. Gearty, 'Something to Declare', *Rationalist Association*, 5 November 2008 – http://rationalist.org.uk/articles/1901/something-to-declare.

11 T. S. Eliot, Letter to Bonamy Dobree, February 1928, in *Letters of T. S. Eliot, Volume 4: 1928–1929*, ed. V. Eliot and J. Haffenden. London: Faber & Faber, 2013, p. 30.

12 In P. Mishra, *From the Ruins of Empire: The Revolt Against the West and the Remaking of Asia*. London: Allen Lane, 2012, p. 111.

13 T. Friend, *Woman, Man, and God in Modern Islam*. Grand Rapids, MI: Eerdmans, 2013, p. 248.

14 In Mishra, *From the Ruins of Empire*, p. 128.

15 In R. Guha, *Gandhi Before India*. New York: Knopf, 2014, p. 103.

16 Mishra, *From the Ruins of Empire*, p. 254.

17 A. Tunzelmann, *Indian Summer: The Secret History of the End of an Empire*. New York: Henry Holt, 2007, p. 61.

18 J. Nehru, *The Discovery of India*. London: Penguin, 2004, p. 420.

19 Nehru, *Discovery of India*, p. 534.

20 Nehru, *Discovery of India*, p. 603.

21 Nehru, *Discovery of India*, p. 571.

22 Nehru, *Discovery of India*, p. 618.

23 M. Hasan (ed.), *Will Secular India Survive?*. Gurgaon: ImprintOne, 2004, p. 58.

24 S. Qutb, 'Commentary on Surah 5', in P. Berman, *Terror and Liberalism*. New York: Norton, 2004, p. 95.

25 S. Qutb, 'Milestones', in Mishra, *From the Ruins of Empire*, p. 270.

6 In our time

1 Quoted in N. Spencer, *Atheists: The Evolution of the Species*. London: Bloomsbury, 2014, p. 225.

2 J. Sartre, 'Existentialism is a Humanism', in R. Norman, *On Humanism*. London: Routledge, 2012, p. 6.

3 A. Camus, *The Plague*, trans S. Gilbert. New York: Vintage, 1991, pp. 127–8.

4 In M. Burleigh, *Small Wars, Far Away Places*. London: Macmillan, 2013, p. 60.

5 W. E. Du Bois, 'Of Our Spiritual Strivings', in W. E. Du Bois, *The Souls of Black Folk*. New York: Dover, 1994, p. 7.

6 M. L. King, Sermon of 7 April 1957, in M. L. King, *'In a Single Garment of Destiny': A Global Vision of Justice*, ed. L. V. Baldwin. Boston: Beacon Press, 2012, p. 60.

7 King, Sermon of 7 April 1957, p. 71.

8 King, Sermon of 7 April 1957, p. 75.

9 Letter to Mr. M. Bernard Resknikoff, 17 September 1961, in King, *'In a Single Garment of Destiny'*, p. 197.

10 M. L. King, Letter from Birmingham Jail – <www.africa.upenn.edu/Articles_Gen/Letter_Birmingham.html>.

11 King, Address to European Baptist Assembly, Amsterdam, 6 August 1964, in King, 'In a Single Garment of Destiny', p. 15.

12 'My Jewish Brother!', article in New York Amsterdam News, in King, 'In a Single Garment of Destiny', p. 206.

13 Letter to Dr Harold E. Fay, 23 June 1962, in King, 'In a Single Garment of Destiny', p. 201.

14 'Beyond Vietnam: A Time to Break Silence', Riverside Church New York, 4 April 1967, in King, 'In a Single Garment of Destiny', p. 179.

15 S. Moyn, The Last Utopia: Human Rights in History. Cambridge MA: Harvard University Press, 2010, p. 130.

16 Moyn, Last Utopia, p. 131.

17 Quoted in Moyn, Last Utopia, p. 155.

18 Wall Street, 20th Century Fox, 1987.

19 F. Fukuyama, The End of History and the Last Man. New York: Hamish Hamilton, 1992, p. xi.

20 Fukuyama, End of History, p. 211.

21 Fukuyama, End of History, p .216.

22 Fukuyama, End of History, p. 334.

23 Fukuyama, End of History, p. 337.

24 Fukuyama, End of History, p. 337.

25 S. P. Huntington, The Clash of Civilizations and the Remaking of the World Order. New York: Simon & Schuster, 1996, p. 183.

26 Huntington, Clash of Civilizations, pp. 20–1.

27 Huntington, Clash of Civilizations, p. 46.

28 L. Siedentop, Democracy in Europe. London: Penguin, 2000, p. 82.

29 Siedentop, Democracy in Europe, p. 165.

30 Siedentop, Democracy in Europe, p. 213.

31 R. Scruton, The West and the Rest: Globalization and the Terrorist Threat. London: Continuum, 2002, p. 57.

32 J. Gray, Straw Dogs: Thoughts on Humans and Other Animals. London: Granta, 2002, p. 26.

33 Gray, Straw Dogs, p. xii.

34 J. Gray, Black Mass: Apocalyptic Religion and the Death of Utopia. New York: Farrar, Straus & Giroux, 2007, p. 192.

35 Gray, Black Mass, p. 197.

36 J. Gray, The Silence of the Animals: On Progress and Other Modern Myths. London: Allen Lane, 2013, p. 76.

37 B. Lévy, Left in Dark Times: A Stand against the New Barbarism, trans. B. Moser. New York: Random House, 2008, p. 193.

38 Lévy, Left in Dark Times, p. 197.

39 Lévy, Left in Dark Times, p. 193.

40 Lévy, Left in Dark Times, p. 205.

41 B. Lévy and M. Houellebecq, *Public Enemies: Duelling Writers Take on Each other and the World*. New York: Random House, 2011, pp. 159–60.

42 B. Obama, *Change We Can Believe In*. Edinburgh: Canongate, 2008, p. 211.

43 Obama, *Change We Can Believe In*, p. 67.

44 R. Williams, 'Has Secularism Failed?', in R. Williams, *Faith in the Public Square*. London: Bloomsbury, 2013, p. 128.

45 R. Williams, 'Reconnecting Human Rights and Religious Faith', in *Faith in the Public Square*, p. 161; emphasis in original.

46 Williams, 'Reconnecting Human Rights and Religious Faith', p. 162; emphasis in original.

47 Williams, 'Reconnecting Human Rights and Religious Faith', p. 172.

48 Z. Williams, 'Katie Hopkins calling migrants vermin recalls the darkest events of history', *The Guardian*, 19 April 2015.

49 M. Parris, 'Millions of us honestly don't know what our duty is to migrants – and Christianity doesn't help', *Spectator*, 5 September 2015.

50 P. Singer, *Practical Ethics*, 3rd edn. Cambridge: Cambridge University Press, 2011, p. 5.

51 Singer, *Practical Ethics*, p. 10.

52 Singer, *Practical Ethics*, p. 11.

53 Singer, *Practical Ethics*, p. 277.

54 W. MacAskill, *Doing Good Better: Effective Altruism and a Radical New Way to Make a Difference*. London: Guardian Books and Faber & Faber, 2015, p. 15.

55 D. Marquand, *Mammon's Kingdom: An Essay on Britain, Now*. London: Allen Lane, 2014, p. 207.

56 Marquand, *Mammon's Kingdom*, p. 220.

57 R. Brand, *Revolution*. London: Century, 2014, p. 73.

58 Brand, *Revolution*, p. 122.

59 Brand, *Revolution*, p. 301.

60 Brand, *Revolution*, p. 305.

61 Brand, *Revolution*, p. 306.

62 J. Milbank, 'The Name of Jesus', in J. Milbank, *The Word Made Strange: Theology, Language, Culture*. Oxford: Blackwell, 1997, p. 154.

63 C. Taylor, *A Secular Age*. Cambridge, MA: Harvard University Press, 2007, p. 637.

64 L. Siedentop, *Inventing the Individual: The Origins of Western Liberalism*. London: Allen Lane, 2014, p. 1.

65 Siedentop, *Inventing the Individual*, p. 2.

66 Siedentop, *Inventing the Individual*, p. 63.

67 Siedentop, *Inventing the Individual*, p. 352.

68 Siedentop, *Inventing the Individual*, p. 349.

69 Siedentop, *Inventing the Individual*, p. 360.

70 Siedentop, *Inventing the Individual*, p. 362.

71 Siedentop, *Inventing the Individual*, p. 362.

72 R. D. Woodberry, 'The Missionary Roots of Liberal Democracy', in the *American Political Science Review*, 2012, quoted in *Christianity Today* 2014 – <www.christianitytoday.com/ct/2014/january-february/world-missionaries-made.html?start=4>.

73 A. Ritchie and N. Spencer, 'The Case for Christian Humanism: Why Christians Should Believe in Humanism, and Humanists in Christianity', Foreword by Rowan Williams. London: Theos, 2014 – <www.theosthinktank.co.uk/files/files/Christian%20Humanism%20FINAL%20combined.pdf>.

74 D. Erdozain, *The Soul of Doubt: The Religious Roots of Unbelief from Luther to Marx*. Oxford: Oxford University Press, 2016, pp. 5–6.

75 Erdozain, *Soul of Doubt*, p. 263.

7 So what? How is Christianity credible?

1 Ps. 73.11.

2 2 Cor. 4.18.

3 2 Cor. 5.7.

4 M. Luther, *Sermons 1*, ed. and trans. J. W. Doberstein, Issue 51 of Luther's Works. Philadelphia, PA: Fortress Press, 1959, p. 37.

5 M. Luther, *Table Talk*, in R. Marius, *Martin Luther: The Man Between God and Death*. Cambridge, MA: Harvard University Press, 1999, p. 465.

Further reading

Berlinerbauer, J., *How to be Secular: A Call to Arms*. Boston: Houghton Mifflin Harcourt, 2012.

Burleigh, M., *Earthly Powers: Religion and Politics in Europe from the French Revolution to the Great War*. London: Harper Collins, 2005.

Damrosch, L., *Jean-Jacques Rousseau: Restless Genius*. New York: Houghton Mifflin, 2005.

Desmond, A. and J.Moore, *Darwin's Sacred Cause: How a Hatred of Slavery Shaped Darwin's Views on Human Evolution*. Boston: Houghton Mifflin Harcourt, 2009.

Eagleton, T., *Reason, Faith and Revolution: Reflections on the God Debate*. New Haven, CT: Yale University Press, 2009.

Erdozain, D., *The Soul of Doubt: The Religious Roots of Unbelief from Luther to Marx*. Oxford: Oxford University Press, 2016.

Gray, J., *Black Mass: Apocalyptic Religion and the Death of Utopia*. New York: Farrar, Straus & Giroux, 2007.

Haught, J. F., *God and the New Atheism: A Critical Response to Dawkins, Harris, and Hitchens*. Louisville, KY: Westminster John Knox Press, 2008.

Himmelfarb, G., *The Roads to Modernity: The British, French, and American Enlightenments*. New York: Knopf, 2004.

Hochschild, A., *Bury the Chains: Prophets and Rebels in the Fight to Free an Empire's Slaves*. New York: Houghton Mifflin, 2005.

Mayer, H., *All on Fire: William Lloyd Garrison and the Abolition of Slavery*. New York: Norton, 1998.

Mishra, P., *From the Ruins of Empire: The Revolt Against the West and the Remaking of Asia*. London: Allen Lane, 2012.

Moyn, S., *The Last Utopia: Human Rights in History*. Cambridge, MA: Harvard University Press, 2010.

Pearson, R., *Voltaire Almighty: A Life in Pursuit of Freedom*. London: Bloomsbury, 2005.

Siedentop, L., *Inventing the Individual: The Origins of Western Liberalism*. London: Allen Lane, 2014.

Spencer, N., *Atheists: The Evolution of the Species*. London: Bloomsbury, 2014.

Taylor, C., *A Secular Age*. Cambridge, MA: Harvard University Press, 2007.

Williams, R., *Faith in the Public Square*. London: Bloomsbury, 2013.

Index

Index

Index

Tyler's Story

A little story about learning to read in prison

It's probably my drinking that got me into prison. That and not having a proper job.

I wasn't bothered about school, but in prison I had a chance to join a reading group. The books are interesting but not too hard to read.

In one book, *Forty-six Quid and a Bag of Dirty Washing*, we read about Barry, a guy who got mixed up with a drug dealer, but has now just left prison. I saw how he had to make good choices every day – and fill in lots of forms – to stay out of prison. I don't want to end up back inside again, so I've decided that I'm not going to drink on my way home. I won't get home drunk before the evening's even started – that just makes me drink more. And I'm going to get better at reading so I can fill in forms when I get out.

Inspired by a true story. Names have been changed.

Help us to tell more stories like Tyler's. Support the Diffusion Fiction Project. Just £4.99 puts an easy-to-read book in prisoners' hands, to help them to improve their reading confidence while encouraging them to think about life's big questions. Visit www.spck.org.uk to make a donation or, to volunteer to run a reading group in a prison, please contact prisonfiction@spck.org.uk.